CATALOGUE
OF THE
BABYLONIAN COLLECTIONS
AT YALE

2

CDL Press Bethesda, Maryland

OLD BABYLONIAN ARCHIVAL TEXTS IN THE NIES BABYLONIAN COLLECTION

GARY BECKMAN

Preface by William W. Hallo

Edited by Ulla Kasten

Published with assistance from the James B. Nies Trust Fund.

© 1995 Yale University

All rights reserved. This book may not be reproduced, in whole or in part, in any form (beyond that copying permitted by Sections 107 and 108 of the U.S. Copyright Law and except by reviewers for the public press), without written permission from the publishers.

Designed by Ulla Kasten
Published by CDL Press, POB 34454, Bethesda, MD 20827
Printed by Bookcrafters, Fredericksburg, Virginia

ISBN 1-883053-11-0

Library of Congress Cataloging-in-Publication Data

Nies Babylonian Collection (Yale University)
   Old babylonian archival texts in the Nies Babylonian Collection / Gary Beckman; edited by Ulla Kasten.
      p. cm. — (Catalogue of the Babylonian Collections at Yale; 2)
   Includes bibliographical references and index.
   ISBN 1-883053-11-0
    1. Akkadian language—Texts—Catalogs.   2. Nies Babylonian Collection (Yale University)—Catalogs. I. Beckman, Gary M. II. Kasten, Ulla. III. Title. IV. Series.
PJ3711.N54 1995
016.492′1—dc20
                                                                                                    95-21149
                                                                                                      CIP

Dedicated to the Memory
of Albrecht Goetze
(1897-1971)

CONTENTS

Preface	ix
Abbreviations	xi
Introduction	1
Catalogue	9
Indices	157

PREFACE

After the appearance of CBCY 1 by Paul-Alain Beaulieu, it is fitting that the first sequel be the present volume by Gary Beckman. Dr. Beckman was the first coordinator of the project for cataloguing the holdings of the Babylonian Collections at Yale (1988–1992). Together with Ulla Kasten and Mary S. Glynn (Yale Computer Center), he designed the program for creating the data base, and helped to select those elements which were to be published in book form. Since moving to Ann Arbor, he has continued to advise the project from there, and he has been spending each summer in New Haven to complete his own assignments. CBCY 2 is the first fruit of these labors.

William W. Hallo

ABBREVIATIONS*

AbB	Altbabylonische Briefe
ActaSum	*Acta Sumerologica*
BiMes 11	R. M. Sigrist, *Les* sattukku *dans l'Ešumeša durant la période d'Isin et Larsa* (Malibu 1984)
BiOr	*Bibliotheca Orientalis*
BIN	Babylonian Inscriptions in the Collection of James B. Nies:
	BIN 2—J. B. Nies and C. Keiser, *Historical, Religious, and Economic Texts and Antiquities* (New Haven, 1920)
	BIN 7—J. Alexander, *Early Babylonian Letters and Economic Texts* (New Haven, 1943)
	BIN 9—V. Crawford, *Sumerian Economic Texts from the First Dynasty of Isin* (New Haven, 1954)
	BIN 10—M. Van De Mieroop, *Sumerian Administrative Documents from the Reigns of Išbi-Erra and Šu-ilišu* (New Haven, 1987)
ENES	B. Buchanan, *Early Near Eastern Seals in the Yale Babylonian Collection* (New Haven, 1981)
JCS	*Journal of Cuneiform Studies*
NABU	*N.A.B.U. Nouvelles Assyriologiques Brèves et Utilitaires*
NBC	*siglum* for objects in the Nies Babylonian Collection
Or	*Orientalia, Nova Series*
PN(s)	Personal name(s)
RA	*Revue d'assyriologie et d'archéologie orientale*
RAI	Rencontre assyriologique internationale
RN	Royal name
TIM	*Texts in the Iraqi Museum*
YBC	*siglum* for objects in the Yale Babylonian Collection
YNER 4	S. D. Walters, *Water for Larsa*, Yale Near Eastern Researches 4 (New Haven, 1970)

---

* Abbreviations for royal names and dynasties are discussed in the Introduction below.

YOS	Yale Oriental Series, Babylonian Texts:
	YOS 10—A. Goetze, *Old Babylonian Omen Texts* (New Haven, 1947)
	YOS 12—S. Feigin, *Legal and Administrative Texts of the Reign of Samsu-iluna* (New Haven, 1979)
	YOS 13—J.J. Finkelstein, *Late Old Babylonian Documents and Letters* (New Haven, 1972)
	YOS 14—S. Simmons, *Early Old Babylonian Documents* (New Haven, 1978)
ZA	*Zeitschrift für Assyriologie und vorderasiatische Archäologie*

INTRODUCTION

Catalogued in this volume are the 3334 cuneiform tablets of archival character in the Nies Babylonian Collection dating to the Old Babylonian period (twentieth through sixteenth centuries B.C.).[1] 1926 (58%) of these texts remain unpublished. With the exception of the 165 items bearing museum numbers between NBC 10535 and 10777 and between NBC 11124 and 11340, which were excavated at Nippur, all of this material was acquired from antiquities dealers or through private donations. While only the most basic details about each item are presented here, much fuller information is contained in the database created and maintained in the Yale Babylonian Collection with the support of an Access and Preservation Grant of the National Endowment for the Humanities.

These texts are practical documents, which originally belonged to what Assyriologists loosely term "archives"—that is, "records accumulated during the time a particular task was performed by an institution or person,"[2] or the miscellaneous groups of private records—sales of property, adoptions, testaments, letters,[3] etc.—collected by an individual or family over the course of years.[4]

The single largest group of texts housed in the Nies Babylonian Collection is the bulk of the Isin Craft Archive, published in BIN 9 and 10.[5] Other well-studied archives represented here are that of Gidānum, son of Ipiq-Adad of Šaduppûm (43 texts in NBC);[6] that of Lu-igisa, an official concerned

---

[1] Only a handful of these texts are dated to the reign of Abī-ešuḫ or later—see Indices—while almost half of all pieces included here can be assigned by date, prosopography, or script to the reigns of Warad-Sîn or earlier. See the database for the period of each item.

By far the greatest numbers of dated documents assignable to individual reigns belong to Rīm-Sîn (384–368 unpublished) and Samsuiluna (340–297 unpublished). The very important rule of Ḫammurabi is represented by a mere 42 dated texts (36 unpublished). Note that these statistics are based on the presence of year names or on the use of the unusual month system of Rīm-Sîn's bureaucracy—see note 18 below—and do not include material which can be assigned to these rulers by other criteria.

[2] K. R. Veenhof, "Cuneiform Archives—An Introduction," in *Cuneiform Archives and Libraries*, 30e RAI 1983 (Leiden, 1986) p. 7.

[3] There are 717 Old Babylonian letters in NBC, 210 still unpublished. Most of the published items of correspondence have been re-edited and translated by M. Stol in *Letters from Yale*, AbB 9 (Leiden, 1981).

[4] Cf. Veenhof, "Cuneiform Archives," pp. 9-10.

[5] Approximately 825 items in NBC. See Marc Van De Mieroop, *Crafts in the Early Isin Period. A Study of the Isin Craft Archive from the Reigns of Išbi-Erra and Šū-Ilišu*, Orientalia Lovaniensia Analecta 24 (Leuven, 1987). Add now NBC 6831 and unpublished 8126.

[6] See S. Simmons, "Early Old Babylonian Tablets from Harmal and Elsewhere," JCS 13 (1959) pp. 72-73, and add unpublished NBC 6811, 9321, 9723, 9743, 9754, 9761, and 9829.

with irrigation works in the kingdom of Larsa under Abī-sarē and Sumu-el (about 150 items);[7] that of the "provisions office" of the Ešumeša temple in Nippur in the earlier Old Babylonian period (157 pieces, mostly fragmentary);[8] and that of Šamaš-ḫāzir, an administrator installed by Ḫammurabi in the newly-annexed territory of Larsa (22 texts).[9]

The current cataloguing project has led to the identification of numerous further corpora of texts.[10] Among these are several interrelated archives from Lagaba, particularly that of one Marduk-muballiṭ, whose distribution of barley and related products—and other activities as well—are documented primarily for years 6 through 8 of Samsuiluna (more than 225 records);[11] of the businessman Dada, son of Kubbulum,[12] attested for the most part during the second half of the reign of the same king (perhaps 50 texts);[13] and of the office responsible for the supply of the *naptanum*, or royal table, of Rīm-Sîn during his fourth decade (47 tablets).[14]

Further work in the database will certainly allow the reconstruction of additional archives whose constituent texts have been separated during their long journey through the hands of illicit diggers, antiquities dealers, and museum curators.[15]

Catalogue

DATE

In fullest form, the date is made up of five elements in the following order: RULER.DYNASTY.YEAR.MONTH.DAY (e.g., AMSA.BA.17.02.10). Abbreviations for these elements are explained below.

---

[7] Analyzed by S. Walters, YNER 4. See pp. 168-70 for a list of published texts—mostly from BIN 7—constituting this archive, to which should be added unpublished NBC 9556 and 10407.

[8] Edited by R. M. Sigrist, BiMes 11. The museum numbers of the texts are given on p. 204.

[9] Thirteen letters from the monarch to his subordinate appeared in BIN 7, and two unpublished pieces of this correspondence (NBC 7858 and 7885) will be included in the posthumous YOS 15 by A. Goetze. To these should be added unpublished non-epistolary documents NBC 5312, 9292, 9576, 10230, 10231, 10394, and 10450.

[10] See D. Charpin, "La Babylonie de Samsu-iluna à la lumière de nouveaux documents," BiOr 38 (1981) pp. 517-47, for an exemplary effort to reconstitute archives from the material published in YOS 12. My work has allowed me to assign numerous tablets, from both the Nies Babylonian Collection and the Yale Babylonian Collection proper, to many of the archives identified by Charpin.

[11] For a listing of the NBC tablets in question, see O. Tammuz, "Archives from Lagaba," (Ph. D. diss. Yale University, 1993) pp. 47-58.

[12] Also written Kunbulum and Kumbulum.

[13] NBC 5327, 5353, 5360*-61*, 5365*, 5385*, 5391*-93*, 5532*, 5534, 5540*, 5564*-65*, 6329, 6333, 6761*, 6830, 8577, 8584, 8642, 8801, 9222, 9225-26*, 9264*, 9297, 9467, 9478, 9490*, 9561*, 9581, 9583, 9617, 9654, 9690*, 9692, 9699, 9709, 9726, 9735, 9737, 9744, 9777*, 9795, 9810, 9813, 9832*, 10351, 10363. Those texts marked with an asterisk contain the patronymic and are thus certainly part of this archive. On the basis of preliminary consideration of content, date, and tablet layout the others seem to belong here, but further study is necessary, since the name Dada is not at all uncommon.

[14] The relevant texts are listed sub no. 8799 of this Catalogue. It is possible that many *naptanum* texts without year names, such as NBC 9567, 9600, 9661, and 9683, also belong here.

[15] In some instances material from other Yale collections, in particular the Yale Babylonian Collection, can be recognized as belonging together with NBC texts. Cf. note 10 above.

"??" indicates that a month or year cannot yet be assigned a place in the annual calendar or within the reign of a ruler. "xx" indicates that an element is present, but is to a greater or lesser degree illegible, while "—" indicates that it is absent. Where a date is so badly damaged that it is not possible to determine which elements had originally been included by the writer, it is described as "illegible." When inspection of a damaged tablet and generic or archival considerations suggest that a date had once been present, it is referred to as "lost." A question mark at the end of the date means that interpretation of one or more of its elements, most often the reading of the numeral for the day, is uncertain.

For some entries additional information concerning the date is provided. Such information includes full transliteration of year names encountered here for the first time and of those presenting unusual orthography or significant lexical or grammatical variants. I have also remarked on those instances when a date appears only within the body of a text, and when a tablet has been assigned to a reign because of the presence of a royal name in an oath or sealing, or because it belongs to an archive otherwise dated.

(1) Ruler

The following abbreviations for names of rulers have been used here. For the abbreviations following the royal names see the next section.

ABER	=	Abdi-Eraḫ (TU)
ABEŠ	=	Abī-ešuḫ (LA)
ABSA	=	Abī-sarē (LA)
AMDI	=	Ammiditana (BA)
AMSA	=	Ammiṣaduqa (BA)
APSI	=	Apil-Sîn (BA)
BUSI	=	Būr-Sîn (IS)
DABA	=	Dadbanaya (IS)
DADU	=	Daduša (EŠ, ŠA)
DAIL	=	Damiq-ilišu (IS)
DATA	=	Dannum-taḫaz (EŠ, NE, ŠA)
ENBA	=	Enlil-bāni (IS)
GUNG	=	Gungunum (LA)
HADU	=	Ḫammi-dušur (ŠA)
HARA	=	Ḫammurabi (BA)
IBŠA	=	Ibni-šadum (KA)
IDDA	=	Iddin-Dagan (IS)
IPAD	=	Ipiq-Adad (EŠ)
IPAD2	=	Ipiq-Adad II (ŠA)
IPE2	=	Ibāl-pī-el II (ŠA)
IQTI	=	Iqīš-Tišpak (ŠA)
IRIM	=	Irra-imittī (IS)
IŠDA	=	Išme-Dagan (IS)
IŠIR	=	Išbi-Irra (IS)
ITPI	=	Itēr-pīša (IS)
ITŠA	=	Itūr-Šamaš (KI)
LIEN	=	Lipit-Enlil (IS)
LIIŠ	=	Lipit-Ištar (IS)

MABA	=	Manabaltiel (KI)
MANA	=	Manana (MN)
NASI	=	Narām-Sîn (ŠA)
NUAD	=	Nūr-Adad (LA)
RISI	=	Rīm-Sîn (LA)
RISI2	=	Rīm-Sîn II (LA)
SABI	=	Sabium (BA)
SADI	=	Samsuditana (BA)
SAIL	=	Samsuiluna (BA)
SIAD	=	Ṣilli-Adad (LA)
SIER	=	Sîn-erībam (LA)
SIID	=	Sîn-iddinam (LA)
SIIQ	=	Sîn-iqīšam (LA)
SIIR	=	Sîn-irībam (UK)
SIMA	=	Sîn-māgir (IS)
SIMU	=	Sîn-muballiṭ (BA)
SUAB	=	Sumu-abum (LA)
SUEL	=	Sumu-el (LA)
SULA	=	Sumu-la-el (BA)
SUYA	=	Sumu-Yamutbala (MN)
ŠUIL	=	Šū-ilišu (IS)
UBAY	=	Ubaya (KI)
UN	=	Unknown
URDU	=	Urdukuga (IS)
URNI	=	Ur-Ninurta (IS)
WAQR	=	Waqrum (ŠA)
WASI	=	Warad-Sîn (LA)
ZAMB	=	Zambia (IS)

(2) Dynasty

The following abbreviations have been employed for names of dynasties or for ad-hoc groups of rulers whose dates have been found on texts from particular sites, such as Šaduppûm (Tell Ḫarmal):

BA	=	Babylon
EŠ	=	Ešnunna
IS	=	Isin
KA	=	Kazallu
KI	=	Kisurra
LA	=	Larsa
MN	=	Manana
NE	=	Nerebtum
ŠA	=	Šaduppûm
ŠL	=	Šadlaš
TU	=	Tutub
UK	=	Uruk
UN	=	Unknown

For the convenience of the reader I repeat here the names of rulers, organized by dynasty, in chronological order within each group.

Isin (IS)

IŠIR	=	Išbi-Irra
ŠUIL	=	Šū-ilišu
IDDA	=	Iddin-Dagan
IŠDA	=	Išme-Dagan
LIIŠ	=	Lipit-Ištar
URNI	=	Ur-Ninurta
BUSI	=	Būr-Sîn
LIEL	=	Lipit-Enlil
IRIM	=	Irra-imittī
ENBA	=	Enlil-bāni
ZAMB	=	Zambia
ITPI	=	Itēr-pīša
URDU	=	Urdukuga
SIMA	=	Sîn-māgir
DAIL	=	Damiq-ilišu
DABA	=	Dadbanaya

Larsa (LA)

GUNG	=	Gungunum
ABSA	=	Abī-sarē
SUEL	=	Sumu-el
NUAD	=	Nūr-Adad
SIID	=	Sîn-iddinam
SIER	=	Sîn-erībam
SIIQ	=	Sîn-iqīšam
SIAD	=	Ṣilli-Adad
WASI	=	Warad-Sîn
RISI	=	Rīm-Sîn
RISI2	=	Rīm-Sîn II

Babylon (BA)

(The kings whose names are in parentheses are not represented by texts in the Nies Babylonian Collection.)

SUAB	=	Sumu-abum
SULA	=	Sumu-la-el
SABI	=	Sabium
(APSI	=	Apil-Sîn)
SIMU	=	Sîn-muballiṭ
HARA	=	Ḫammurabi
SAIL	=	Samsuiluna
ABEŠ	=	Abī-ešuḫ
AMDI	=	Ammiditana
AMSA	=	Ammiṣaduqa
(SADI	=	Samsuditana)

Ešnunna (EŠ)
  IPAD = Ipiq-Adad
  NASI = Narām-Sîn
  DATA = Dannum-taḫaz

Kazallu (KA)
  IBŠA = Ibni-šadum

Kisurra (KI)
  ITŠA = Itūr-Šamaš
  MABA = Manabaltiel
  UBAY = Ubaya

Manana (MN)
  MANA = Manana
  SUYA = Sumu-Yamutbala

Nerebtum (NE)
  DATA = Dannum-taḫaz

Šaduppûm (ŠA)
  WAQR = Waqrum
  HADU = Ḫammi-dušur
  IPAD2 = Ipiq-Adad II
  NASI = Narām-Sîn
  IQTI = Iqīš-Tišpak
  DATA = Dannum-taḫaz
  DADU = Dadūša
  IPE2 = Ibāl-pī-el II

Tutub (TU)
  ABER = Abdi-Eraḫ

Uruk (UK)
  SIIR = Sîn-irībam

(3) Year

In general I have employed the identification and numeration of year names compiled by M. Sigrist and P. Damerow,[16] but for years Išbi-Irra 24 through Šū-ilišu 3 of the Isin dynasty I have followed M. Van De Mieroop.[17] The later years of Rīm-Sîn of Larsa call for special attention:

---

[16] M. Sigrist and P. Damerow, *Mesopotamian Yearnames. Neo-Sumerian and Old Babylonian Date Formulae*, forthcoming. Dr. Sigrist kindly allowed me to utilize this work in manuscript and discussed many problematic year names in the texts of the Nies Babylonian Collection with me. Most of the newly discovered year names found in the present Catalogue will be included in the book of Sigrist and Damerow and have been designated here with the *sigla* which that listing will employ.

[17] M. Van De Mieroop, *Crafts in the Early Isin Period*, pp. 120-28, and BIN 10, pp. 1-3.

Damaged dates of the "Isin era" are designated as "30+," or as "31+," "32+" etc., depending upon how much of the formula or the numeral can be read.

(4) Month

Months have been assigned the numerals 1 through 12 according to their place in the Babylonian calendar. Intercalary *Elūlu* is designated 06D (diri), and intercalary *Addaru* 12D. I have cited a number of aberrant (or Akkadian) writings of the usual month names, and have given the full spelling of designations of non-standard months. Where these latter cannot yet be placed within the year, they are indicated as "??," as are the peculiar months employed in the second half of the reign of Rīm-Sîn.[18]

(5) Day

Days are expressed in numerals from 1 through 30. "+" means that the damaged numeral indicating the day may in fact be higher than read.

DESCRIPTION

Here the reader will find a concise description of the type of object[19] and the contents[20] of the text; an indication as to whether the record was sealed;[21] occasional additional remarks, most frequently indicating some relationship to texts at Yale or in other collections; and the *editio princeps*. The excavation numbers of the texts found at Nippur (NBC 10535 through 10777 and NBC 11124 through 11340) have also been given here. The character of the primary publication has been indicated utilizing the following abbreviations: (C) = Copy; (T) = Transliteration; (Tr) = Translation; (P) = Photograph.

---

[18] See F. R. Kraus, "Ungewöhnliche Datierungen aus der Zeit des Königs Rim-Sin von Larsa," ZA 53 (1959) pp. 136-67; J. F. Robertson, "An Unusual Dating System from Isin-Larsa Period Nippur: New Evidence," ActaSum 5 (1983) pp. 147-59; and M. Van De Mieroop, "The Reign of Rim-Sin," RA 87 (1993) pp. 64-66.

[19] Unless otherwise specified—as "tag," "bulla," "case," etc.—all items catalogued here are clay tablets. "Fragmentary" refers to the condition of the inscribed object itself and not to the degree of legibility of the text.

[20] Here I have been only as specific as the nature of the record and its state of preservation allow. Thus on one extreme I differentiate between "loan" and "promissory note," for example, depending on whether the commodity in question is actually conveyed at the time of the drawing up of the document, and between "delivery" (most frequently employing the verb mu-túm) and "consignment" (*paqādum*) of livestock. At the other extreme, I content myself with such general designations as "list" or "record concerning ..." when a document is badly damaged or when its bureaucratic purpose cannot be determined without placing it in its archival context, the very task which the compilation of this Catalogue is intended to facilitate.

"Ration list" is used here only for texts in which small amounts of a foodstuff or foodstuffs are issued to individuals usually indicated by name. An "account" is either a record of both income and expenditure of a commodity or commodities—whether "balanced" or not—or alternately, a tabulation of receipt or disbursement over an extended period of time.

I designate a damaged text as a "contract" if witnesses are present, and as "administrative" if it is clear—usually from the presence of the seal impressions of known officials or through comparison of its shape and layout with better-preserved records—that it is the product of a bureaucratic organization.

"?" means that an entire description is uncertain and "(?)" that only the immediately preceding noun or phrase is in doubt.

[21] For convenience I have included references to the sealings studied by Buchanan and Hallo in ENES even where the object has not otherwise been published.

Indices

The texts have been indexed by date within each dynasty, and the dynasties ordered according to the schema given above. Texts with no year or an unclear year name have not been included in the indices.

CATALOGUE

NBC	Date	Description
1233	Lost	Loan of barley; BIN 2, 92 (C)
1233A	—.09.—	Fragmentary receipt of foodstuff
1234	SAIL.BA.19.04.01	Receipt of dates; sealed; BIN 2, 96 (C)
1235	RISI.LA.14.—.—	Hire of person(?); BIN 2, 83 (C)
1236	SULA.BA.31.04.—	Loan (šu-lá) of silver and barley; sealed; BIN 2, 74 (C)
1237	SAIL.BA.25.03.—	Receipt of silver; BIN 2, 93 (C)
1238	ABEŠ.BA.K.08.05	Payment of barley; sealed; BIN 2, 90 (C)
1239	SAIL.BA.26.10.01	Loan of barley to be repaid in dates; sealed; BIN 2, 88 (C)
1240	No date	Loan of barley; sealed; BIN 2, 105 (C)
1241	Lost	Loan of barley; BIN 2, 89 (C)
1242	??.09.—	Agreement concerning interest; sealed; mu-ús-sa tukul(?)-me ^{d}Utu; BIN 2, 87 (C)
1243	SAIL.BA.10.12.20	Guarantee of person; sealed; BIN 2, 81 (C)
1244	SABI.BA.14.03.20	Receipt of barley; BIN 2, 97 (C)
1245	ABEŠ.BA.01.07.21	Receipt of silver, price of bran; BIN 2, 95 (C)
1246	MANA.MN.F.—.—	Sale of improved residential property; sealed; BIN 2, 86 (C)
1247	SIMU.BA.16.06.—	Seizure of field *ana ridûtišu*; sealed; BIN 2, 98 (C)
1248	SAIL.BA.04.08.22	Loan (*ḫubuttātum*) of silver; BIN 7, 82 (C)
1249	RISI2.LA.02.12.30	Receipt of barley for *sattukku* offerings; sealed; BIN 2, 73 (C)
1250	HARA.BA.05.07.08	Record concerning weapons(?); sealed; BIN 2, 99 (C)
1255	SAIL.BA.28.09.10	Loan of barley; sealed; BIN 2, 84 (C)
1256	SAIL.BA.27.02.10	Loan of silver, interest to be paid in dates; BIN 2, 85 (C)
1259	SAIL.BA.27.04.22	Sale of slave-girl; sealed; BIN 2, 80 (C)
1260	No date	Record concerning silver (ledger); BIN 2, 104 (C)
1261	SAIL.BA.04.12.20	Receipt of dates; BIN 2, 94 (C)

NBC	Date	Description
1262	SAIL.BA.28.02.11	Rental of field and orchard; BIN 2, 91 (C)
1263	SAIL.BA.05.05.22	Receipt of barley; fingernail impressions; BIN 2, 101 (C)
1264	SAIL.BA.06.10.26	Ration list; BIN 2, 103 (C)
1266	No date	Letter to Rīm-Sîn from Awīltum concerning barley shipment and slaves; BIN 2, 69 (C)
1267	No date	Letter to Qurdi-Ištar and Ubayatum from Ibbi-ilī concerning wages of workers; BIN 2, 70 (C)
1268	No date	Letter to Beya and Ibbi-Ilabrat from Ilī-apīlī concerning orchard; BIN 2, 71 (C)
1269	SAIL.BA.—.07.20	Manumission; sealed; RN in oath; BIN 2, 76 (C)
1271	HARA.BA.36.03.01	Tablet and portion of case—rental of field; sealed; BIN 2, 79 (C)
1272	SAIL.BA.07.04.30	Adoption; sealed; BIN 2, 75 (C)
1273	Lost	Rental of field; sealed; BIN 2, 78 (C); ENES 1003
1274	No date	Record concerning foodstuffs and silver; BIN 2, 100 (C)
1275	SAIL.BA.02.11.21	Receipt of dates; BIN 2, 102 (C)
1276	SAIL.BA.02.09.20?	Rental of orchard; sealed; BIN 2, 77 (C)
1280	No date	Account of barley; BIN 2, 68 (C)
1980	No date	Ration list
2104	RISI.LA.24.09.27	Disbursement of barley
4082	SAIL.BA.24.03.—	Ration list—barley
4088	No date	List of PNs
4109	No date	List of PNs and quantities of foodstuff
4117	SAIL.BA.24.10.04	Account of silver and foodstuffs (ledger)
4118	SAIL.BA.03.—.—	Ration list—dates
4120	No date	Ration list
4121	No date	List of PNs and numbers of sheep (ledger)
4122	No date	Ration list

NBC	Date	Description
4124	No date	Ration list
4129	SAIL.BA.04.—.—	Ration list—dates
4133	No date	List of PNs and towns
4150	No date	Fragmentary list of numerals
4150A	No date?	Fragmentary memorandum concerning disbursements of silver(?)
4216	xx.08.—	Tablet and portion of case—promissory note—silver; mu erin$_2$(?) x x x x
4217	SULA.BA.30.11.—	Loan of silver; sealed; YOS 14, 141 (C)
4218	SULA.BA.30.07.24	Tablet and case—loan (šu-lá) of barley; sealed; YOS 14, 140 (C)
4956	—.xx.—	Record of harvest labor(?); sealed
4958	—.06.10	List of PNs and quantities of foodstuff
4961	xx.11.07	Disbursement of foodstuff for *naptanum*; mu gu-za x x
4962	No date	Memorandum concerning vessels
4979	No date	List of PNs
4986	AMDI.BA.05.04.01	Rental of fields; sealed; YOS 13, 368 (C)
4987	—.05.25	Account of various foodstuffs
5026	No date	Account of barley and silver (ledger)
5033	??.11.—	Unopened case—promissory note—dates; mu ^{urudu}x ki-bé gi$_4$-a-a
5066	SULA.BA.28.07.—	List of PNs and quantities of silver; mu Bar-sí-pa^{ki} ba-an-ku$_4$
5156	No date	List of field acreages
5284	No date	Letter to Šamaš-ḫāzir from Lu-Ninurta concerning assignment of field; BIN 7, 13 (C)
5285	No date	Letter to Šamaš-ḫāzir from Ḫammurabi concerning possession of field; BIN 7, 2 (C)

NBC	Date	Description
5286	No date	Letter to Šamaš-ḫāzir, Sîn-mušallim, and associates from Ḫammurabi concerning assignment of field; BIN 7, 8 (C)
5287	No date	Letter to Lu-Ninurta, Balmunamḫe, Ipqu-Irra, and Mannum-kīma-Sîn from Rīm-Sîn concerning punishment of slave; BIN 7, 10 (C)
5288	No date	Letter to Šamaš-ḫāzir from Lu-Ninurta concerning dispute over field; BIN 7, 12 (C)
5289	No date	Letter to "my mother" from Šamaš-bāni concerning welfare of third party; BIN 7, 43 (C)
5290	SAIL.BA.04.12.24	Rental of orchard; sealed; BIN 7, 182 (C)
5291	No date	Letter to Šamaš-ḫāzir from Munawwirum concerning assignment of field; BIN 7, 11 (C)
5292	No date	Letter to Aḫulap-[...] from Šamaš-ša-ta-[...] requesting silver
5293	No date	Letter to Šamaš-ḫāzir from Ḫammurabi concerning maintenance of canal; BIN 7, 7 (C)
5294	AMSA.BA.17.02.10	Rental of field; sealed; BIN 7, 211 (C)
5295	No date	Letter to Lu-igisa from Banum concerning legal case about field; BIN 7, 27 (C)
5296	No date	Letter to Šamaš-ḫāzir from Ḫammurabi concerning field; BIN 7, 1 (C)
5297	No date	Letter to Šamaš-ḫāzir from Ḫammurabi concerning field; BIN 7, 3 (C)
5298	No date	Letter to Šamaš-ḫāzir from Ḫammurabi concerning field; BIN 7, 9 (C)
5299	HARA.BA.32.03.—	Rental of fields; sealed; BIN 7, 177 (C)
5300	No date	Letter to Šamaš-ḫāzir from Ḫammurabi concerning barley tax; BIN 7, 5 (C)
5301	AMSA.BA.13.12D.04	Sale of cow; sealed; BIN 7, 208 (C)
5302	No date	Receipt of barley; BIN 7, 219 (C)
5303	RISI.LA.58.05.01	Division of inheritance; sealed; BIN 7, 171 (C)

NBC	Date	Description
5304	IPE2.ŠA.08.—.—?	Legal case concerning slaves; sealed; YOS 14, 72 (C)
5305	RISI.LA.24.09.29	Legal case
5306	RISI.LA.28.06.18	Rental of orchard; BIN 7, 166 (C)
5307	No date	Letter to Amat-Ea from Marduk-nāṣir concerning ox; BIN 7, 42 (C)
5308	No date	Letter to Nūr-Šamaš from Irra-bāni concerning boundary of field; BIN 7, 47 (C)
5309	No date	Letter to Šamaš-ḫāzir from Ḫammurabi concerning field; BIN 7, 6 (C)
5310	SAIL.BA.15.06.04	Testament; sealed; BIN 7, 190 (C)
5311	RISI.LA.46.01.—	Tablet and portion of case—sale of neglected residential property; sealed; BIN 7, 170 (C)
5312	No date?	Legal case concerning silver left on deposit; sealed
5313	No date	Letter to Ma-ZI-KI from Rīm-Sîn-qarrād concerning marriage
5314	DAIL.IS.05.12D.—	Sale of temple office; sealed; BIN 7, 65 (C)
5315	SAIL.BA.12.08.—	Tablet and case—sale of improved residential property; sealed; cf. NBC 5334
5316	RISI.LA.45.05.—	Sale of uncultivated field; sealed; BIN 7, 168 (C)
5317	No date	Receipt of animals, garments, and slaves
5318	DAIL.IS.06.01.—	Tablet and fragments of case—sale of temple offices; sealed; BIN 7, 66 (C)
5319	No date	Letter to "my father" from Annum-pî-Ilabrat concerning disputed sale of slave; BIN 7, 44 (C)
5320	HARA.BA.34.06.—	Sale of house to partnership; sealed; BIN 7, 178 (C)
5321	RISI.LA.46.05.—	Sale of temple office; sealed; BIN 7, 169 (C)
5322	ZAMB.IS.A.04.—	Sale of improved residential property; sealed; BIN 7, 62 (C)
5323	No date	Letter to Šamaš-ḫāzir from Ḫammurabi concerning field; BIN 7, 4 (C)

NBC	Date	Description
5324	SAIL.BA.27.05.01	Legal case concerning sale of temple office; sealed
5325	DAIL.IS.13.03.—	Sale of improved residential property; sealed; BIN 7, 64 (C)
5326	DAIL.IS.A.04.—	Sale of reed field; sealed; BIN 7, 67 (C)
5327	SAIL.BA.23.05.15	Sale of uncultivated field
5328	RISI2.LA.03.09.10	Sale of temple office; sealed; BIN 7, 175 (C)
5329	No date	Tablet and case—letter to Išar-kubi from Lu-igisa concerning allotment field; sealed; BIN 7, 25 (C)
5330	SUEL.LA.12.12.—	Sale of vacant lot; sealed; BIN 7, 106 (C)
5331	No date	Letter to Lu-igisa from Nanna-mansum concerning seizure of silver; BIN 7, 31 (C)
5332	No date	Letter to Banum from Nūr-Sîn concerning sacrifice of sheep; YNER 4, no. 69 (C, T, Tr)
5333	SAIL.BA.12.03.07	Sale of improved residential property; sealed; BIN 7, 186 (C)
5334	SAIL.BA.11.08.—	Tablet and portion of case—sale of improved residential property; sealed; cf. NBC 5315
5335	NASI.ŠA.F.—.—	Tablet and portion of case—loan of silver; sealed; BIN 7, 83 (C)
5336	RISI.LA.59.08.—	Sale of girl; sealed; BIN 7, 173 (C)
5337	SUEL.LA.15.02.—	Ration list—barley; BIN 7, 112 (C)
5338	ABSA.LA.10.12.—	Tablet and case—receipt of barley tax; sealed; BIN 7, 97 (C)
5339	—.05.17	Fragmentary ration list—beer
5339A	No date?	Fragmentary ration list
5340	No date	Letter to Nūr-Sîn from Išar-kubi concerning corvée labor; YNER 4, no. 70 (C, T, Tr)
5341	DAIL.IS.C.03.—	Division of inheritance; sealed; BIN 7, 71 (C)
5342	No date	Letter to Banum and Ilum-nāṣir from Nūr-Sîn concerning wages; BIN 7, 49 (C)

NBC	Date	Description
5343	No date	Letter to Adad-tillatī from Lu-igisa concerning work crew; YNER 4, no. 54 (C, T, Tr)
5344	No date	Marriage agreement; sealed
5345	No date	Letter to Sîn-ni from Akatiya concerning field; BIN 7, 41 (C)
5346	No date	Letter to Šumi-ilišu and Šērum-ilī from Aplum concerning report; BIN 7, 37 (C)
5347	NASI.ŠA.I.—.—	Tablet and case—loan of barley; sealed; BIN 7, 72 (C); ENES 765
5348	SAIL.BA.04.12.05	Tablet and fragments of case—sale of improved residential property; sealed; BIN 7, 183 (C)
5349	DAIL.IS.01.03.—	Sale of uncultivated field; sealed; BIN 7, 63 (C)
5350	Lost?	Payments of barley; sealed
5351	RISI.LA.59.09.17	Sale of uncultivated field; sealed; BIN 7, 174 (C)
5352	ENBA.IS.F.03.—	Sale of field; sealed; BIN 7, 61 (C)
5353	SAIL.BA.16.09.12	Partnership agreement for cultivation of field; sealed; BIN 7, 191 (C)
5354	No date	Letter to Namram-šarūr and Sîn-imguranni from Gimil-Gula concerning field; BIN 7, 50 (C)
5355	AMSA.BA.15.12.06	Loan of slave-girl; sealed; BIN 7, 210 (C); ENES 1013
5356	RISI.LA.58.05.01	Sale of house, field, and orchard; sealed; BIN 7, 172 (C)
5357	Lost	Sale of temple offices; sealed; BIN 7, 214 (C)
5358	SAIL.BA.05.05.—	Loan of barley; sealed; BIN 7, 184 (C)
5359	DATA.NE..03.—.—	Tablet and portion of case—loan of barley; sealed; mu bàd dumu-a-ni ba-dù; BIN 7, 85 (C)
5360	SAIL.BA.27.12D.22	Loan of copper; sealed; BIN 7, 205 (C)
5361	SAIL.BA.24.10.23	Contract concerning production of bricks; sealed; BIN 7, 198 (C)
5362	No date	Letter to "my son" from Zu-ra-x-[...] concerning payment of barley or silver

NBC	Date	Description
5363	SAIL.BA.04.05.17	Sale of improved residential property; sealed; BIN 7, 181 (C)
5364	No date	Loan of barley and silver; BIN 7, 88 (C)
5365	SAIL.BA.24.06.08	Loan of barley; sealed; BIN 7, 199 (C)
5366	No date	Letter to Ibli-Eraḫ from Dumuzi-sumu concerning distrainee
5367	NASI.ŠA.B.—.—	Loan of barley; BIN 7, 80 (C)
5368	NASI.ŠA.F.—.—	Loan of barley and silver; BIN 7, 84 (C)
5369	HARA.BA.40.07.23	Receipt of barley
5370	No date?	List of PNs and quantities of silver(?)
5371	No date	Loan of silver; BIN 7, 89 (C)
5372	xx.—.—	Loan of barley; mu uš-ša-x(-)[...]; BIN 7, 90 (C)
5373	NASI.ŠA.J.03.—	Tablet and fragments of case—loan of barley; sealed; BIN 7, 75 (C)
5374	No date	Tablet and fragments of case—loan of barley; sealed; BIN 7, 91 (C)
5375	No date	List of PNs and quantities of silver; list of PNs and numbers of harvest workers
5376	NASI.ŠA.F.—.—	Loan of barley and silver; BIN 7, 78 (C)
5377	No date	Letter to Gidānum from Erissum-mātum concerning payment; BIN 7, 58 (C)
5379	No date	Letter to Lipit-Irra from Nūriya concerning slave-girls; YNER 4, no. 76 (C, T, Tr)
5380	No date	Letter to Šū-Tišpak and Šamaš-gāmil from Puzriya concerning cultivation of sesame; BIN 7, 57 (C)
5381	—.12.—	Disbursement of barley over three months; ITIKi-in-kum; BIN 7, 92 (C)
5382	DATA.NE.03.—.—	Tablet and fragments of case—loan of barley and silver; sealed; BIN 7, 86 (C); ENES 730
5383	NASI.ŠA.F.—.—	Tablet and portion of case—loan of silver; sealed; BIN 7, 79 (C)

NBC	Date	Description
5384	No date	List of property—slave-girl, field, small cattle,
5385	SAIL.BA.27.11.04	Loan of barley and silver; sealed; BIN 7, 203 (C)
5386	NASI.ŠA.E.—.—	Loan of barley and silver; BIN 7, 81 (C)
5387	RISI.LA.09.07.—	Loan of barley; sealed; BIN 7, 164 (C)
5388	NASI.ŠA.I.—.—	Loan of barley; BIN 7, 73 (C)
5389	No date	List of PNs and quantities of silver
5390	RISI.LA.09.07.—	Tablet and fragments of case—loan of barley; sealed; BIN 7, 165 (C)
5391	SAIL.BA.26.10.18	Hire of teams of oxen; sealed; BIN 7, 201 (C)
5392	SAIL.BA.11.05.20?	Hire of harvest workers; sealed; BIN 7, 185 (C)
5393	No date	Ration list—barley
5394	No date	Letter to Nūr-Sîn from Lu-igisa concerning distrainees; BIN 7, 24 (C)
5395	No date	Letter to Banum from Lu-igisa concerning small cattle; YNER 4, no. 57 (C, T, Tr)
5396	No date	Letter to Ilum-nāṣir from Lu-igisa concerning silver and wool as wages; BIN 7, 220 (C)
5397	No date	Letter to Ṭaridum from Irra-bāni concerning arrears; BIN 7, 39 (C)
5398	No date	Letter to Lu-igisa from Batūlum requesting assistance for third party; BIN 7, 32 (C)
5399	No date	Letter to Nūr-Sîn from Lu-igisa concerning large quantity of barley; YNER 4, no. 66 (C, T, Tr)
5400	No date	Letter to Lipit-Sîn from Lu-igisa concerning pasturage; BIN 7, 18 (C)
5401	No date	Letter to Lu-igisa from Nūr-Sîn concerning field; BIN 7, 20 (C)
5402	No date	Letter to Lu-igisa from Nūr-Sîn concerning detaining of soldiers/workers; BIN 7, 34 (C)
5403	NASI.ŠA.J.—.—	Tablet and case—loan of barley flour and silver; sealed; BIN 7, 76 (C)

NBC	Date	Description
5404	No date	Ration list
5405	No date?	Ration list—sesame and oil
5406	No date	Letter to Lu-igisa from Ku-Nanna concerning dispatch of third party; BIN 7, 26 (C)
5407	SAIL.BA.07.12.17	Loan of dates; sealed; cf. YBC 8681 = YOS 12, 237
5408	ABSA.LA.10.12.—	Receipt of barley tax; fingernail impressions; BIN 7, 94 (C)
5409	ABSA.LA.10.12.—	Receipt of barley tax; sealed; BIN 7, 96 (C)
5410	SUEL.LA.13.09.—	Delivery of earth; sealed; BIN 7, 108 (C)
5411	ABSA.LA.10.12.—	Receipt of barley tax; sealed; BIN 7, 95 (C)
5412	ABSA.LA.10.12.—	Receipt of barley tax; sealed; BIN 7, 98 (C)
5413	HARA.BA.42.06.01	Rental of field; sealed; BIN 7, 179 (C)
5414	xx.09.—	Sale of improved residential property; sealed
5415	SUEL.LA.06.07.19	Tag—record of workers; sealed; BIN 7, 135 (C)
5416	SUEL.LA.04.05.10	Tag—record of workers; sealed; BIN 7, 118 (C)
5417	SUEL.LA.06.10.09	Tag—record of workers; sealed; BIN 7, 128 (C)
5418	SUEL.LA.06.07.08	Tag—record of workers; sealed; BIN 7, 136 (C)
5419	SUEL.LA.14.08.—	Tag—receipt of fodder for oxen; sealed; BIN 7, 143 (C)
5420	SUEL.LA.15.08.—	Tag—receipt of fodder for oxen; sealed; BIN 7, 145 (C)
5421	SUEL.LA.15.04.17	Tag—receipt of fodder for sheep; BIN 7, 146 (C)
5422	SUEL.LA.03.08.01	Tag—record of workers; sealed; BIN 7, 115 (C)
5423	SUEL.LA.14.09.—	Tag—receipt of fodder for sheep; BIN 7, 139 (C)
5424	SUEL.LA.14.12.15	Tag—receipt of fodder for sheep; sealed; BIN 7, 140 (C)
5425	SUEL.LA.15.06.07	Tag—receipt of fodder for sheep; sealed; BIN 7, 144 (C)
5426	SUEL.LA.14.12.24	Tag—receipt of fodder for sheep; sealed; BIN 7, 141 (C)
5427	xx.09.10?	Loan (šu-lá) of silver; sealed

NBC	Date	Description
5428	ABSA.LA.10.12.—	Tablet and fragment of case—receipt of barley tax; sealed; BIN 7, 101 (C)
5431	SUEL.LA.04.06.02?	Tag—record of workers; sealed; BIN 7, 127 (C)
5432	SUEL.LA.06.07.22	Tag—record of workers; sealed; BIN 7, 129 (C)
5433	SUEL.LA.03.06.06	Tag—record of workers; sealed; BIN 7, 116 (C)
5434	SUEL.LA.04.06.10	Tag—record of workers; sealed; BIN 7, 119 (C)
5435	—.06.—	Tag—record of boats; sealed; BIN 7, 148 (C)
5436	SUEL.LA.06.06.28	Tag—record of workers; sealed; BIN 7, 137 (C)
5437	SUEL.LA.06.07.15	Tag—record of workers; sealed; BIN 7, 130 (C)
5438	SUEL.LA.04.06.11	Tag—record of workers; sealed; BIN 7, 120 (C)
5439	—.01.15	Tag—record of workers; sealed; BIN 7, 147 (C)
5440	SUEL.LA.06.10.06	Tag—record of workers; sealed; BIN 7, 131 (C)
5441	SUEL.LA.04.06.07	Tag—record of workers; sealed; BIN 7, 121 (C)
5442	SUEL.LA.06.07.05	Tag—record of workers; sealed; BIN 7, 132 (C)
5443	No date	Tag—seal impression only; BIN 7, 149 (C)
5444	SUEL.LA.06.07.12	Tag—record of workers; sealed; BIN 7, 133 (C)
5445	SUEL.LA.03.07.24	Tag—record of workers; sealed; BIN 7, 117 (C)
5446	SUEL.LA.06.07.24	Tag—record of workers; sealed; BIN 7, 134 (C)
5447	SUEL.LA.04.06.19	Tag—record of workers; sealed; BIN 7, 125 (C)
5448	SUEL.LA.04.06.20	Tag—record of workers; sealed; BIN 7, 122 (C)
5449	No date	Letter concerning obligations in barley; YNER 4, no. 77 (C, T, Tr)
5450	No date?	List of PNs and numbers of workers; list of PNs and quantities of silver
5451	No date	Letter to Mīnam-ēpuš-ilam from Inaṭṭal-ilī concerning slave-girl; BIN 7, 36 (C)
5453	HARA.BA.30.05.14	Legal case concerning house; sealed; BIN 7, 176 (C)
5454	RISI.LA.45.11.—	Sale of temple office; sealed; BIN 7, 167 (C)

NBC	Date	Description
5455	No date	Letter to Puzur-Šamaš from Nergal-nišu concerning field; BIN 7, 56 (C)
5456	AMSA.BA.13.12D.04	Sale of cow; sealed; BIN 7, 209 (C); ENES 1012x
5457	Lost	Sale of field; sealed
5458	SAIL.BA.23.03.01	Rental of field; sealed; BIN 7, 197 (C)
5459	DAIL.IS.A.05.—	Sale of uncultivated field; sealed; BIN 7, 70 (C)
5460	RISI.LA.07.06.—	Division of inheritance; sealed
5461	No date	Tablet and fragments of case—letter to La-[...] from Mušširu
5462	SUEL.LA.14.11.07	Record of number of workers assigned to supervisors; YNER 4, no. 111 (C, T)
5463	Illegible	Sale of house; sealed
5464	SUEL.LA.14.05.29	Record of number of workers assigned to supervisors of irrigation construction; BIN 7, 155 (C)
5465	No date	Letter to Lu-igisa from Bulalum concerning feeding of oxen; YNER 4, no. 63 (C, T, Tr)
5466	No date	Letter to Wuttur-dunnī from Aḫumma concerning trial for theft; YNER 4, no. 75 (C, T, Tr)
5467	NASI.ŠA.F.—.—	Tablet and portion of case—loan of silver; sealed; BIN 7, 87 (C)
5468	xx.02.—	Sale of real property
5469	ABSA.LA.10.12.—	Tablet and case—receipt of barley tax; sealed; BIN 7, 99 (C)
5470	No date	Receipt of various objects, mostly of wood or reed; BIN 7, 218 (C)
5471	SUEL.LA.10.12.—	Sale of vacant lot; sealed; BIN 7, 104 (C)
5472	No date	Letter to Šimat-Sîn from Ilī-apilšunu concerning activities of woman; BIN 7, 38 (C)
5473	SUEL.LA.14.09.—	Disbursement of sheep; BIN 7, 109 (C)
5474	SUEL.LA.14.07.—	Record of bricks for irrigation construction; BIN 7, 153 (C)

NBC	Date	Description
5476	No date	Tablet and case—letter to Warad-kubi from Lu-igisa concerning construction materials; sealed; BIN 7, 23 (C)
5477	SUEL.LA.12.—.—?	Ration list—barley; BIN 7, 150 (C)
5478	—.05.28	Ration list
5479	SUEL.LA.14.09.—	Disbursement of foodstuffs; BIN 7, 158 (C)
5480	SUEL.LA.14.05.—	Record of bricks; YNER 4, no. 112 (C, T)
5481	No date	Letter to Sîn-šemi from Ilī-iddina concerning cattle trade; BIN 7, 55 (C)
5482	No date	Letter to "my lord" from Irra-bāni concerning reassignment of fields; BIN 7, 45 (C)
5483	No date?	Ration list
5484	No date	Letter to Banum from Iku-pî-Sîn concerning maintenance of canals; BIN 7, 40 (C)
5485	No date	Letter to Nūr-Sîn from Lu-igisa concerning loan of barley; BIN 7, 28 (C)
5486	No date	Receipt of barley
5487	DAIL.IS.A.11.—	Sale of temple office; sealed; BIN 7, 68 (C)
5488	No date	Letter to Lu-igisa from Nūr-Sîn concerning hire of workers; BIN 7, 30 (C)
5489	No date	Letter to Nūr-Sîn from Lu-igisa concerning earth work; BIN 7, 35 (C)
5490	No date	Letter to Lu-igisa from Nabi-ilišu concerning silver, work obligation, and field; YNER 4, no. 65 (C, T, Tr)
5491	No date	Letter to Kubbutum and Narām-Adad from Tarīš-mātum requesting aid; BIN 7, 53 (C)
5492	SAIL.BA.21.07.01	Rental of field; sealed; BIN 7, 195 (C)
5493	SAIL.BA.23.12.—	Loan of silver to be repaid in barley; sealed; BIN 7, 196 (C)
5494	IQTI.ŠA.01.—.—	Loan of barley (ḫubuttātum); BIN 7, 82 (C)
5495	No date	Letter to Ṭaridum from Wuttur-dunnī concerning distrainees; BIN 7, 51 (C)

NBC	Date	Description
5496	No date	Letter to Lu-igisa from Aḫum concerning welfare of dependant; BIN 7, 22 (C)
5497	No date	Letter to Šamaš-nāṣir from Ḫāzirum concerning shipment of bag and silver; BIN 7, 52 (C)
5498	NASI.ŠA.F.—.—	Loan of barley and silver; BIN 7, 77 (C)
5499	NASI.ŠA.I.—.—	Tablet and fragments of case—loan of barley and silver; sealed; BIN 7, 74 (C)
5500	SUEL.LA.04.08.—	Receipt; sealed; BIN 7, 126 (C); ENES 751
5501	SUEL.LA.13.12D.—	Receipt of small cattle; BIN 7, 107 (C)
5502	SUEL.LA.03.05.—	Record of workers; sealed; BIN 7, 103 (C)
5503	SUEL.LA.01.07.—	Tag—record of workers; sealed; BIN 7, 114 (C)
5504	SUEL.LA.14.07.—	Record of numbers of workers assigned to supervisors of irrigation construction; BIN 7, 154 (C)
5505	No date	Letter to Irra-qarrād from Lu-igisa concerning earth work; BIN 7, 33 (C)
5506	SUEL.LA.14.11.—	Record of corvée due from various holdings; BIN 7, 110 (C)
5507	No date	List of supervisors of canal workers; YNER 4, no. 94 (C, T)
5508	No date	Receipt of silver and barley flour; YNER 4, no. 96 (C, T, Tr)
5509	SUEL.LA.15.08.—	Loan of barley; BIN 7, 160 (C)
5510	ABSA.LA.10.12.—	Receipt of barley tax; BIN 7, 102 (C)
5511	RISI.LA.47.07.26	Tablet and fragments of case—receipt of ram; sealed
5512	SUEL.LA.16.02.—	Decision of king concerning workers; sealed; BIN 7, 161 (C)
5513	ENBA.IS.C.12D.—	Sale of field; sealed; BIN 7, 215 (C)
5514	RISI.LA.05.03.—?	Sale of empty lot
5515	Lost?	Fragmentary dissolution of adoption; cf. NBC 5516, 6314, 9047, 9436, 9452, and 10089

NBC	Date	Description
5516	No date	Legal case; joined with NBC 5430; cf NBC 5515
5517	SUEL.LA.14.07.—	Receipt of barley; BIN 7, 151 (C)
5518	SUEL.LA.04.05.27	Tag—record of workers; sealed; BIN 7, 123 (C)
5519	SUEL.LA.07.06.29	Tag—record of workers; sealed; BIN 7, 138 (C)
5520	SUEL.LA.04.06.08	Tag—record of workers; sealed; BIN 7, 124 (C)
5521	SUEL.LA.14.07.24	Record of number of workers assigned to supervisors of irrigation construction; cf. NBC 6352; BIN 7, 156 (C)
5522	SUEL.LA.12.08.—	Disbursement of silver; BIN 7, 152 (C)
5523	SUEL.LA.16.02.03	Disbursement of foodstuffs; BIN 7, 113 (C)
5524	—.04.07	Economic record of uncertain character—only date preserved
5525	No date	Record of large quantities of barley; YNER 4, no. 13 (C, T)
5526	No date	Record of numbers of workers; BIN 7, 216 (C)
5527	No date	Letter to Lu-igisa from Banum concerning dispatch of sheep; BIN 7, 21 (C)
5528	ABSA.LA.10.12.—	Record of barley tax; sealed; BIN 7, 100 (C)
5529	SUEL.LA.14.12D.—	Record of barley for entire year; BIN 7, 111 (C)
5530	No date	Ration list—oil
5531	RISI.LA.25.07.18	Payment of sesame
5532	SAIL.BA.27.10.10	Loan of silver; sealed; BIN 7, 202 (C)
5533	NUAD.LA.B.09.—	Loan of wool to be repaid in silver; sealed; BIN 7, 162 (C)
5534	SAIL.BA.24.06.21	Loan of silver to be repaid in barley; sealed; BIN 7, 200 (C)
5535	xx.07.—	Sale of field; sealed
5536	No date	Ration list—beer
5537	Lost	Sale of improved residential property; sealed; BIN 7, 212 (C)
5538	Lost	Sale of improved residential property; sealed; BIN 7, 213 (C)

NBC	Date	Description
5539	No date	Disbursement of barley; BIN 7, 217 (C)
5540	SAIL.BA.19.04.16?	Rental of temple office; sealed; BIN 7, 193 (C)
5541	SAIL.BA.15.05.07	Payment of silver; sealed; BIN 7, 189 (C)
5542	No date	List of PNs and areas of real property
5544	xx.12.—	Promissory note—silver; mu-ús-sa ...
5546	No date	Ration list—barley
5547	SUEL.LA.14.08.—	Tag—receipt of fodder for sheep; sealed; BIN 7, 142 (C)
5549	SUEL.LA.14.04.08	Record of beams for irrigation construction; BIN 7, 157 (C)
5550	No date	Letter to Lu-igisa from Alā concerning bran; YNER 4, no. 58 (C, T, Tr)
5551	No date	Letter to Lu-igisa from Išar-kubi concerning earth work; BIN 7, 15 (C)
5552	No date	Letter to Šumi-aḫiya from Irra-bāni concerning forwarding of documents to king; BIN 7, 46 (C)
5553	No date	Tablet and portion of case—letter to Puzur-Amurrum and Ḫabdiya from Šamaš-ḫāzir concerning pasturing of small cattle; BIN 7, 54 (C)
5554	No date	Letter to Lu-igisa from Nūr-Sîn concerning absent worker; BIN 7, 19 (C)
5555	No date	Letter to Lu-igisa from Išar-kubi concerning distrainee; BIN 7, 14 (C)
5556	No date	Letter to Lu-igisa from Nūr-Sîn concerning excavation of canal; BIN 7, 17 (C)
5557	No date	Letter to Banum from Nārum-rabi concerning misappropriation of funds; BIN 7, 48 (C)
5558	No date	Letter to Banum from Lu-igisa concerning diversion of provisions; YNER 4, no. 64 (C, T, Tr)
5559	No date	Letter to Lu-igisa from Išar-kubi concerning hire of harvest workers; BIN 7, 16 (C)
5560	No date	Letter to Lu-igisa from Šumi-aḫiya concerning neglected labor obligation; BIN 7, 29 (C)

NBC	Date	Description
5561	No date	Letter to Lu-igisa from Šū-Nana concerning distrainees; YNER 4, no. 43 (C, T, Tr)
5562	SUEL.LA.14.12.11?	Record of bricks for irrigation construction; BIN 7, 159 (C)
5563	xx.04.—	Testament; sealed
5564	SAIL.BA.27.12.14	Hire of teams of oxen; sealed; BIN 7, 204 (C)
5565	SAIL.BA.16.06.16	Hire of teams of oxen; sealed; BIN 7, 192 (C)
5566	SUEL.LA.12.—.—	List of PNs and quantities of silver and bricks(?); BIN 7, 105 (C)
5567	SAIL.BA.10.12.—	Sale of house; sealed
5568	SAIL.BA.17.12.14	Sale of field
5569	SAIL.BA.35.06.05?	Adoption; sealed; BIN 7, 206 (C)
5570	WASI.LA.04.01.—	Adoption; sealed; BIN 7, 163 (C)
5571	SAIL.BA.12.10.01	Adoption of woman; sealed; BIN 7, 187 (C)
5572	ABSA.LA.07.12D.—	Legal case; sealed; BIN 7, 93 (C)
5573	SAIL.BA.14.07.23	Sale of temple office; sealed; BIN 7, 188 (C)
5574	HARA.BA.10.—.—	Legal case concerning silver; sealed; mu uru^{ki} á-dam sig$_4$^{ki}
5575	AMSA.BA.10.05.20	Sale of ox; sealed; BIN 7, 207 (C); ENES 1009x
5576	SAIL.BA.03.07.22	Account of barley; BIN 7, 180 (C)
5577	LIEN.IS.B.04.—	Sale of field; sealed; BIN 7, 60 (C)
5578	SAIL.BA.20.08.01	Rental of field; sealed; BIN 7, 194 (C)
5579	No date	Receipt of barley
5580	LIEN.IS.B.04.10	Sale of field; sealed; BIN 7, 59 (C)
5602	IŠIR.IS.13.05.11	Delivery of leather, glue, and bitumen; BIN 9, 27 (C)
5603	IŠIR.IS.33.01.24	Disbursement of glue, leather, and bags; BIN 9, 199 (C)
5604	RISI.LA.08.12.—	Bulla—record concerning small cattle(?)
5608	IŠIR.IS.28.07.—	Receipt of wool; BIN 10, 42 (C)

NBC	Date	Description
5609	IŠIR.IS.13.08.—	Disbursement of reed mats for chairs; BIN 9, 480 (C)
5617	IŠIR.IS.15.—.—	Disbursement of wooden utensils; sealed; BIN 10, 124 (C)
5618	IŠIR.IS.14.09.22	Disbursement of bags and leather; BIN 9, 273 (C)
5619	IŠIR.IS.14.07.22	List of workers; BIN 10, 259 (C)
5620	IŠIR.IS.09.10.—	Delivery of glue; BIN 9, 132 (C)
5621	IŠIR.IS.19.03.05	Disbursement of leather; BIN 9, 244 (C)
5622	IŠIR.IS.14.07.06	List of workers; BIN 10, 258 (C)
5623	IŠIR.IS.15.09.29	List of workers; BIN 10, 268 (C)
5624	IŠIR.IS.15.01.19	List of workers; BIN 10, 264 (C)
5625	IŠIR.IS.14.01.20	Disbursement of bags for letters; BIN 9, 302 (C)
5626	IŠIR.IS.20.01.—	Delivery of hides and skins; BIN 9, 6 (C)
5627	IŠIR.IS.14.03.16	Disbursement of leather; BIN 9, 243 (C)
5628	IŠIR.IS.18.03.—	Receipt of skins; BIN 9, 54 (C)
5629	IŠIR.IS.18.01.03	Receipt of bitumen; BIN 10, 19 (C)
5630	IŠIR.IS.17.12.—	Receipt of bitumen; BIN 10, 18 (C)
5631	IŠIR.IS.06.03.—	Delivery of wood; BIN 10, 88 (C)
5632	IŠIR.IS.24.06.07	Receipt of wool; BIN 10, 35 (C)
5633	IŠIR.IS.22.11.01	Receipt of hides; BIN 9, 20 (C)
5634	IŠIR.IS.30.02.—	Receipt of hides; BIN 9, 19 (C)
5635	ŠUIL.IS.01.09.11	Disbursement of glue and gypsum; BIN 9, 260 (C)
5636	IŠIR.IS.16.12.—	Disbursement of leather; BIN 9, 235 (C)
5637	IŠIR.IS.21.04.04	Disbursement of glue; BIN 9, 456 (C)
5638	IŠIR.IS.22.02.—	Delivery of pomegranate products; BIN 10, 24 (C)
5639	UN.IS.B.06.—	Loan of silver; sealed; mu ^{id}ur-sag-gal-zu mu-un-ba-al
5640	SUEL.LA.09.06.—	Receipt of cattle
5641	IŠIR.IS.23.04.06	Disbursement of skins and bags; sealed; BIN 9, 363

NBC	Date	Description
5642	IŠIR.IS.25.02.—	Receipt of wool; sealed; BIN 9, 501 (C)
5643	IŠIR.IS.07.07.04	List of workers; BIN 10, 210 (C)
5644	SIID.LA.06.07.07	Receipt of dates and barley; Hallo, JCS 21, 1967, p. 95 (Tr)
5645	IŠIR.IS.19.06.07	Disbursement of bitumen for repair of boats; sealed; BIN 10, 129 (C)
5646	UN.EŠ.AB.11.—	Loan of barley; sealed; mu-ús-sa má-gur$_8$ mah ^{d}Nanna ba-dím
5647	IŠIR.IS.33.03.11	Disbursement of door; BIN 9, 349 (C)
5648	IŠIR.IS.22.01.—	Disbursement of doors and their fittings; BIN 9, 442 (C)
5649	IŠIR.IS.28.12.—	Receipt of wool; BIN 10, 43 (C)
5650	IŠIR.IS.12.04.—	Disbursement of wooden object; BIN 9, 494 (C)
5651	IŠIR.IS.08.12D.08	List of workers; BIN 19, 229 (C)
5653	IŠIR.IS.09.11.—	Disbursement of skins, leather, reed mats, thread, and bitumen; BIN 9, 332 (C)
5654	IŠIR.IS.17.05.17	List of workers; BIN 10, 272 (C)
5655	IŠIR.IS.08.—.—	Disbursement of hides; BIN 9, 331 (C)
5656	IŠIR.IS.21.06.—	Receipt of skins; BIN 9, 8 (C)
5657	IŠIR.IS.25.08.—	Receipt of various leather objects for (re-)gluing; BIN 9, 106 (C)
5663	IŠIR.IS.17.04.17	Disbursement of leather; BIN 9, 175 (C)
5664	ŠUIL.IS.02.06.21	Disbursement of bags; BIN 9, 230 (C)
5665	IŠIR.IS.05.08.—	Disbursement of glue; BIN 9, 145 (C)
5666	IŠIR.IS.16.01.09	Receipt of hides; BIN 9, 69 (C)
5667	IŠIR.IS.22.01.01	Receipt of hides; BIN 9, 11 (C)
5669	IŠIR.IS.12.12.10	Disbursement of flutes and reed containers; BIN 10, 103 (C)
5670	IŠIR.IS.17.12D.01	Disbursement of leather; BIN 9, 170 (C)
5671	IŠIR.IS.16.06.28	Receipt of leather; BIN 10, 13 (C)

NBC	Date	Description
5672	RISI.LA.30.04.05	Disbursement of foodstuff; mu Ì-si-i-in^{ki}
5673	IŠIR.IS.13.02.11	Disbursement of bag and skins; BIN 9, 274 (C)
5674	IŠIR.IS.23.04.—	Disbursement of leather; BIN 9, 468 (C)
5675	IŠIR.IS.13.07.13	Disbursement of vessels; BIN 9, 320 (C)
5676	IŠIR.IS.17.04.—	Disbursement of leather; BIN 9, 171 (C)
5677	IŠIR.IS.15.10.—	Disbursement of leather; BIN 9, 186 (C)
5678	IŠIR.IS.13.04.23	Disbursement of leather; BIN 9, 237 (C)
5679	IŠIR.IS.20.07.17	Receipt of hides and skins; BIN 9, 5 (C)
5680	IŠIR.IS.12.10.—	Disbursement of chair; BIN 9, 340 (C)
5681	IŠIR.IS.15.03.16	Disbursement of bags; BIN 9, 277 (C)
5682	IŠIR.IS.16.12.—	Disbursement of bitumen; BIN 9, 465 (C)
5683	IŠIR.IS.13.04.11	Disbursement of skin; BIN 9, 330 (C)
5684	IŠIR.IS.13.08.—	Disbursement of musical instruments; BIN 9, 352 (C)
5685	IŠIR.IS.13.10.13	Disbursement of reed mat; BIN 9, 358 (C)
5686	IŠIR.IS.13.08.—	Disbursement of hides; BIN 9, 464 (C)
5687	IŠIR.IS.13.05.10	Disbursement of leather; BIN 9, 256 (C)
5688	IŠIR.IS.09.09.26	List of workers; BIN 10, 234 (C)
5774	IŠIR.IS.13.02.10	Disbursement of leather and glue; BIN 9, 372 (C)
5983	No date	Cylinder—record of wool
6252	xx.12.xx	Ration list—beer
6253	SAIL.BA.07.03.27	Ration list—beer
6254	No date	Letter to Marduk-muballiṭ from Unnubtum concerning garments
6255	—.03.—	List of PNs and commodities measured in gín
6256	SUEL.LA.13.08.—	Ration list—barley and fodder; YOS 14, 244 (C)
6257	No date	Draft of seal inscription; Beckman, NABU 1988/72

NBC	Date	Description
6258	SUEL.LA.14.05.—	List of workers
6259	—.01.—	Ration list
6260	—.—.08	List of workers
6261	SAIL.BA.04.07.23	Record concerning registration of transactions in barley; sealed
6262	No date	Ration list—barley
6263	UN.EŠ.AB.08.—	Loan of barley; sealed; mu-ús-sa má-gur$_8$ maḫ ^{د}Nanna ba-dù
6264	No date	Letter to Marduk-muballiṭ from Saggil-mansum concerning field
6265	No date	Ration list
6266	—.01.23	Receipt of harvest workers(?)
6267	No date	Letter to Ilī-u-Šamaš from Dummuq-Marduk concerning silver
6268	No date	Letter to Nūr-Sîn from Ipquša concerning field and labor obligation; YNER 4, no. 35 (C, T, Tr)
6269	No date	Letter to Marduk-dayyān from Etel-pî-Marduk concerning dispute over dates
6270	No date	Letter to Marduk-muballiṭ from Saggil-mansum concerning field
6271	No date	Ration list—beer; cf. NBC 6274
6272	No date	Letter to Sîn-eribam, Sîn-iddinam, and Marduk-nāṣir from Ibni-^{d}BU concerning shipment of barley; cf. NBC 6289
6273	No date	Letter to the overseers of the Amorites from Lipit-Ištar concerning contingent of men
6274	No date	Ration list—beer; cf. NBC 6271
6275	No date	Record of workers assigned to supervisors; YNER 4, no. 114 (C, T)
6276	No date	Letter to Marduk-muballiṭ from Unnubtum concerning shipment of garments

NBC	Date	Description
6277	No date	Letter to "the man whom Gula and Marduk preserve" from Sîn-imguranni concerning dispute
6278	No date	Letter from the *kārum* of Isin to their overseer concerning legal case
6279	No date	Payment for workers; YNER 4, no. 27 (C, T)
6280	No date	Fragmentary letter concerning silver
6280A	No date	Fragmentary letter to Marduk-muballiṭ from Saggil-mansum concerning shipment of agricultural product
6281	SUEL.LA.04.06.—	Record of workers for two months
6282	No date	Letter to Itḫiya from Išme-Sîn concerning bricks
6283	SUEL.LA.14.11.29	Record of bricks for irrigation construction; YNER 4, no. 109 (C, T)
6284	No date	Letter to Ilī-u-Šamaš from Bēlšunu concerning field
6285	No date	Ration list—oil
6286	Lost?	Account of silver, dates, barley, and emmer
6287	No date	Letter to "the overseer" from Aḫī-wēdim concerning boat
6288	—.—.06?	Disbursement of beer, oil, and barley
6289	No date	Letter to Sîn-iddinam, Marduk-nāṣir, and Sîn-iqīšam from Nanna-mansum concerning sale of barley; cf. NBC 6272
6290	SAIL.BA.08.—.—	Letter to Marduk-muballiṭ from Saggil-mansum concerning records; year in context
6291	ABSA.LA.10.12.—	Receipt of barley tax; sealed; YNER 4, no. 15 (C, T)
6292	SUEL.LA.04.06.—	Receipt of sesame; sealed; YNER 4, no. 80 (C, T)
6293	ABSA.LA.11.12.—	Payment of silver; sealed; YNER 4, no. 17 (C, T, Tr)
6294	No date	List of numerals and PNs
6295	—.04.08	Record of number of workers assigned to supervisors; YNER 4, no. 107 (C, T)

NBC	Date	Description
6296	ABSA.LA.10.12.—	Tablet and fragment of case—receipt of barley tax; sealed; YNER 4, no. 16 (C, T)
6297	SUEL.LA.13.12.—	Receipt of silver by nine persons; sealed; YNER 4, no. 95 (C, T, Tr)
6298	ABSA.LA.10.12.—	Receipt of barley tax; YNER 4, no. 9 (C, T)
6299	No date	Record of corvée due; YNER 4, no. 97 (C, T)
6300	SUEL.LA.17.11.—	Receipt and disbursement of large cattle; YNER 4, no. 25 (C, T)
6301	No date	Letter to "the man whom Marduk preserves" from Awīl-Sîn concerning return of property
6302	xx.07.20+	Sale of house; sealed
6303	SUEL.LA.14.08.13	Record of number of workers assigned to supervisors of irrigation construction; YNER 4, no. 108 (C, T)
6304	SUEL.LA.14.11.—?	Disbursement of foodstuffs; YNER 4, no. 84 (C, T, Tr)
6305	AMDI.BA.26.08.22	Rental of field; sealed; YOS 13, 369 (C)
6306	No date	Letter to Marduk-muballiṭ from Saggil-mansum concerning servants
6307	No date	Letter to Nadān-Marduk-rabi and Marduk-iddinam from Maratum concerning maintenance of field
6308	No date	Letter to Marduk-muballiṭ from Saggil-mansum concerning dispatch of third party
6309	No date	Letter to Marduk-muballiṭ from Nidin-Ištar concerning sale of Elamite slaves
6309A	No date	Three letter fragments
6310	No date	Letter to Marduk-muballiṭ from Unnubtum concerning business in the palace and shipment of garments
6311	No date	Letter to "the man whom Marduk preserves" from Awīl-Sîn concerning dispute over produce of field
6312	No date	Letter to Marduk-muballiṭ from Saggil-mansum concerning division of barley

NBC	Date	Description
6313	No date	Letter to Marduk-muballiṭ from Saggil-mansum concerning shipment of livestock and distrainees; BIN 7, 223 (C)
6314	No date	Adoption of slave; cf. NBC 5515
6315	No date	Rental of field
6316	No date	Loan (ḫubuttātum) of barley; YOS 14, 52 (C)
6317	RISI.LA.28.??.—	Account of sesame; ^{iti}udra ki-9
6318	SUAB.BA.01.11.—	Loan (ḫubuttātum) of silver and barley; sealed
6319	No date	"Dowry" of qadištum priestess
6320	No date	Letter to Marduk-muballiṭ from Saggil-mansum concerning legal case
6322	SUEL.LA.17.10.—	Account of grain; YOS 14, 257 (C)
6323	SUEL.LA.17.05.—	Account of grain; YOS 14, 256 (C)
6324	SAIL.BA.19.10.22	Receipt of implements; sealed; mu ^{giš}gu-za bara$_2$ kù-sig$_{17}$ 2-bi; cf. NBC 6325
6325	SAIL.BA.19.07.12	Receipt of implements; sealed; cf. NBC 6324
6326	—.06.—	Record of hired men; YNER 4, no. 28 (C, T)
6327	ABSA.LA.10.12.—	Receipt of barley tax; YNER 4, no. 12 (C, T)
6328	No date	Receipt of silver, barley, and beer
6329	SAIL.BA.24.10.21	Loan of silver to be repaid in barley; sealed
6330	No date	Letter to Alā from Lu-igisa concerning pea flour; YNER 4, no. 59 (C, T, Tr)
6331	ABSA.LA.10.12.—	Receipt of barley tax; YNER 4, no. 10 (C, T)
6332	No date	Letter to Urdukuga from Būr-Sîn concerning sustenance of third party
6333	SAIL.BA.21.04.01	Record concerning consumption of bran; sealed
6334	ABSA.LA.10.12.—	Receipt of barley tax; YNER 4, no. 13 (C, T)
6335	RISI.LA.50.03.—	Disbursement of small cattle; sealed
6336	IŠIR.IS.14.07.03	Disbursement of wooden cover; BIN 10, 116 (C)

NBC	Date	Description
6337	SAIL.BA.17.06.20	Hire of teams of oxen; sealed
6338	ENBA.IS.E.01.—	Division of inheritance; sealed
6339	SUEL.LA.14.07.02	Record of bricks and workers for irrigation construction; YNER 4, no. 101 (C, T)
6340	WASI.LA.09.09.xx	Sale of improved residential property; sealed
6341	RISI.LA.07.06.—	Sale of house; sealed
6342	No date	Letter to Narāmtum from Unnubtum concerning reception of third party at palace; BIN 7, 221 (C)
6345	No date	Disbursement of silver; YNER 4, no. 95 (C, T)
6346	No date	Letter to Marduk-muballiṭ from Saggil-mansum concerning shipment of flour; BIN 7, 222 (C)
6347	Illegible	Record of workers assigned to supervisors; YNER 4, no. 115 (C, T)
6348	SAIL.BA.07.10.19	Disbursement of fodder
6350	SAIL.BA.07.xx.10	Disbursement of beer and bran
6351	No date	Letter to Lu-igisa from Ilum-nāṣir concerning harvest labor; YNER 4, no. 49 (C, T, Tr)
6352	SUEL.LA.14.07.20	Record of number of workers assigned to supervisors of irrigation construction; cf. NBC 5521; YNER 4, no. 102 (C, T)
6353	No date	Letter to Adad-šarrum and Tarībatum from Mannašu concerning fish
6354	—.06.15	Record of sheep for temples of Sîn and Inanna
6355	IŠIR.IS.07.08.—	Receipt of hides; BIN 9, 110 (C)
6356	No date	Disbursement of skins; BIN 9, 261 (C)
6357	IŠIR.IS.21.04.—	Letter ordering disbursement of glue; sealed; BIN 9, 486 (C)
6358	IŠIR.IS.13.07.—	Disbursement of reed tables; BIN 10, 108 (C)
6360	IŠIR.IS.19.06.—	Receipt of hides to wrap skins; BIN 9, 114 (C)
6361	IŠIR.IS.14.06.03	List of workers; BIN 10, 255 (C)

NBC	Date	Description
6362	IŠIR.IS.14.12.18	List of workers; BIN 10, 262 (C)
6363	IŠIR.IS.16.01.—	Disbursement of wool; BIN 9, 526 (C)
6364	IŠIR.IS.10.07.28	Disbursement of *zamītum*-instruments; BIN 9, 38 (C)
6365	IŠIR.IS.22.03.11	Disbursement of rope; BIN 10, 136 (C)
6366	IŠIR.IS.26.05.28	Disbursement of bags and leather; BIN 9, 400 (C)
6367	IŠIR.IS.07.01.—	Disbursement of bitumen; BIN 9, 516 (C)
6368	IŠIR.IS.12.09.—	Receipt of hides and skins; BIN 9, 41 (C)
6369	IŠIR.IS.15.02.28	List of workers; BIN 10, 265 (C)
6370	IŠIR.IS.22.04.16	Disbursement of bitumen; BIN 10, 138 (C)
6371	IŠIR.IS.23.12.—	Receipt of hides and skins; BIN 9, 91 (C)
6372	IŠIR.IS.25.07.—	Disbursement of wool; sealed; BIN 10, 69 (C)
6373	IŠIR.IS.14.03.04	Disbursement of sandals; BIN 9, 427 (C)
6374	IŠIR.IS.13.06.17	Receipt of bitumen and wool; BIN 10, 106 (C)
6375	RISI.LA.32+.11.—	Promissory note—foodstuff
6376	IŠIR.IS.25.04.24	Receipt of alum; BIN 9, 104 (C)
6377	IŠIR.IS.33.12D.25	Disbursement of leather bag; BIN 10, 165 (C)
6378	IŠIR.IS.23.10.—	Receipt of alum, gypsum, and madder; BIN 9, 80 (C)
6379	IŠIR.IS.23.11.—	Receipt of hides; BIN 9, 18 (C)
6381	IŠIR.IS.30.02.—	Receipt of hides and skins; BIN 9, 21 (C)
6382	IŠIR.IS.25.08.—	Receipt of skins and hides; BIN 10, 39 (C)
6383	IŠIR.IS.23.09.—	Receipt of hides and skins; BIN 9, 96 (C)
6384	IŠIR.IS.19.02.17	Disbursement of mattress; BIN 9, 351 (C)
6385	IŠIR.IS.19.02.17	Disbursement of bags; BIN 9, 216 (C)
6386	IŠIR.IS.06.06.—	Disbursement of glue; BIN 10, 90 (C)
6387	IŠIR.IS.10.06.26	List of workers; BIN 10, 239 (C)

NBC	Date	Description
6388	IŠIR.IS.22.03.12	Disbursement of bitumen, leather, and bags; dupl. NBC 6438; BIN 9, 376 (C)
6389	IŠIR.IS.16.04.—	Delivery of combed wool; BIN 9, 32 (C)
6390	IŠIR.IS.07.07.24	List of workers; BIN 10, 213 (C)
6391	IŠIR.IS.25.12.14?	Disbursement of bag and leather; BIN 9, 268 (C)
6393	IŠIR.IS.08.05.10	List of workers; BIN 10, 224 (C)
6394	IŠIR.IS.18.06.27	List of workers; BIN 9, 504 (C)
6395	IŠIR.IS.25.12.—	Receipt of hides and skins; BIN 9, 102 (C)
6396	SIIQ.LA.04.01.—	Loan (šu-lá?) of barley; sealed
6397	IŠIR.IS.21.09.26	List of workers; sealed; BIN 10, 274 (C)
6398	IŠIR.IS.14.12D.—	Receipt of hides and skins; BIN 9, 56 (C)
6399	IŠIR.IS.26.08.—	Receipt of skins; BIN 9, 100 (C)
6400	IŠIR.IS.14.06.10	Disbursement of bags; BIN 9, 276 (C)
6401	IŠIR.IS.24.09.—	Receipt of hides; BIN 9, 92 (C)
6402	IŠIR.IS.26.11.26	Disbursement of bags and leather; BIN 9, 275 (C)
6403	IŠIR.IS.25.03.—	Receipt of hides and skins; BIN 9, 42 (C)
6404	IŠIR.IS.19.12.—	Receipt of hides; BIN 9, 474 (C)
6405	IŠIR.IS.19.10.29	Disbursement of sandals; sealed; BIN 9, 422 (C)
6407	IŠIR.IS.16.06.—	Receipt of hides and skins; BIN 9, 87 (C)
6408	IŠIR.IS.21.06.17	Receipt of hides; BIN 9, 3 (C)
6409	IŠIR.IS.21.07.—	Receipt of skins; BIN 9, 9 (C)
6410	IŠIR.IS.21.05.—	Receipt of skins; BIN 9, 86 (C)
6411	IŠIR.IS.19.11.—	Receipt of alum and other leatherworking materials; BIN 9, 82 (C)
6412	IŠIR.IS.19.06.20	Disbursement of bags and bowls; dupl. NBC 7582; BIN 9, 403 (C)
6414	IŠIR.IS.08.05.09	List of workers; BIN 10, 223 (C)

NBC	Date	Description
6416	IŠDA.IS.N.07.03	Receipt of bran for fodder; sealed
6417	IŠIR.IS.19.08.—	Disbursement of hides; BIN 10, 68 (C)
6418	IDDA.IS.02.12.—	Economic record of uncertain character
6421	IŠIR.IS.28.01.—	Disbursement of hides for shields; sealed; BIN 9, 111 (C)
6422	IŠIR.IS.06.10.—	Disbursement of bitumen; BIN 10, 92 (C)
6423	IŠIR.IS.04.11.—	Receipt of hides and skins; BIN 9, 127 (C)
6424	IŠIR.IS.22.02.10	Disbursement of bitumen; BIN 10, 134 (C)
6425	IŠIR.IS.15.07.—	Disbursement of glue, skins, and bitumen; BIN 9, 262 (C)
6426	IŠIR.IS.25.xx.10	Disbursement of bags, containers, and sandals; sealed; BIN 9, 421 (C)
6427	SIID.LA.06.05.19	Account of foodstuffs and livestock; YOS 14, 286 (C)
6428	IŠIR.IS.09.08.23	List of workers; BIN 9, 533 (C)
6429	LIIŠ.IS.B.02.—	Letter to Ur-Ninurta concerning issue of barley and garments; sealed; YOS 14, 317 (C)
6430	LIIŠ.IS.A.11.14	Fragmentary list of animal offerings to various deities; YOS 14, 315 (C)
6431	IDDA.IS.A.04.—	Delivery of sheep; YOS 14, 313 (C)
6432	SIID.LA.06.11.26	List of groups of workers, their rations, and overseers; sealed; YOS 14, 291 (C)
6433	SIID.LA.07.01.01	Ration list—barley; YOS 14, 292 (C)
6435	IŠIR.IS.25.03.15	Disbursement of bags for tablets; BIN 9, 413 (C)
6436	IŠIR.IS.06.08.—	Disbursement of wool; BIN 10, 91 (C)
6438	IŠIR.IS.22.03.12	Disbursement of bitumen, leather, and bags; dupl. NBC 6388; BIN 9, 377 (C)
6439	IŠIR.IS.09.10.26	Disbursement of lyre, bags, leather, and reed container; BIN 9, 441 (C)
6440	IŠIR.IS.33.03.05	Disbursement of bags; BIN 9, 224 (C)
6441	IŠIR.IS.07.—.—	Delivery of glue; BIN 9, 130 (C)
6442	IŠIR.IS.07.07.06	List of workers; BIN 10, 211 (C)

NBC	Date	Description
6443	IŠIR.IS.22.01.29	Disbursement of chariot part; BIN 9, 446 (C)
6444	IŠIR.IS.17.—.—	List of workers paid per month; BIN 9, 495 (C)
6445	IŠIR.IS.10.02.06	Disbursement of doors, bags, and leather; sealed; BIN 9, 345 (C)
6446	IŠIR.IS.16.10.07	List of workers; BIN 10, 271 (C)
6447	IŠIR.IS.25.02.03	Disbursement of various commodities; BIN 10, 153 (C)
6448	—.10.10	List of workers; BIN 10, 291 (C)
6449	UN.UN.AQ.06.23	Account of barley; mu alam(?) DU
6450	IŠIR.IS.11.07.17	List of workers; BIN 10, 244 (C)
6451	SIMA.IS.A.03.—	Division of inherited temple office; sealed; YOS 14, 328 (C)
6452	IŠIR.IS.22.03.—	Receipt of hides; BIN 9, 1 (C)
6453	IŠIR.IS.09.08.—	Disbursement of materials for royal shoes; BIN 9, 385 (C)
6454	IŠIR.IS.22.10.03	Disbursement of thread; BIN 10, 140 (C)
6455	—.—.08	Disbursement of foodstuff
6456	No date	Disbursement of oil
6459	IŠIR.IS.25.06.—	Disbursement of bags; BIN 9, 278 (C)
6460	Lost	Receipt of hides and skins; BIN 9, 45 (C)
6461	IŠIR.IS.13.11.—	Receipt of reed containers; BIN 10, 8 (C)
6462	—.01.—	Receipt of hides and skins; BIN 9, 55 (C)
6463	IŠIR.IS.22.11.01	Receipt of skins; BIN 9, 22 (C)
6466	SAIL.BA.20.08.02	Tag—label for tablet basket
6469	IŠIR.IS.20.02.—	Disbursement of oil; BIN 9, 512 (C)
6470	IŠIR.IS.22.04.—	Receipt of hides; BIN 9, 2 (C)
6471	No date	Delivery of glue; BIN 9, 135 (C)
6472	ŠUIL.IS.01.04.10	Disbursement of glue and flour; BIN 9, 191 (C)
6473	IŠIR.IS.17.09.08	Receipt of bitumen; BIN 10, 16 (C)

NBC	Date	Description
6474	IŠIR.IS.17.09.05	Receipt of bitumen; BIN 9, 493 (C)
6475	IŠIR.IS.13.05.14	Disbursement of bags and leather; BIN 9, 279 (C)
6476	IŠIR.IS.13.08.—	Disbursement of bitumen; BIN 10, 109 (C)
6477	IŠIR.IS.13.05.24	List of workers; BIN 10, 247 (C)
6479	IŠIR.IS.22.05.—	Receipt of bitumen; BIN 10, 28 (C)
6480	IŠIR.IS.22.06.08	Disbursement of leather; BIN 9, 200 (C)
6482	IŠIR.IS.18.xx.16	Receipt of bitumen; BIN 10, 20 (C)
6483	IŠIR.IS.14.xx.09	Disbursement of bags; BIN 9, 284 (C)
6484	—.08.08	Disbursement of beer
6485	No date	Basket tag(?)—inventory of stones(?); BIN 9, 487 (C)
6486	—.06.05	Disbursement of leather; BIN 9, 180 (C)
6487	—.10.04	Disbursement of glue; BIN 10, 176 (C)
6488	IDDA.IS.09.02.—	Disbursement of beer
6489	—.12D.24	Receipt of wool; BIN 9, 481 (C)
6491	IŠIR.IS.13.04.—	Receipt of skins; BIN 9, 66 (C)
6493	DABA.IS.A.—.—	Sale of field; sealed; mu Da-ad-ba-na-a lugal-e ba-ug$_6$-a
6494	NUAD.LA.I.10.29	Tag—account of large cattle; sealed
6495	NUAD.LA.I.04.—	Delivery of barley
6496	LIIŠ.IS.01.—.—	Economic record of uncertain character
6497	IŠDA.IS.I.09.14	Record concerning fattened sheep
6498	IDDA.IS.09.12.—	Record of dates for temple
6499	IŠDA.IS.H.07.02	Disbursement; sealed
6505	IŠIR.IS.21.05.30	Disbursement of wooden and reed objects; dupl. NBC 6513; BIN 9, 449 (C)
6506	URDU.IS.B.09.—	Sale of uncultivated field; sealed; YOS 14, 327 (C)

NBC	Date	Description
6507	IŠDA.IS.N.07.01	Fragmentary receipt of barley flour for regular offerings for priestess of Ninurta; YOS 14, 312 (C)
6508	IŠIR.IS.23.03.15	Disbursement of bags and leather; BIN 9, 281 (C)
6509	LIIŠ.IS.A.05.30	Record concerning beer
6510	ITPI.IS.01.08.—	Sale of temple offices; sealed; YOS 14, 326 (C)
6511	RISI.LA.09.07.—	Tablet and case—loan of barley; sealed
6512	DAIL.IS.A.01.—	Sale of improved residential property; sealed; BIN 7, 69 (C)
6513	IŠIR.IS.21.05.30	Disbursement of wooden and reed objects; sealed; dupl. NBC 6505; BIN 9, 448 (C)
6521	IŠIR.IS.23.03.—	Receipt of hides and skins; BIN 9, 101 (C)
6522	IŠIR.IS.23.07.—	Receipt of hides and skins; BIN 9, 98 (C)
6523	IDDA.IS.xx.02.—	Receipt of barley; sealed
6524	IŠIR.IS.15.—.—	Disbursement of bags; BIN 9, 389 (C)
6727	ABSA.LA.11.03.—	Tag—delivery of beer for *naptanum*; sealed
6745	No date	Ration list
6746	RISI.LA.06.08.—	Account of hides (ledger)
6747	SIER.LA.01.10.27	Tablet and case—guarantee of debt; sealed; YOS 14, 299 (C); ENES 761xx
6748	RISI.LA.53.06.30	Unopened case—delivery of dead sheep; sealed
6749	SAIL.BA.08.03.01	Rental of fields
6750	SUEL.LA.24.12.—	Tablet and case—delivery of barley; sealed; YOS 14, 330 (C—case only)
6751	NASI.ŠA.J.10.08	Loan of barley; sealed; ^{ITI}*Ma-mi-tum*; YOS 14, 20 (C); ENES 768a
6752	SAIL.BA.07.12.01	Tablet and case—loan (šu-lá) of silver and barley; sealed
6753	RISI.LA.18.10.—	Loan of silver; sealed
6754	RISI.LA.47.12.—	Sale of temple office; sealed

NBC	Date	Description
6755	RISI.LA.47.01.—	Account of small cattle (ledger)
6756	—.06.15	Record of foodstuff (ledger)
6757	RISI.LA.??.02.—	Tablet and case—legal case; sealed; mu dumu-munus lugal ša a-na Di-ir i-ni-ku₄-re; RN in oath
6758	SAIL.BA.12.06.—	Adoption; sealed
6759	HARA.BA.39.01.24?	Record concerning small cattle; mu-ús-sa ma-da Èš-nun^{ki}
6760	ITPI.IS.A.05.—	Sale of field in stubble; sealed; YOS 14, 325 (C)
6761	SAIL.BA.34.05.01?	Sale of field; sealed
6762	No date	Letter to Enlil-mudammiq from Lipit-Ištar concerning payments of barley
6763	RISI.LA.38.11.08	Record of dimensions and volumes of soil excavated (ledger)
6764	SAIL.BA.04.03.08	Sale of vacant lot; sealed
6765	—.06.05	Record of foodstuff over several days
6766	SIID.LA.06.06.—	Delivery of barley; YOS 14, 287 (C)
6767	SIER.LA.01.02.—	Receipt of foodstuff; mu-ús-<sa> bàd Maš-kán-šabra
6768	No date	List of PNs
6769	—.10.30	Account of barley
6770	SUEL.LA.20.02.—	Tablet and fragments of case—loan of barley; sealed; YOS 14, 261 (C)
6771	No date	List of field acreages
6772	RISI.LA.38.02.01	Record of workers and barley rations
6773	RISI.LA.59.01.—	Account of barley
6774	No date	Letter to Dada from Marduk-nišu concerning division of field
6775	MANA.MN.A.11.—	Sale of field; sealed; YOS 14, 105 (C)
6776	No date	Letter to Dada from Nūr-Šamaš concerning loan of barley

NBC	Date	Description
6777	SAIL.BA.13.05.18	Sale of temple office; sealed
6779	No date	List of PNs
6780	No date	Letter to Inbi-ilišu from Šamaš-mušēzib concerning barley of *napṭarum*-house
6781	No date	Letter to Ipiq-elletim and Sîn-iddinam from Gimil-Gula concerning fields; cf. NBC 5354
6782	No date	Letter to A-ru-[...] from Awīl-[...] concerning hire of oxen
6783	No date	Letter to Sîn-iddinam from Awiyatum concerning field
6784	No date	Letter to "the man whom [Marduk] preserves" from Sîn-nāṣir concerning fodder
6785	—.—.14	Record of dates over two days (ledger); day in text
6786	SAIL.BA.17.06.05	List of PNs and quantities of silver for several days; sealed
6787	RISI.LA.32.12.—	Disbursement of foodstuff
6788	No date	Letter to "my lord" from Nanna-barazi concerning measuring of barley
6789	SAIL.BA.08.05.01	Hire of person; sealed
6790	No date	Disbursement of barley
6791	UN.ŠA.N.—.—	Loan of barley; mu ^{d}En-ki bí-in-sa$_4$; Simmons, JCS 13, 1959, p. 71, n. 5 (T, Tr)
6792	No date	Loan of barley; sealed
6793	RISI.LA.10.04.10?	Receipt of slaves; sealed
6794	RISI.LA.19.11.20	Account of silver; sealed
6795	SAIL.BA.24.11.30	Consignment of small cattle; sealed
6796	NUAD.LA.01.05.—	Sale of orchard; sealed; YOS 14, 283 (C)
6797	No date	Letter concerning legal case
6798	SAIL.BA.07.11.xx	Tablet and fragments of case—loan of barley and silver; sealed

NBC	Date	Description
6799	SAIL.BA.08.06.21	Receipt of silver reward for apprehending of fugitive slave; sealed
6800	SUEL.LA.04.11.xx	Loan of silver; YOS 14, 221 (C)
6801	SIID.LA.07.03.22	Record of barley deficit; Goetze, JCS 4, 1950, pp. 70-72 (C, T, Tr)
6802	HARA.BA.43.01.15	Account of small cattle
6803	No date	List of payments of barley and silver
6804	HARA.BA.36.12.17	Tablet and case—division of inheritance; sealed
6805	SIER.LA.01.12D.—	Institutional cultivation record; YOS 14, 301 (C)
6806	No date	Letter to Sîn-andullī from Sîn-pāṭer concerning oak trees/acorns(?)
6807	No date	Letter to Isinītum from Aplatum
6808	SIER.LA.01.06.—	Record concerning woolen textiles; YOS 14, 296 (C)
6809	No date	Letter to Warad-Amurrum from Awīl-ili concerning payment
6810	SIER.LA.01.12D.—	Institutional cultivation record; YOS 14, 302 (C)
6811	No date	Letter to Amatum from Gidānum concerning distribution of barley; sealed
6812	SIER.LA.02.01.14	Institutional cultivation record; YOS 14, 305 (C)
6813	SIER.LA.01.12D.—	Institutional cultivation record; YOS 14, 300 (C)
6814	SIER.LA.01.06.26	Tag—record of garments; YOS 14, 295 (C)
6815	SIER.LA.01.06.21	List of votive gifts to Nanna; YOS 14, 298 (C)
6816	SIER.LA.01.12D.—	Institutional cultivation record; YOS 14, 304 (C)
6817	ŠUIL.IS.10.—.—	Legal case concerning inheritance; sealed; mu-ús-sa ^{giš}gu-za kù-sig$_{17}$ é ^{d}Nin-gal
6818	HARA.BA.07.08.—?	Tablet and fragments of case—loan (šu-lá) of barley
6819	SAIL.BA.xx.02.10	Loan of boat; sealed
6820	ABER.TU.A.06.—	Tablet and case—sale of field; sealed; cf. NBC 6821; YOS 14, 107 (C)

NBC	Date	Description
6821	ABER.TU.A.06.—	Tablet and case—sale of field; sealed; cf. NBC 6820; YOS 14, 106 (C)
6822	No date	Letter to Sîn-kāšid from Sîn-iqīšam concerning distribution of flour
6823	SAIL.BA.27.08.17	Loan of barley; sealed
6824	SAIL.BA.24.02.01	Rental of field; sealed
6825	No date	Letter to Sîn-[...] from Sumu-[...]
6826	No date	Letter to Sîn-[...] from Lu-[...]
6827	SAIL.BA.08.10.01	Loan of silver and barley; sealed
6828	No date	Letter to Adaša from Sumutbalim concerning provisions
6829	No date	Letter to Arurum from Sîn-wēdi concerning distraint
6830	SAIL.BA.26.08.01	Receipt of beer and silver; sealed
6831	No date	Disbursement of skins and household furnishings; Van De Mieroop, ActaSum 16, 1994, pp. 202-05 (C, T, Tr)
6832	No date	Letter to Duššuptum and Sîn-izzu from Apil-ilišu concerning foodstuffs
6833	No date	Letter to "the overseer of the Amorites whom Marduk preserves" from Ibbi-Šaḫan concerning provisions
6834	SIIQ.LA.02.04.19?	Promissory note—barley; YOS 14, 309 (C)
6835	No date	Record of quantities of silver and equivalents in bricks
6836	No date	Loan of silver
7043	IŠIR.IS.22.05.—	Receipt of bitumen; BIN 10, 29 (C)
7044	No date	Letter to Puzur-Kiš concerning shipment of foodstuff; sealed; BIN 9, 475 (C)
7045	IŠIR.IS.22.07.—	Receipt of hides and skins; BIN 9, 113 (C)
7046	IŠIR.IS.28.04.02	Disbursement of skins and thread; BIN 9, 254 (C)
7047	IŠIR.IS.22.07.—	Receipt of skins; BIN 9, 117 (C)

NBC	Date	Description
7048	ŠUIL.IS.01.11.14	Disbursement of skins and thread; BIN 9, 264 (C)
7049	IŠIR.IS.22.10.—	Receipt of bitumen; BIN 10, 31 (C)
7050	IŠIR.IS.15.05.—	Receipt of hide and skins; BIN 9, 43 (C)
7051	IŠIR.IS.25.07.04	Disbursement of leather vessels; BIN 9, 313 (C)
7052	IŠIR.IS.13.02.08	Disbursement of sandals and bags; BIN 9, 39 (C)
7053	IŠIR.IS.28.07.—	Disbursement of skins; BIN 9, 239 (C)
7054	IŠIR.IS.23.10.—	Receipt of copper and leather for royal shoes; BIN 9, 107 (C)
7055	IŠIR.IS.25.04.03	Receipt of skins and woolen thread; BIN 9, 303 (C)
7056	IŠIR.IS.19.06.—	Receipt of hides and skins; BIN 9, 64 (C)
7057	IŠIR.IS.27.07.—	Disbursement of shield; BIN 9, 119 (C)
7058	IŠIR.IS.24.08.—	Receipt of skins; BIN 9, 95 (C)
7059	IŠIR.IS.25.11.29	Receipt of glue and leather; BIN 9, 28 (C)
7060	IŠIR.IS.16.08.12	Disbursement of glue; BIN 9, 167 (C)
7062	IŠIR.IS.11.03.—	Receipt of bitumen; BIN 10, 2 (C)
7063	IŠIR.IS.20.07.—	Disbursement of copper; BIN 10, 132 (C)
7064	IŠIR.IS.11.03.—	Receipt of bitumen; BIN 9, 511 (C)
7065	IŠIR.IS.22.11.18	Disbursement of thread; BIN 10, 142 (C)
7066	IŠIR.IS.15.—.—	Disbursement of reed doormat; BIN 9, 525 (C)
7067	IŠIR.IS.21.10.—	Receipt of skins; BIN 9, 10 (C)
7068	IŠIR.IS.16.12.03	Delivery of leather; BIN 9, 137 (C)
7069	IŠIR.IS.18.12.—	Receipt of hides and skin; BIN 9, 70 (C)
7070	IŠIR.IS.17.06.—	Receipt of bitumen; BIN 10, 15 (C)
7071	IŠIR.IS.16.12D.13	Disbursement of bitumen; BIN 9, 204 (C)
7072	IŠIR.IS.16.01.15	Receipt of hides; BIN 9, 75 (C)
7073	IŠIR.IS.17.03.22	Disbursement of glue; BIN 10, 126 (C)

NBC	Date	Description
7074	IŠIR.IS.13.01.—	Delivery of hide and skins; BIN 9, 44 (C)
7075	IŠIR.IS.13.10.02	Disbursement of glue for royal boots; BIN 9, 469 (C)
7076	IŠIR.IS.13.09.—	Disbursement of bitumen, reed mat, and leather; BIN 9, 259 (C)
7077	IŠIR.IS.22.05.—	Receipt of bitumen; BIN 10, 30 (C)
7078	IŠIR.IS.06.—.—	Disbursement of doors; BIN 10, 94 (C)
7079	IŠIR.IS.19.02.—	Receipt of hides and skins; BIN 9, 46 (C)
7080	IŠIR.IS.21.12D.—	Receipt of hides; BIN 9, 4 (C)
7081	IŠIR.IS.12.09.—	Receipt of skins; BIN 9, 60 (C)
7082	IŠIR.IS.12.06.—	Receipt of bitumen; BIN 9, 478 (C)
7083	IŠIR.IS.09.05.14	Disbursement of leather and glue; BIN 9, 189 (C)
7085	IŠIR.IS.12.10.29	Receipt of bitumen; BIN 10, 6 (C)
7086	IŠIR.IS.22.11.—	Disbursement of leather containers; BIN 9, 314 (C)
7087	IŠIR.IS.24.10.—	Disbursement of leather objects—weapon holders(?); sealed; BIN 9, 108 (C)
7088	IŠIR.IS.19.08.—	Receipt of hides; BIN 9, 126 (C)
7089	IŠIR.IS.25.—.—	Disbursement of reed baskets(?); BIN 9, 506 (C)
7090	SIIQ.LA.04.06.08	Receipt of barley
7091	IŠIR.IS.25.02.—	Receipt of bitumen; BIN 10, 36 (C)
7092	IŠIR.IS.14.08.22	List of workers; BIN 10, 261 (C)
7093	ENBA.IS.D.12.29	Disbursement of barley flour
7094	IŠIR.IS.13.06.19	Receipt of bitumen; BIN 10, 107 (C)
7095	IŠIR.IS.13.05.—	Receipt of skins, wool, glue, and bitumen; BIN 9, 30 (C)
7096	IŠIR.IS.24.09.—	Receipt of hides and skins; BIN 9, 93 (C)
7097	IŠIR.IS.33.01.06	Disbursement of reed items; BIN 9, 530 (C)
7098	IŠIR.IS.16.01.21	Receipt of wool; BIN 10, 11 (C)
7099	IŠIR.IS.15.12.—	Disbursement of copper utensils; BIN 10, 67 (C)

NBC	Date	Description
7100	IŠIR.IS.24.09.—	Receipt of hides and skins; BIN 9, 94 (C)
7101	IŠIR.IS.16.01.19	Receipt of hides; BIN 9, 73 (C)
7102	IŠIR.IS.20.03.—	Disbursement of skins; BIN 9, 245 (C)
7103	IŠIR.IS.25.02.—	Receipt of skins; BIN 9, 97 (C)
7104	IŠIR.IS.14.02.08	Receipt of sandals and leather; BIN 9, 323 (C)
7105	IŠIR.IS.16.04.—	Receipt of skins; BIN 9, 62 (C)
7107	IŠIR.IS.13.01.12	Delivery of skins, glue, and woolen thread; BIN 9, 31 (C)
7108	IŠIR.IS.27.11.—	Disbursement of vessels; BIN 9, 322 (C)
7109	IŠIR.IS.14.06.22	Disbursement of reed tables; BIN 10, 115 (C)
7110	IŠIR.IS.33.05.10	Memorandum of no activity; dupl. NBC 7629; BIN 10, 199 (C)
7111	IŠIR.IS.24.07.—	Receipt of bitumen; BIN 9, 479 (C)
7112	IŠIR.IS.23.06.—	Disbursement of leather; BIN 9, 471 (C)
7113	IŠIR.IS.16.07.13	Receipt of hides; BIN 9, 77 (C)
7114	IŠIR.IS.21.06.05	Receipt of skins; BIN 9, 7 (C)
7115	IŠIR.IS.16.04.—	Disbursement of copper objects and leather shields; BIN 9, 338 (C)
7116	IŠIR.IS.23.09.—	Receipt of hide and skins; BIN 9, 47 (C)
7117	IŠIR.IS.24.08.06	Delivery of glue; BIN 9, 131 (C)
7118	IŠIR.IS.33.04.—	Receipt of oil; BIN 10, 44 (C)
7119	IŠIR.IS.10.12D.—	Receipt of hides and skins; BIN 9, 48 (C)
7120	IŠIR.IS.22.04.—	Receipt of bitumen; BIN 10, 27 (C)
7121	IŠIR.IS.21.06.06	Receipt of skins; BIN 10, 22 (C)
7122	IŠIR.IS.22.11.—	Receipt of chairs; BIN 10, 143 (C)
7123	IŠIR.IS.12.06.—	Receipt of hides and skins; BIN 9, 49 (C)
7124	IŠIR.IS.28.—.—	Disbursement of glue and leather; BIN 9, 266 (C)
7125	IŠIR.IS.22.02.10	Disbursement of bitumen; BIN 9, 485 (C)

NBC	Date	Description
7126	IŠIR.IS.14.11.—	Disbursement of bag and leather; BIN 9, 304 (C)
7127	IŠIR.IS.28.09.11	Disbursement of wool and skins; BIN 9, 246 (C)
7128	IŠIR.IS.12.03.—	Receipt of hides and skins; BIN 9, 52 (C)
7129	IŠIR.IS.25.09.09?	Disbursement of combed wool; mu ^{urudu}gu-za ba-dím; BIN 9, 524 (C)
7130	IŠIR.IS.19.11.06	Disbursement of leather, bitumen, gypsum, and thread; BIN 9, 249 (C)
7131	IŠIR.IS.23.12.—	Receipt of skins; BIN 10, 34 (C)
7132	No date	Disbursement of hides and various commodities; BIN 9, 181 (C)
7133	IŠIR.IS.19.10.24	Disbursement of chairs and material for their repair; sealed; BIN 9, 434 (C)
7134	IŠIR.IS.21.07.22	Disbursement of leather and sandals; sealed; BIN 9, 383 (C)
7135	IŠIR.IS.13.06.27	List of workers; BIN 10, 250 (C)
7136	IŠIR.IS.08.12D.12	List of workers; BIN 10, 228 (C)
7137	No date	Account of various objects, including leather goods and small cattle; BIN 9, 150 (C)
7139	IŠIR.IS.21.03.—	Receipt of alum and other materials; BIN 9, 83 (C)
7140	IŠIR.IS.25.09.19	Disbursement of reed products; BIN 10, 158 (C)
7141	IŠIR.IS.24.09.—	Receipt of hides and skins; BIN 9, 50 (C)
7142	IŠIR.IS.23.07.16	Disbursement of bitumen; BIN 10, 151 (C)
7143	IŠIR.IS.19.11.—	Receipt of hides and skins; BIN 9, 63 (C)
7144	IŠIR.IS.14.06.28	List of workers; BIN 10, 257 (C)
7145	Lost	Disbursement of bags; BIN 9, 280 (C)
7147	ŠUIL.IS.01.09.29	Disbursement of chair and felt; BIN 9, 341 (C)
7149	IŠIR.IS.15.02.—	Disbursement of skins; BIN 9, 152 (C)
7150	IŠIR.IS.20.12.16	Disbursement of leather and glue; BIN 9, 252 (C)
7151	IŠIR.IS.19.05.14	Disbursement of leather; BIN 9, 174 (C)

NBC	Date	Description
7152	ŠUIL.IS.03.06.06	Disbursement of sandals; BIN 9, 232 (C)
7153	IŠIR.IS.23.10.—	Disbursement of glue; sealed; BIN 9, 124 (C)
7154	IŠIR.IS.19.01.08	Disbursement of reed baskets; dupl. NBC 7188; BIN 9, 356 (C)
7155	No date	Disbursement of wood; BIN 10, 183 (C)
7156	IŠIR.IS.15.10.11	List of workers; BIN 10, 270 (C)
7157	—.06.23	Disbursement of glue and meal; BIN 9, 169 (C)
7158	IŠIR.IS.13.12D.02	List of workers; BIN 10, 254 (C)
7159	—.10.19	Disbursement of chairs and leather; BIN 9, 342 (C)
7160	IŠIR.IS.18.06.27	Disbursement of beds and mattresses; BIN 9, 348 (C)
7161	—.01.16	Delivery of thread, bitumen, and glue; BIN 9, 134 (C)
7162	IŠIR.IS.17.12.12	Disbursement of thread; BIN 9, 482 (C)
7163	IŠIR.IS.23.03.—	Disbursement of leather for throne; BIN 9, 184 (C)
7164	IŠIR.IS.11.05.—	Receipt of wool; BIN 10, 3 (C)
7165	IŠIR.IS.10.03.—	Disbursement of leather for wrapping silver; BIN 9, 386 (C)
7166	IŠIR.IS.21.12.20	Disbursement of reed containers and bags; BIN 9, 390 (C)
7167	—.xx.22	List of workers; BIN 10, 305 (C)
7168	IŠIR.IS.07.07.xx	List of workers; BIN 10, 215 (C)
7169	xx.06.24	Disbursement of chair and reed containers; BIN 9, 436 (C)
7170	—.07.16	List of workers; BIN 10, 277 (C)
7171	IŠIR.IS.19.02.—	Disbursement of door and reed objects; sealed; BIN 9, 443 (C)
7172	No date	Disbursement of skins; BIN 9, 312 (C)
7173	—.03.29	List of tablets; BIN 10, 206 (C)
7175	IŠIR.IS.09.11.14	List of workers; BIN 10, 235 (C)
7176	ŠUIL.IS.01.10.11	Disbursement of reed objects and container, and vessels; BIN 9, 452 (C)

NBC	Date	Description
7177	IŠIR.IS.07.06.16?	List of workers; ^{iti}kin-^{d}Nanna; BIN 10, 208 (C)
7178	IŠIR.IS.23.04.—	Disbursement of oil and red paste for manufacture of furniture; BIN 10, 150 (C)
7179	UN.KI.A.12.—	Loan of silver; sealed; mu Ú-ba-a-a ba-ug$_6$
7180	IŠIR.IS.07.06.16	List of workers; BIN 9, 515 (C)
7181	IŠIR.IS.19.02.11	Disbursement of doors and their fittings, reed containers, and bowl; sealed; BIN 9, 350 (C)
7182	IŠIR.IS.25.12.—	Disbursement of oil and leather; sealed; BIN 9, 371 (C)
7183	IŠIR.IS.07.06.—?	Disbursement of wood; ^{iti}kin-^{d}Nanna; BIN 10, 96 (C)
7184	No date	List of wood and leather objects; BIN 9, 183 (C)
7185	—.11.30	List of workers; BIN 10, 301 (C)
7186	—.08.05	List of workers and professional designations; ^{iti}šu-eš-ša
7187	IŠIR.IS.33.10.—	Delivery of reeds; BIN 10, 47 (C)
7188	IŠIR.IS.19.01.08	Disbursement of reed baskets; sealed; dupl. NBC 7154; BIN 9, 357 (C)
7189	—.09.28	List of workers; dupl. NBC 8028; BIN 10, 289 (C)
7190	IŠIR.IS.22.09.26	Disbursement of thread; BIN 10, 139 (C)
7191	IŠIR.IS.13.06.—	Disbursement of copper for dyeing; BIN 9, 460 (C)
7192	IŠIR.IS.23.04.26	Disbursement of glue, leather, and woolen garments; BIN 9, 378 (C)
7193	—.10.—	List of PNs and numerals
7194	IŠIR.IS.20.03.—	Disbursement of leather objects—weapon holders(?); sealed; BIN 9, 507 (C)
7195	IŠIR.IS.12.12.—	Disbursement of garment and bed; BIN 9, 453 (C)
7196	IŠIR.IS.21.04.29	Disbursement of chair, bed, wooden items, bags, containers, and leather; BIN 9, 435 (C)
7197	IŠIR.IS.25.03.07	Disbursement of doors with their equipment and reed containers; BIN 10, 155 (C)

NBC	Date	Description
7198	IŠIR.IS.19.—.—	Disbursement of reed and leather containers; BIN 9, 361 (C)
7199	IŠIR.IS.11.06.—	List of workers; BIN 10, 242 (C)
7201	IŠIR.IS.08.12.—	Receipt of wool; sealed; BIN 10, 72 (C)
7202	ŠUIL.IS.01.04.03	Disbursement of bags; BIN 9, 416 (C)
7203	IŠIR.IS.07.07.01	List of workers; BIN 10, 209 (C)
7204	IŠIR.IS.33.10.—	Receipt of felt, wool, and linen; sealed; BIN 9, 129 (C)
7205	IŠIR.IS.22.04.14	Disbursement of bitumen; sealed; BIN 10, 137 (C)
7206	ŠUIL.IS.02.02.14	Disbursement of bags and bowls; BIN 9, 405 (C)
7207	IŠIR.IS.19.01.17	Disbursement of doors; sealed; BIN 9, 347 (C)
7208	ŠUIL.IS.02.09.—	List of days on which tablets were written; BIN 9, 521 (C)
7209	IŠIR.IS.21.11.06	Disbursement of bags and reed objects; BIN 9, 412 (C)
7210	IŠIR.IS.26.02.—	Disbursement of bag; BIN 9, 308 (C)
7211	IŠIR.IS.19.02.10	Disbursement of doors; sealed; BIN 9, 346 (C)
7213	ŠUIL.IS.01.08.—	Disbursement of vessels; BIN 10, 167 (C)
7214	IŠIR.IS.14.11.12	Disbursement of sandals, bags, and woolen garments; BIN 9, 324 (C)
7215	—.09.24+	List of workers; BIN 10, 287 (C)
7216	—.08.11	List of workers; BIN 10, 283 (C)
7217	IŠIR.IS.07.07.26	List of workers; BIN 10, 214 (C)
7218	IŠIR.IS.25.02.11	Disbursement of reed containers; BIN 10, 154 (C)
7219	ŠUIL.IS.03.04.16	Disbursement of leather, glue, and thread; BIN 9, 366 (C)
7220	IŠIR.IS.33.11.15	Disbursement of leather, madder, and alum; BIN 9, 470 (C)
7221	IŠIR.IS.14.03.14	Receipt of rope; BIN 10, 75 (C)
7222	IŠIR.IS.16.01.14	Disbursement of thread, leather, and glue; BIN 9, 194 (C)
7223	—.12.25	Delivery of hides and glue; BIN 9, 147 (C)

NBC	Date	Description
7224	IŠIR.IS.15.04.24	Disbursement of bags and leather; BIN 9, 283 (C)
7225	No date	List of unspecified articles by month; BIN 10, 207 (C)
7226	No date	Delivery of glue; BIN 9, 133 (C)
7227	IŠIR.IS.16.01.26	Disbursement of wood; BIN 10, 125 (C)
7228	IŠIR.IS.21.06.—	Record of debit records and copies; BIN 9, 535 (C)
7230	IŠIR.IS.22.06.—	Disbursement of leather; BIN 9, 198 (C)
7231	IŠIR.IS.19.05.—	Receipt of hides and skins; BIN 9, 59 (C)
7232	IŠIR.IS.16.01.17	Disbursement of hide, skins, and glue; BIN 9, 195 (C)
7233	ŠUIL.IS.02.11.13	Disbursement of baskets; BIN 10, 171 (C)
7234	IŠIR.IS.33.05.22	Memorandum of no activity; sealed; BIN 10, 202 (C)
7235	IŠIR.IS.xx.xx.xx	Disbursement of leather, glue, and thread; BIN 9, 258 (C)
7236	No date	List of various products; BIN 10, 184 (C)
7237	IŠIR.IS.33.02.—	Disbursement of reed items; BIN 9, 529 (C)
7238	IŠIR.IS.17.04.13	Disbursement of leather; BIN 9, 176 (C)
7239	ŠUIL.IS.01.10.—?	Receipt of fat, glue, and red paste; BIN 10, 51 (C)
7240	IŠIR.IS.12.04.—	Receipt of skins; BIN 9, 68 (C)
7241	—.12.23	Delivery of hides; BIN 9, 148 (C)
7242	IŠIR.IS.17.11.18	Disbursement of skins; BIN 9, 196 (C)
7244	IŠIR.IS.28.02.20	Disbursement of rope; BIN 10, 161 (C)
7245	IŠIR.IS.33.04.02	Disbursement of bags and lids; BIN 9, 217 (C)
7246	IŠIR.IS.12.07.—	Receipt of hides; BIN 9, 71 (C)
7248	—.12D.08	Disbursement of thread; BIN 9, 483 (C)
7249	IŠIR.IS.12.08.—	Receipt of hides; BIN 9, 74 (C)
7250	IŠIR.IS.13.12.06	Receipt of rope; BIN 10, 84 (C)
7251	IŠIR.IS.13.10.08	Disbursement of vessels; BIN 9, 321 (C)
7252	IŠIR.IS.17.09.25	Receipt of bitumen; BIN 10, 17 (C)

NBC	Date	Description
7253	IŠIR.IS.19.11.30	Disbursement of bitumen, gypsum, and leather; BIN 9, 251 (C)
7254	IŠIR.IS.13.11.02	Disbursement of musical instruments and reed mats; BIN 9, 354 (C)
7255	IŠIR.IS.12.06.—	Receipt of glue and red paste; BIN 10, 5 (C)
7256	IŠIR.IS.22.03.—	Disbursement of bags and skins; BIN 9, 211 (C)
7257	IŠIR.IS.14.01.—	Disbursement of bags and leather; BIN 9, 285 (C)
7258	IŠIR.IS.13.04.02	Disbursement of leather; BIN 9, 335 (C)
7259	IŠIR.IS.13.01.08	Disbursement of leather; BIN 9, 242 (C)
7260	IŠIR.IS.30.02.—	Receipt of hides; BIN 9, 23 (C)
7261	IŠIR.IS.13.01.22	Disbursement of leather; BIN 9, 337 (C)
7262	—.07.27	List of workers; BIN 10, 279 (C)
7264	IŠIR.IS.26.08.15	Disbursement of leather, reed and wooden containers, and sandals; BIN 9, 395 (C)
7265	IŠIR.IS.33.12.30	Disbursement of tarpaulin; BIN 9, 37 (C)
7266	IŠIR.IS.08.07.01	List of workers; BIN 10, 226 (C)
7267	IŠIR.IS.25.03.—	Disbursement of sandals and bags; BIN 9, 425 (C)
7268	IŠIR.IS.10.08.21	List of workers; BIN 10, 240 (C)
7269	IŠIR.IS.10.03.04+	List of workers; BIN 10, 236 (C)
7272	No date	Disbursement of foodstuff over six days (ledger)
7273	No date	Record of field acreages
7274	RISI.LA.18.??.16	Record of gold, silver, and sheep (ledger); ^{iti}<...> u_4-16-kam
7275	RISI.LA.59.02.—	Account of barley
7276	SAIL.BA.27.05.16	Ration list
7277	RISI.LA.47.01.—	Record concerning small cattle
7278	RISI.LA.55.02.05	Division of property among members of three generations

NBC	Date	Description
7279	—.08.30	Disbursement of barley rations
7280	No date	Ration list—oil
7281	No date	Record of field acreages
7282	RISI.LA.53.07.18	Tablet and case—delivery of large and small cattle over 25 days; sealed
7283	RISI.LA.47.08.—	Receipt of barley, sesame, and dates
7284	RISI.LA.58.10.30	Receipt of sesame and oil
7285	RISI.LA.59.05.—	Account of barley and sesame (ledger)
7286	RISI.LA.47.11.27	Account of sesame
7287	RISI.LA.60.02.—	Record of barley and date rations; cf. NBC 7289
7288	RISI.LA.31.03.—	Tablet and portion of case—promissory note—silver
7289	RISI.LA.50.01.—	Record of barley and date rations; cf. NBC 7287
7290	SIAD.LA.01.09.01	Record of work of female clothing workers; YOS 14, 310 (C)
7291	RISI.LA.59.07.—	Ration list—barley
7292	No date	List of payments of silver
7293	RISI.LA.59.02.—	Ration list—barley
7294	RISI.LA.58.10.—	Ration list—barley for fodder
7295	RISI.LA.59.01.14	Account of foodstuff
7296	No date	Tablet and fragment of case—sale of slave
7297	RISI.LA.49.09.30	Account of barley
7298	RISI.LA.58.12.30	Account of wool
7299	RISI.LA.58.04.08	Account of barley
7300	RISI.LA.59.08.—	Disbursement of barley
7301	RISI.LA.20.12.30	Account of disbursement of silver over one year
7302	SUYA.MN.??.06.03	List of slaves; mu *Su-mu-e-mu-ut-ba-lim*
7303	RISI.LA.51.04.—	Tablet and case—receipt of barley and wheat; sealed

NBC	Date	Description
7304	RISI.LA.53.07.—	Unopened case—receipt of barley; sealed; cf. NBC 7303
7305	MABA.KI.J.—.—	Sale of house; sealed; YOS 14, 345 (C)
7307	SAIL.BA.07.05.20	Tablet and case—agreement to repair wall; sealed
7308	HARA.BA.43.10.02	Tablet and case—"dowry" of *nadītum* priestess(?); sealed
7309	IPAD2.ŠA.J.—.—	Tablet and case—loan of boards and silver; sealed; YOS 14, 50 (C); ENES 762
7310	RISI.LA.52.04.—	Record of provision of substitute soldiers/workers
7311	No date	Memorandum concerning deed for field
7312	RISI.LA.49.06.10	Disbursement of silver for grave
7313	RISI.LA.19.09.—	Account of barley and silver; sealed
7314	No date	List of workers and supervisors
7315	RISI.LA.36.04.10	Sale of improved residential property; sealed
7316	RISI.LA.28.03.16?	Account of silver
7317	RISI.LA.56.06.01	List of votive gifts for Sumuqan
7318	No date	Letter to Irra-bašti from Lu-i-tum concerning barley and cultivation of field
7319	No date	Payment of silver
7320	No date	List of payments of silver
7321	No date	Loan of silver; YOS 14, 54 (C)
7322	No date	Loan of barley; YOS 14, 49 (C)
7323	RISI.LA.24.06.—	Loan (šu-lá) of silver
7324	SAIL.BA.06.10.—	Promissory note—bricks; sealed
7325	IPE2.ŠA.08.—.—	Loan of barley; sealed; YOS 14, 38 (C)
7327	SIIR.UK.01.09.10	Promissory note—silver; YOS 14, 297 (C)
7328	No date	List of payments of silver
7329	No date	List of PNs

NBC	Date	Description
7330	UN.MN.A.—.—	Legal case concerning sale of house; mu bàd gal Ka-x-x^{ki}; YOS 14, 335 (C)
7331	No date	Letter to Wēdi-[...] from Išum-[...]
7333	RISI.LA.23.05.—	Loan of barley and silver; sealed
7335	RISI.LA.37.06.—	Agreement for management of orchard; sealed
7337	—.01.15	Disbursement of barley
7339	IŠIR.IS.19.04.01?	List of numbers of workers, quantities of barley(?), and overseers(?)
7340	RISI.LA.58.04.10	Consignment of large cattle; sealed
7341	Lost	Sale of improved residential property; sealed
7342	IBŠA.KA.F.—.—	Tablet and case—adoption; sealed; YOS 14, 344 (C)
7348	No date	Letter to Lu-Ninurta and Balmunamḫe from Rīm-Sîn
7349	SAIL.BA.07.05.13	Sale of improved residential property
7350	SIMU.BA.13.08.—	Receipt of silver
7351	No date	Letter to Kubburum from Nabium-malik concerning oil
7353	No date	Letter to Ikūn-pî-Adad from Maratum concerning herdsmen and garments
7354	IŠIR.IS.12.04.27	Disbursement of leather containers; BIN 9, 318 (C)
7355	IŠIR.IS.15.02.15	List of workers; BIN 9, 527 (C)
7356	IŠIR.IS.16.05.29	Disbursement of glue; BIN 9, 163 (C)
7357	IŠIR.IS.10.08.04	Disbursement of tablet basket; BIN 10, 100 (C)
7358	IŠIR.IS.26.12.06	Disbursement of musical instruments and bags; BIN 9, 359 (C)
7359	IŠIR.IS.24.01.—	Receipt of skins; BIN 9, 99 (C)
7360	IŠIR.IS.19.09.08	Disbursement of glue, leather, bitumen, and gypsum; BIN 9, 178 (C)
7361	IŠIR.IS.13.03.19	Delivery of glue, gypsum, and skins; BIN 9, 35 (C)
7362	ŠUIL.IS.01.07.17	Disbursement of bitumen; BIN 10, 169 (C)

NBC	Date	Description
7363	IŠIR.IS.26.12.—	Receipt of hides and skins; BIN 9, 65 (C)
7364	IŠIR.IS.11.03.—	Receipt of hides and skins; BIN 9, 51 (C)
7365	IŠIR.IS.16.12D.—	Receipt of bitumen; BIN 10, 14 (C)
7366	ŠUIL.IS.01.04.—	Receipt of oil; BIN 10, 49 (C)
7367	IŠIR.IS.12.02.—	Receipt of shields; BIN 9, 85 (C)
7368	IŠIR.IS.15.06.28	Disbursement of baskets; BIN 10, 122 (C)
7369	IŠIR.IS.16.12.07	Disbursement of thread; BIN 9, 205 (C)
7370	IŠIR.IS.19.02.12	Disbursement of reed containers; sealed; BIN 9, 362 (C)
7371	ŠUIL.IS.02.02.—	Receipt of wool; BIN 9, 517 (C)
7372	IŠIR.IS.26.10.—	Receipt of wool and other materials; BIN 9, 81 (C)
7373	IŠIR.IS.16.12.03	Delivery of thread; BIN 9, 141 (C)
7374	IŠIR.IS.16.12.21	Disbursement of glue; BIN 9, 161 (C)
7375	IŠIR.IS.12.07.27	Disbursement of glue; BIN 9, 374 (C)
7376	IŠIR.IS.20.01.—	Disbursement of leather and linen; BIN 9, 455 (C)
7377	IŠIR.IS.16.11.25	Delivery of oil; BIN 9, 505 (C)
7378	IŠIR.IS.16.11.22+	Disbursement of leather; BIN 9, 173 (C)
7379	IŠIR.IS.23.07.04?	Disbursement of bags and musical instruments; BIN 9, 394 (C)
7380	IŠIR.IS.31.02.12	Disbursement of reed container; BIN 9, 523 (C)
7381	IŠIR.IS.16.10.17	Disbursement of bags; BIN 9, 271 (C)
7382	IŠIR.IS.27.07.—	Delivery of glue; sealed; BIN 9, 146 (C)
7383	IŠIR.IS.20.02.18	Disbursement of bags; BIN 9, 406 (C)
7384	IŠIR.IS.26.11.22	Disbursement of bags and leather; BIN 9, 282 (C)
7385	IŠIR.IS.13.02.10	Disbursement of leather containers; BIN 9, 319 (C)
7386	IŠIR.IS.25.01.—	Disbursement of wool; BIN 9, 500 (C)
7387	IŠIR.IS.23.06.—	Disbursement of leather objects—weapon holders(?); sealed; BIN 9, 109 (C)

NBC	Date	Description
7388	IŠIR.IS.07.08.17	List of workers; BIN 10, 217 (C)
7389	IŠIR.IS.14.07.12	Disbursement of leather; BIN 9, 240 (C)
7390	ŠUIL.IS.03.05.—	List of workers; BIN 9, 520 (C)
7391	ŠUIL.IS.01.06.—	Disbursement of vessels; BIN 10, 168 (C)
7392	ŠUIL.IS.02.09.10	Disbursement of boots; BIN 9, 328 (C)
7393	IŠIR.IS.33.05.30	Disbursement of leather; BIN 9, 367 (C)
7394	IŠIR.IS.21.12.22	List of workers; sealed; BIN 10, 275 (C)
7395	IŠIR.IS.26.09.—	Disbursement of skins, bags, and reed objects; BIN 9, 393 (C)
7396	IŠIR.IS.21.12D.12	Disbursement of flutes and bags; sealed; BIN 10, 133 (C)
7397	IŠIR.IS.22.01.10	Disbursement of leather, bitumen, and glue; BIN 9, 212 (C)
7398	No date	List of reed containers and sieves; BIN 10, 185 (C)
7399	IŠIR.IS.16.01.18	Delivery of thread, bitumen, and leather; BIN 9, 136 (C)
7400	No date	Receipt of wood from fir trees; BIN 10, 57 (C)
7401	IŠIR.IS.14.03.—	Disbursement of musical instruments; BIN 9, 496 (C)
7402	IŠIR.IS.18.03.—	Disbursement of goat skin; sealed; BIN 9, 13 (C)
7403	IŠIR.IS.15.12.—	Disbursement of leather bags; BIN 9, 34 (C)
7404	ŠUIL.IS.03.03.29	Disbursement; BIN 10, 172 (C)
7405	IŠIR.IS.14.04.06	Disbursement of woolen cloth; BIN 9, 257 (C)
7406	IŠIR.IS.22.04.28	Receipt of hides and skins; BIN 9, 72 (C)
7407	IŠIR.IS.14.06.03	Disbursement of bags and leather; BIN 9, 272 (C)
7409	IŠIR.IS.16.06.08	Disbursement of glue; BIN 9, 164 (C)
7410	IŠIR.IS.14.02.24	Disbursement of leather and glue; BIN 9, 253 (C)
7411	No date	Disbursement of shoes; sealed; BIN 9, 88 (C)
7412	IŠIR.IS.11.07.—	Receipt of wool; BIN 10, 4 (C)
7413	IŠIR.IS.13.11.23	Disbursement of leather and bags; BIN 9, 241 (C)

NBC	Date	Description
7414	IŠIR.IS.16.07.15	Record concerning glue; BIN 9, 154 (C)
7415	IŠIR.IS.16.06.16	Disbursement of glue; BIN 9, 153 (C)
7416	IŠIR.IS.15.03.10+	List of workers; BIN 10, 266 (C)
7417	IŠIR.IS.22.12.07	Disbursement of thread; BIN 10, 145 (C)
7418	IŠIR.IS.22.12.05	Disbursement of thread; BIN 10, 144 (C)
7420	IŠIR.IS.17.03.15	Disbursement of leather and glue; BIN 9, 158 (C)
7421	IŠIR.IS.24.08.—?	Receipt of skin; BIN 9, 76 (C)
7422	IŠIR.IS.28.04.01	Disbursement of skins and wool; BIN 9, 255 (C)
7423	IŠIR.IS.19.11.17	Disbursement of leather, bitumen, gypsum, and thread; BIN 9, 250 (C)
7424	—.06.05	Disbursement of bags; BIN 9, 218 (C)
7425	IŠIR.IS.22.12.20?	Disbursement of thread; BIN 9, 518 (C)
7426	IŠIR.IS.16.08.10	Disbursement of glue; BIN 9, 166 (C)
7427	IŠIR.IS.16.06.13	Disbursement of leather; BIN 9, 236 (C)
7428	IŠIR.IS.12.12.06	Disbursement of leather; BIN 9, 457 (C)
7429	IŠIR.IS.25.09.—?	Disbursement of wooden object; BIN 10, 163 (C)
7430	IŠIR.IS.15.02.—	Disbursement of hides; sealed; BIN 9, 125 (C)
7432	IŠIR.IS.25.08.13	Disbursement of bags; BIN 9, 287 (C)
7433	IŠIR.IS.33.05.18	Record of no transactions; sealed; BIN 9, 528 (C)
7434	IŠIR.IS.14.12.01	Disbursement of sandals and bags; BIN 9, 325 (C)
7436	IŠIR.IS.07.10.12	List of workers; BIN 9, 514 (C)
7438	IŠIR.IS.23.01.05+	Disbursement of reed doormats and wooden objects; BIN 9, 534 (C)
7440	IŠIR.IS.26.01.11	Disbursement of bags and skins; BIN 9, 270 (C)
7441	IŠIR.IS.09.05.02	Disbursement of containers and bitumen; BIN 9, 447 (C)
7442	No date	List of doors; BIN 10, 186 (C)
7443	IŠIR.IS.14.07.21	Disbursement of bags and mats; BIN 9, 307 (C)

NBC	Date	Description
7444	IŠIR.IS.xx.02.09	Disbursement of leather and glue; BIN 9, 454 (C)
7445	IŠIR.IS.33.01.08	Disbursement of bags; BIN 9, 219 (C)
7446	IŠIR.IS.33.11.21	Disbursement of bags; BIN 9, 228 (C)
7447	ŠUIL.IS.03.03.24	Disbursement of bags; BIN 9, 220 (C)
7448	—.06.16	Disbursement of sandals; BIN 9, 420 (C)
7449	IŠIR.IS.33.12D.27	Disbursement of leather; BIN 9, 187 (C)
7450	—.09.09	List of workers; BIN 10, 285 (C)
7451	IŠIR.IS.20.02.—	Receipt of skins; BIN 9, 120 (C)
7452	IŠIR.IS.33.05.04	Memorandum of no activity; dupl. NBC 7743; BIN 10, 197 (C)
7453	—.09.18	Disbursement of skins; BIN 9, 207 (C)
7454	IŠIR.IS.07.—.—	Disbursement of bitumen; BIN 10, 97 (C)
7455	ŠUIL.IS.02.04.21	Disbursement of bags; BIN 9, 215 (C)
7456	IŠIR.IS.15.04.23	Disbursement of containers and beams; BIN 10, 120 (C)
7457	No date	List of furniture and other objects; BIN 10, 187 (C)
7458	ŠUIL.IS.01.10.15	Disbursement of bags; BIN 9, 229 (C)
7459	IŠIR.IS.19.03.08	Receipt of rope; BIN 10, 76 (C)
7460	—.10.11	Disbursement of leather; BIN 9, 488 (C)
7461	IŠIR.IS.14.06.17	Receipt of skins, glue, and wool; BIN 9, 29 (C)
7462	—.01.12	Disbursement of thread and glue; BIN 9, 466 (C)
7463	IŠIR.IS.07.05.—	Disbursement of wood; BIN 10, 95 (C)
7464	IŠIR.IS.16.01.20	Disbursement of leather, thread, and bitumen; BIN 9, 463 (C)
7465	IŠIR.IS.25.07.—	Receipt of hides, skins, and wool; BIN 9, 112 (C)
7466	IŠIR.IS.15.01.20	Disbursement of sandals; BIN 9, 231 (C)
7467	No date	Disbursement of barley
7468	IŠIR.IS.33.09.—	Delivery of wooden objects; BIN 10, 46 (C)

NBC	Date	Description
7469	ŠUIL.IS.03.06.—	Receipt of glue; BIN 9, 121 (C)
7470	ŠUIL.IS.03.06.—	Receipt of glue; BIN 9, 122 (C)
7471	IŠIR.IS.33.09.—	Receipt of bowls; BIN 10, 164 (C)
7472	—.11.19	List of workers; BIN 10, 297 (C)
7473	IŠIR.IS.19.01.23	Disbursement of doors; BIN 10, 127 (C)
7474	—.11.22	List of workers; BIN 10, 298 (C)
7475	IŠIR.IS.07.09.22	List of workers; BIN 10, 219 (C)
7476	IŠIR.IS.32.11.—	Deliveries of chairs; BIN 9, 151 (C)
7477	—.11.xx	Account of small cattle and skins
7478	IŠIR.IS.18.03.04	Disbursement of reed door and leather goods; BIN 9, 343 (C)
7479	—.12D.07	List of workers; BIN 10, 303 (C)
7480	IŠIR.IS.33.09.30	Delivery of reeds; BIN 10, 45 (C)
7481	IŠIR.IS.14.04.06	Disbursement of reed objects and leather containers; BIN 9, 360 (C)
7482	IŠIR.IS.22.07.07	Disbursement of bags, leather, and musical instruments; BIN 9, 396 (C)
7483	IŠIR.IS.07.10.04	List of workers; BIN 10, 220 (C)
7484	IŠIR.IS.07.07.21	List of workers; BIN 10, 212 (C)
7485	IŠIR.IS.25.02.10	Disbursement of lyre and leather; BIN 9, 445 (C)
7486	IŠIR.IS.14.06.17+	List of workers; BIN 10, 256 (C)
7487	ŠUIL.IS.03.04.18	Disbursement of sandals and bag; BIN 9, 423 (C)
7488	IŠIR.IS.32.04.—	Disbursement of glue and leather; BIN 9, 192 (C)
7489	IŠIR.IS.18.12D.08	Disbursement of door and its materials; BIN 9, 179 (C)
7490	—.12D.02	Delivery of glue; BIN 9, 140 (C)
7491	IŠIR.IS.16.05.19	Disbursement of glue; BIN 9, 155 (C)
7492	IŠIR.IS.33.03.—	Disbursement of glue, leather, and cord; BIN 9, 193 (C)

NBC	Date	Description
7493	IŠIR.IS.15.10.07	List of workers; BIN 10, 269 (C)
7495	IŠIR.IS.33.11.11	Disbursement of thread, bitumen, and skins; BIN 9, 206 (C)
7496	IŠIR.IS.16.01.24+	Disbursement of leather, bitumen, and thread; BIN 9, 197 (C)
7497	—.12D.04	Delivery of bitumen and thread; BIN 9, 139 (C)
7498	IŠIR.IS.15.04.28	Disbursement of reed baskets; BIN 10, 121 (C)
7499	IŠIR.IS.08.12.—	Disbursement of skins and sandals; BIN 9, 369 (C)
7500	IŠIR.IS.25.09.—	Receipt of madder; BIN 9, 84 (C)
7501	—.12.22	Delivery of thread; BIN 9, 143 (C)
7503	IŠIR.IS.16.12D.13	Disbursement of glue; BIN 9, 159 (C)
7504	IŠIR.IS.32.12.—	Disbursement of beer and flour; BIN 9, 509 (C)
7505	IŠIR.IS.11.02.—	Disbursement of wool; sealed; BIN 10, 60 (C)
7506	ŠUIL.IS.03.03.10	Receipt of glue; BIN 9, 16 (C)
7507	IŠIR.IS.33.12D.23	Disbursement of leather; BIN 9, 472 (C)
7508	—.??.—	Disbursement of bitumen; $^{iti}gu_4$-zag-a; BIN 10, 181 (C)
7509	IŠIR.IS.16.08.14	Disbursement of glue; BIN 9, 168 (C)
7511	IŠIR.IS.18.06.26	Disbursement of bag; BIN 9, 288 (C)
7513	—.12D.06	Delivery of thread; BIN 9, 144 (C)
7514	IŠIR.IS.13.09.—	Receipt of skins; BIN 9, 67 (C)
7515	IŠIR.IS.21.06.—	Disbursement of glue, leather, and thread; BIN 9, 462 (C)
7516	IŠIR.IS.30.02.—	Receipt of hide; BIN 9, 24 (C)
7517	IŠIR.IS.33.01.06	Disbursement of bags and accessories; BIN 9, 227 (C)
7518	IŠIR.IS.33.09.11	Disbursement of materials for reed containers; BIN 9, 490 (C)
7519	IŠIR.IS.22.04.—	Archival label; BIN 10, 196 (C)
7520	IŠIR.IS.16.11.24	Delivery of leather and beer; BIN 9, 149 (C)

NBC	Date	Description
7521	IŠIR.IS.13.06.05	Disbursement of reed containers; BIN 9, 364 (C)
7522	IŠIR.IS.16.01.25	Delivery of hides; BIN 10, 12 (C)
7523	IŠIR.IS.14.02.10	Disbursement of reed mats; BIN 9, 497 (C)
7524	IŠIR.IS.15.01.13	Receipt of hides and skins; BIN 9, 58 (C)
7525	IŠIR.IS.16.01.07	Disbursement of bitumen; BIN 9, 208 (C)
7526	IŠIR.IS.13.05.17	Disbursement of leather; BIN 9, 336 (C)
7527	IŠIR.IS.13.05.20	Disbursement of bitumen; BIN 10, 105 (C)
7528	IŠIR.IS.16.12.26	Disbursement of glue; BIN 9, 160 (C)
7529	—.07.16	Disbursement of glue and flour; BIN 9, 172 (C)
7531	ŠUIL.IS.01.10.16	Disbursement of glue and gypsum; BIN 9, 202 (C)
7532	ŠUIL.IS.03.06.03	Disbursement of bags; BIN 9, 221 (C)
7533	ŠUIL.IS.01.03.18	Disbursement of bags; BIN 9, 289 (C)
7534	IŠIR.IS.25.05.26	Disbursement of bitumen; BIN 10, 156 (C)
7535	ŠUIL.IS.01.07.—	Receipt of oil; BIN 10, 50 (C)
7536	Lost	List of workers; BIN 10, 310 (C)
7537	Lost	Disbursement of door parts; BIN 10, 193 (C)
7538	xx.xx.20	Disbursement of leather; BIN 9, 334 (C)
7540	IŠIR.IS.19.10.18	Disbursement of bags, leather, musical instruments, boots, and sandals; sealed; BIN 9, 397 (C)
7541	IŠIR.IS.25.02.17	Disbursement of harness equipment, leather, and vessels; BIN 9, 429 (C)
7542	IŠIR.IS.27.03.02	Disbursement of bags and bowls; BIN 9, 407 (C)
7543	xx.xx.06	Disbursement of chairs, containers, and leather; BIN 9, 437 (C)
7544	No date	Receipt of reeds; BIN 10, 58 (C)
7545	ŠUIL.IS.03.01.22	Disbursement of bags and leather; BIN 9, 388 (C)
7547	IŠIR.IS.24.02.21	Disbursement of bags, mattresses, and reed objects; BIN 9, 417 (C)

NBC	Date	Description
7548	IŠIR.IS.13.09.14	List of workers; sealed; BIN 10, 253 (C)
7549	IŠIR.IS.15.07.—	Disbursement of bags; BIN 9, 316 (C)
7550	IŠIR.IS.15.09.20?	Disbursement of sandals, boots, reed containers, tables, and door bolts; BIN 9, 426 (C)
7551	IŠIR.IS.19.07.16	Disbursement of leather, sandals, and bags; sealed; BIN 9, 382 (C)
7552	IŠIR.IS.21.10.25	Disbursement of chairs, reed mats, doors, and reed objects; BIN 9, 439 (C)
7553	IŠIR.IS.26.01.29	Disbursement of oil and leather; sealed; BIN 9, 370 (C)
7554	ŠUIL.IS.02.03.23	Disbursement of leather, musical instruments, and bags; BIN 9, 368 (C)
7555	No date	List of workers' absences; BIN 10, 314 (C)
7556	IŠIR.IS.10.05.06	List of workers; BIN 10, 237 (C)
7557	IŠIR.IS.13.05.30	List of workers; BIN 10, 248 (C)
7558	IŠIR.IS.12.11.24	List of workers; BIN 10, 246 (C)
7559	IŠIR.IS.11.05.23	List of workers; BIN 10, 241 (C)
7560	IŠIR.IS.10.—.15	List of workers; BIN 9, 492 (C)
7561	IŠIR.IS.21.12.02	Disbursement of sandals and bags; BIN 9, 424 (C)
7562	—.??.15	Disbursement of barley; ^{m}Sà-ḫa-ra-t[um]
7563	ŠUIL.IS.03.04.16	Disbursement of table for fattening shed(?); BIN 9, 234 (C)
7564	IŠIR.IS.33.12D.30?	Disbursement of bags; BIN 9, 392 (C)
7565	IŠIR.IS.09.06.10	Disbursement of leather, reed tables, thread, and sandals; BIN 9, 238 (C)
7566	IŠIR.IS.26.11.—	Disbursement of sandals; sealed; BIN 9, 123 (C)
7567	No date	List of bags; BIN 9, 214 (C)
7568	IŠIR.IS.22.xx.xx	Receipt of baskets; sealed; BIN 10, 147 (C)
7569	IŠIR.IS.14.02.—	Disbursement of barley flour and beer
7570	IŠIR.IS.07.10.09	List of workers; BIN 9, 513 (C)

NBC	Date	Description
7571	IŠIR.IS.06.03.—	Delivery of door and its equipment; BIN 10, 89 (C)
7572	IŠIR.IS.15.03.—	Receipt of wool; BIN 10, 10 (C)
7573	ŠUIL.IS.01.04.11	Disbursement of alum, madder, leather, and glue; BIN 9, 467 (C)
7574	—.11.23	List of workers; BIN 10, 299 (C)
7575	xx.11.—	Exchange of real property; sealed
7576	ŠUIL.IS.02.09.30	Disbursement of bags; BIN 9, 286 (C)
7577	ŠUIL.IS.02.07.—	Disbursement of reed tables and containers; BIN 10, 170 (C)
7578	IŠIR.IS.22.—.—	Disbursement of Amorite slave-girl; BIN 10, 146 (C)
7579	ŠUIL.IS.03.01.09	Disbursement of leather and glue; BIN 9, 379 (C)
7580	ŠUIL.IS.03.05.05	Disbursement of bitumen and glue; BIN 9, 381 (C)
7581	IŠIR.IS.19.01.05	Disbursement of bags; sealed; BIN 9, 36 (C)
7582	IŠIR.IS.19.06.20	Disbursement of bags and bowls; dupl. NBC 6412; BIN 9, 404 (C)
7583	ŠUIL.IS.03.05.13	Disbursement of glue; BIN 9, 380 (C)
7584	IŠIR.IS.11.12.—	Disbursement of bags; BIN 9, 269 (C)
7585	IŠIR.IS.16.12.22	Delivery of leather; BIN 9, 138 (C)
7586	ŠUIL.IS.01.08.03	Disbursement of glue and flour; BIN 9, 203 (C)
7587	IŠIR.IS.13.12.18	Disbursement of leather containers; BIN 9, 315 (C)
7588	IŠIR.IS.12.10.—	Disbursement of musical instruments; BIN 9, 353 (C)
7589	IŠIR.IS.16.12.01	Disbursement of thread; BIN 9, 210 (C)
7590	IŠIR.IS.22.01.13	Receipt of hides; BIN 9, 15 (C)
7591	IŠIR.IS.26.07.13	Disbursement of bags; BIN 9, 290 (C)
7592	IŠIR.IS.29.05.—	Disbursement of glue; BIN 9, 263 (C)
7593	IŠIR.IS.25.04.23	Receipt of bitumen; BIN 10, 37 (C)
7594	—.10.03	Disbursement of leather object; BIN 9, 213 (C)

NBC	Date	Description
7595	IŠIR.IS.21.09.—	Delivery of glue and leather; BIN 9, 33 (C)
7596	IŠIR.IS.19.06.05	Delivery of glue; BIN 9, 12 (C)
7597	IŠIR.IS.10.09.28	Disbursement of thread; BIN 10, 131 (C)
7598	IŠIR.IS.22.xx.xx	Disbursement of hide; BIN 10, 148 (C)
7599	IŠIR.IS.08.11.—	Receipt of bitumen; BIN 10, 1 (C)
7600	IŠIR.IS.13.10.20	Disbursement of leather and bed; BIN 9, 473 (C)
7601	—.09.—	Disbursement of glue, skins, and thread; BIN 9, 247 (C)
7602	IŠIR.IS.33.12D.—	Archival label; BIN 10, 204 (C)
7603	—.07.13	Record concerning barley
7604	No date	Receipt of barley over several months
7605	No date	List of PNs
7606	ŠUIL.IS.03.04.16	Disbursement of palm spines and fronds; BIN 9, 519 (C)
7607	ŠUIL.IS.01.10.—	Disbursement of materials for throne of deity; BIN 9, 182 (C)
7608	IŠIR.IS.12.10.—	Disbursement of hides; BIN 10, 102 (C)
7609	IŠIR.IS.22.10.18	Disbursement of thread; BIN 10, 141 (C)
7610	xx.04.22?	Disbursement of leather; BIN 9, 461 (C)
7611	IŠIR.IS.23.01.27	Disbursement of reed objects, doormat, bags, and flutes; BIN 9, 532 (C)
7612	ŠUIL.IS.01.10.12	Disbursement of glue, gypsum, and flour; BIN 9, 201 (C)
7613	IŠIR.IS.19.09.21	Disbursement of bags and bowls; BIN 9, 410 (C)
7614	ŠUIL.IS.03.05.24	Disbursement of bags; BIN 9, 222 (C)
7615	IŠIR.IS.16.05.22	Disbursement of glue; BIN 9, 156 (C)
7616	IŠIR.IS.22.02.—	Receipt of rope; BIN 9, 25 (C)
7617	No date	Receipt of barley; sealed
7618	IŠIR.IS.25.10.25	Receipt of bitumen; BIN 9, 498 (C)
7619	IŠIR.IS.24.09.—	Receipt of hides and skins; BIN 9, 90 (C)

NBC	Date	Description
7620	No date	Receipt of wool; BIN 10, 79 (C)
7621	IŠIR.IS.33.06.10	Memorandum of no activity; sealed; BIN 10, 203 (C)
7622	IŠIR.IS.14.03.05+	Disbursement of bag and leather; BIN 9, 291 (C)
7623	ŠUIL.IS.01.06.16	Disbursement of bags; BIN 9, 310 (C)
7624	IŠIR.IS.33.05.12	Memorandum of no activity; BIN 10, 201 (C)
7625	IŠIR.IS.33.04.18	Disbursement of bags; BIN 9, 311 (C)
7626	IŠIR.IS.11.01.—	Receipt of skins; BIN 9, 89 (C)
7627	IŠIR.IS.15.—.—	Receipt of wool; sealed; BIN 9, 484 (C)
7629	IŠIR.IS.33.05.10	Memorandum of no activity; sealed; dupl. NBC 7110; BIN 10, 200 (C)
7630	IŠIR.IS.16.06.01	Disbursement of glue; BIN 9, 162 (C)
7631	IŠIR.IS.14.02.12	Disbursement of glue and woolen rope; BIN 9, 458 (C)
7632	IŠIR.IS.18.01.06	Disbursement of bags; BIN 9, 305 (C)
7633	IŠIR.IS.24.03.16	Disbursement of bags, reed containers, and sandals; BIN 9, 415 (C)
7634	IŠIR.IS.16.12.17	Disbursement of thread; BIN 9, 209 (C)
7637	Lost	Fragmentary sale of house; sealed
7639	IŠIR.IS.14.11.—	Disbursement of copper utensil; BIN 10, 118 (C)
7640	No date	Disbursement of roof beams; BIN 10, 188 (C)
7641	IŠIR.IS.18.06.19	Disbursement of bags; BIN 9, 292 (C)
7643	IŠIR.IS.13.11.—	Disbursement of reed container; BIN 10, 112 (C)
7644	IŠIR.IS.19.12.—	Disbursement of leather and glue; BIN 9, 248 (C)
7645	ŠUIL.IS.03.01.13	Disbursement of bags and leather; BIN 9, 419 (C)
7646	SIID.LA.07.09.23	Receipt of silver; sealed; YOS 14, 288 (C)
7647	IŠIR.IS.33.03.06	Disbursement of wooden and reed objects, and leather; BIN 9, 339 (C)
7648	—.07.08	List of workers; BIN 10, 276 (C)

NBC	Date	Description
7649	IŠIR.IS.13.03.20	Disbursement of reed objects and covers; BIN 9, 355 (C)
7650	ŠUIL.IS.03.01.30	Disbursement of bags; BIN 9, 293 (C)
7651	ŠUIL.IS.03.03.01	Disbursement of musical instruments; BIN 9, 444 (C)
7652	—.11.10	List of workers; BIN 10, 296 (C)
7653	IŠIR.IS.07.08.14	List of workers; BIN 10, 216 (C)
7654	IŠIR.IS.25.12.—	Receipt of hides and skins; sealed; BIN 9, 116 (C)
7655	URNI.IS.G.—.—	Assignment of fields; YOS 14, 318 (C)
7656	No date	Disbursement of reed objects; BIN 10, 189 (C)
7657	—.10.04	List of workers; BIN 10, 290 (C)
7658	IŠIR.IS.09.07.18	List of workers; BIN 10, 232 (C)
7659	IŠIR.IS.33.10.—	Delivery of reeds; BIN 10, 48 (C)
7660	No date	List of PNs
7661	—.10.30	List of workers; BIN 10, 294 (C)
7662	Lost	Disbursement of bags and leather; BIN 9, 306 (C)
7663	IŠIR.IS.22.02.13	Disbursement of reed mats, wooden object, reed container, and bed; sealed; BIN 9, 451 (C)
7664	ŠUIL.IS.03.01.30	List of tablets; BIN 10, 205 (C)
7665	Lost	Sale of real property; sealed
7666	No date	List of households
7667	IŠIR.IS.27.03.23	Disbursement of bags and bowls; BIN 9, 414 (C)
7668	IŠIR.IS.26.03.26	Disbursement of reed container for tablets, bags, leather, and musical instruments; BIN 9, 399 (C)
7669	IŠIR.IS.15.02.03	Disbursement of furniture as wedding gift; BIN 9, 438 (C)
7670	IŠIR.IS.09.07.25	List of workers; BIN 10, 233 (C)
7671	—.05.—	List of supplies for goldsmiths
7672	IŠIR.IS.12.10.26	List of workers; BIN 10, 245 (C)
7673	IŠIR.IS.09.04.—	Receipt of reed baskets; sealed; BIN 10, 59 (C)

NBC	Date	Description
7674	No date	Delivery of cord
7675	IŠIR.IS.28.03.25	Disbursement of harness equipment, sieves, and leather; BIN 9, 433 (C)
7676	IŠIR.IS.21.04.—	Account of leather manufacture; BIN 9, 489 (C)
7677	URNI.IS.J.09.—	Sale of empty lot; sealed
7678	No date	Payments of silver
7684	No date	Letter to Elmēšum and Nidnatum from Sîn-rēmēni concerning barley
7685	No date	Letter to Adda from Iddin-Adad concerning barley
7686	No date	Letter to "the man whom Šamaš preserves" from Šamaš-lamassu concerning possession of field
7687	SIMU.BA.08.01.08	Tablet and case—loan of silver
7692	IŠIR.IS.21.07.26	Disbursement of glue, leather, and bronze object; BIN 9, 459 (C)
7695	WASI.LA.11.12.—	Account of cattle; YOS 14, 311 (C)
7697	UN.UN.AŠ.12.—	Tablet and case—loan of barley; mu-ús-sa šita$_2$ ^{d}Utu-ra
7699	No date	Letter to Ištar-im-[...] from PI-ra-ya-x
7700	No date	Disbursement of garments
7702	No date	Delivery of foodstuffs
7703	No date	Account of barley for four months
7704	No date	Account of barley
7705	No date	Ration list
7706	Lost	Ration list for gardeners
7707	—.02.17	Ration list—barley
7708	xx.04.—	Disbursement of barley
7709	RISI.LA.53.03.—?	Delivery of large cattle
7710	IŠIR.IS.12.04.01?	Receipt of silver(?); mu bàd gal
7711	SIID.LA.07.06.18	Disbursement of dates

NBC	Date	Description
7712	—.07.15	Disbursement of silver
7713	No date	Legal case; YOS 14, 306 (C)
7714	IŠIR.IS.16.04.01?	Disbursement of flour and barley
7715	—.03.—	Ration list
7716	IŠIR.IS.16.10.—?	Disbursement
7717	xx.xx.05	List of workers; BIN 10, 304 (C)
7719	IŠIR.IS.13.11.05	Disbursement of leather; BIN 9, 267 (C)
7720	—.05.21	Disbursement of leather and glue; BIN 9, 188 (C)
7721	—.11.29	Disbursement of thread; BIN 10, 71 (C)
7722	SIID.LA.06.06.—	Delivery of slaves; YOS 14, 289 (C)
7723	UN.UN.I.—.—	Loan of silver; mu Ša-za-ar-za-ru-um i-pu-šu
7724	xx.12.19	Loan?
7725	No date	List of field acreages
7726	Lost?	Record concerning slaves
7727	RISI.LA.38.02.—	Delivery of wheat
7728	xx.09.13	List of PNs and quantities of sesame
7729	SIER.LA.01.12D.—	Institutional cultivation record; YOS 14, 303 (C)
7732	ŠUIL.IS.02.02.—?	Delivery of woven products; BIN 10, 86 (C)
7742	—.12.05	Disbursement of skins and glue; sealed; BIN 10, 177 (C)
7743	IŠIR.IS.33.05.04	Memorandum of no activity; BIN 10, 198 (C)
7745	IŠIR.IS.08.??.—	Disbursement of reed containers; sealed; ^{iti}[. . .] ^{d}Nin-a-zu; BIN 10, 99 (C)
7746	—.12.15	Delivery of leather; BIN 10, 178 (C)
7747	—.12.29	Delivery of leather; BIN 10, 180 (C)
7752	—.—.05	Disbursement of hides, sandals, and reed containers; BIN 10, 182 (C)
7759	Lost?	List of workers

NBC	Date	Description
7760	No date	Disbursement of vessels; BIN 10, 190 (C)
7772	Lost	Record concerning reeds
7783	No date	List of beams
7784	—.12D.—	Receipt of hides and skins; BIN 10, 55 (C)
7791	—.??.—	List of reed workers; ^{iti}síg-^{d}Inanna; BIN 10, 313 (C)
7796	—.12.19	Delivery of leather; BIN 10, 179 (C)
7798	No date?	Ration list—oil
7800A	No date	Fragmentary economic record of uncertain character
7842	No date	Report of an extispicy; YOS 10, 10 (C)
7844	RISI.LA.—.??.21	Account of large and small cattle; iti-24 ki-9(?)
7845	NUAD.LA.B.06.—	Division of inheritance; sealed; YOS 14, 285 (C)
7846	No date	Letter to "the man whom Marduk preserves" from Ikšud-appašu concerning rental of house
7847	SIER.LA.01.12D.—	Institutional cultivation record; cf. YOS 14, 300-05
7848	No date	Receipt of barley; sealed
7849	RISI.LA.17.11.—	Loan (šu-lá) of barley
7850	No date	Letter to Lu-Ninurta, Ipqu-Irra, Mannum-kīma-Sîn, and Si-im-me-me from Rīm-Sîn concerning defenses
7851	No date	Letter to Sîn-iddinam and the accountants from Warad-[...] concerning field
7852	No date	Letter
7853	No date	Letter concerning management of household
7854	No date	Letter to Ḫirutum from Nanna-mansum concerning arrears in taxes
7855	No date	Letter to Marduk-nāṣir from Ibni-Marduk concerning release of distrainee
7856	No date	Letter from Ipqu-^{d}x-x concerning shipment of precious stones
7857	No date	Letter to Warad-Sîn from Amat-Sîn concerning girl

NBC	Date	Description
7858	No date	Letter to Šamaš-ḫāzir from Ḫammurabi concerning filling of canal
7859	No date	Letter from Warad-Sîn
7860	No date	Fragmentary letter
7861	No date	Letter to Ṣilli-^{d}Sag-[...] from Ilšu-nāṣir concerning field
7862	No date	Letter to Ṣilli-Ištar from Tutub-māgir concerning distrainee
7863	No date	Fragmentary letter
7864	No date	Letter to Zizi from Sîn-māgir concerning military matters
7865	No date	Letter to Šamaš-eli-mātim from Nabi-ilišu concerning invitation; sealed
7866	No date	Fragmentary letter
7867	No date	Fragmentary letter to [...]-rēmēni
7868	No date	Letter to Sîn-māgir concerning silver
7869	No date	Fragmentary letter
7870	No date	Letter to Ibnatum from Ikūn-pî-Adad concerning wool and barley
7871	No date	Letter to Bēletum from Aḫuni
7872	No date	Fragmentary letter to Enki-zi-kalama from Sîn-x-lú
7873	No date	Letter to Sîn-uṣelli from Etel-pî-Marduk concerning release of man
7874	No date	Letter to Rīm-Sîn from "the exalted one who loves you" concerning silver
7875	No date	Letter concerning herdsmen
7876	No date	Letter to Šamaš-ayabaš concerning payment of flour
7877	No date	Fragmentary letter to Sîn-rēmēni from Awīl-Adad concerning legal case

NBC	Date	Description
7878	No date	Fragmentary letter concerning copper spade and garments
7879	No date	Fragmentary letter to Sîn-rēmēni and Gimillum from Ātanaḫ-ilī
7880	No date	Letter to Erībam-Sîn from Šamḫum concerning silver
7881	No date	Letter
7882	Illegible	List of PNs and towns
7883	No date	Letter from Andulli-Sîn concerning accounts and straw
7884	No date	Letter to Šamaš-dayyān from Sîn-gāmil
7885	No date	Letter to Šamaš-ḫāzir, Sîn-mušallim, and their associates from Ḫammurabi concerning field
7886	—.06.20	Memorandum concerning sheep
7887	xx.06.24?	Tag—record concerning bovine
7888	No date	Letter to Ilī-tillatī from Uraš-iddinam concerning barley
7889	No date	Letter from Sîn-iddinam concerning transport of wood
7890	No date	Fragmentary letter concerning large cattle
7891	No date	Letter from Itūr-ašdum concerning planting of orchard
7892	No date	Letter from Ṣilli-Šamaš concerning garments
7894	No date	Letter
7895	—.06.01	Disbursements of silver
7896	No date	Letter to Sîn-leqe-[...] from Šamaš-IGI-NI concerning dispute over slave-girl
7898	No date	Letter to Mār-erṣetim from Pirḫi-Marduk concerning *igisûm*-tax
7899	No date	Letter to Imgur-[...] and Sîn-[...] from Erībam-[...]
7900	No date	Letter concerning silver

NBC	Date	Description
7901	No date	Letter
7902	No date	Account of barley (ledger)
7903	No date	Letter to Sîn-puṭram from Sîn-abušu
7904	No date	Fragmentary letter
7905	No date	Letter to [...]-rēmēni from Marduk-mušallim concerning journey to Babylon
7906	—.02.13	List of numerals and days in month of Ayyaru
7907	No date	Letter to Arnabtum from Lu-igisa concerning maintenance of canal; YNER 4, no. 36 (C, T, Tr)
7908	No date	Letter concerning distrainee
7910	—.11.09	Memorandum concerning silver as price of large cattle
7911	SIID.LA.07.06.21	Receipt of silver as price of large cattle
7929	No date	Letter to Sîn-aḫi from Gagum concerning *e'iltu*-obligation
7930	DADU.ŠA.xx.xx.xx	Sale of orchard and well; sealed; date lost, RN in oath
7931	Lost	Fragmentary adoption?; sealed
7932	No date	Letter to Itūr-ašdu from Rīš-Šamaš concerning large cattle
7933	No date	Letter to Rīm-Adad from A-x-am(?)-mu concerning oxen and plowing of field
7973	No date	Letter to Sîn-ubla from Sîn-imittī concerning barley
7995	No date	Account of barley rations for harvest laborers
7997	—.06.09	Disbursement of silver; cf. NBC 9904 and 9920
7998	—.06.06	Exchange of sheep
8002	—.xx.xx	Economic record of uncertain character
8003	No date	Memorandum concerning payment of silver for persons
8004	No date	Memorandum concerning disbursement of silver

NBC	Date	Description
8005	SIID.LA.06.12.30	Delivery of flour; sealed
8006	No date	Tag—record of reed objects(?) for two months; sealed
8007	No date	Tag—record of barley as wages of plowmen; sealed; cf. NBC 8013
8008	No date	Disbursement of foodstuff
8009	—.11.04	Disbursement of large and small cattle
8010	No date	Disbursement of dates
8011	No date	Delivery of reed tables; BIN 10, 80 (C)
8012	—.06.30	Promissory note—barley
8013	—.02.30	Tag—record of barley as wages of plowmen; sealed; ENES 966x; cf. NBC 8007
8014	SIID.LA.06.11.15	Receipt of silver as price of gold; YOS 14, 290 (C)
8015	RISI.LA.11.06.—	Loan (šu-lá) of barley
8016	—.05.07	Disbursement of vessels; BIN 10, 174 (C)
8017	??.??.—	Disbursement of foodstuff; $^{iti}gu_4$(?)-si-sá(?) sig_4-a mu x kù-sig_{17}
8018	No date	Delivery of barley
8020	No date	Record of hides for shields; BIN 9, 329 (C)
8021	No date	Disbursement of bags and leather; BIN 9, 294 (C)
8022	—.10.23	List of workers; BIN 10, 293 (C)
8023	—.10.20	List of workers; BIN 10, 292 (C)
8024	—.07.28	List of workers; BIN 10, 280 (C)
8025	IŠIR.IS.13.06.05	List of workers; BIN 10, 249 (C)
8026	—.07.30	List of workers; BIN 10, 281 (C)
8027	—.08.22	List of workers; BIN 10, 284 (C)
8028	—.09.28	List of workers; dupl. NBC 7189; BIN 10, 288 (C)
8029	No date	List of numerals and PNs; sealed

NBC	Date	Description
8030	SUEL.LA.28.07.—	Sale of field; YOS 14, 267 (C)
8031	—.07.03	Disbursement of foodstuff
8032	SUEL.LA.05.—.—	Receipt of wool of palace; sealed; YOS 14, 225 (C)
8036	ITŠA.KI.F.04.—	Loan of silver; sealed
8039	—.01.—	Disbursement of barley
8078	RISI.LA.30.??.12	Disbursement of dead sheep; sealed; iti-16 ki-2
8079	IŠIR.IS.27.10.—	Receipt; BIN 10, 77 (C)
8103	SIID.LA.07.—.—	Receipt of silver in lieu of barley rations for two months
8114	No date	Fragmentary list of PNs
8126	IŠIR.IS.10.10.—	Receipt of leather scraps
8136	IŠIR.IS.13.11.—	Disbursement of furniture; BIN 10, 113 (C)
8137	IŠIR.IS.13.01.—	Disbursement of leather containers; BIN 9, 317 (C)
8139	IŠIR.IS.10.05.30	List of workers; BIN 10, 238 (C)
8161	RISI.LA.22.03.—	Cadastre; cf. NBC 10916
8169	IŠIR.IS.07.06.30	Disbursement of foodstuffs
8170	RISI.LA.30+.03.—	Cadastre
8180	SAIL.BA.11.09.01?	Disbursement; sealed
8183	No date	List of PNs
8228	SAIL.BA.23.11.01	Tablet and fragments of case—receipt of silver, price of dates
8231	Lost	List of property
8232	No date	Ration list
8233	Lost?	Fragmentary ration list
8234	No date	List of workers
8235	IŠIR.IS.19.07.30	Disbursement of materials for leatherworking; BIN 10, 130 (C)

NBC	Date	Description
8236	WAQR.ŠA.A.—.—	Tablet and fragments of case—loan of silver; sealed; mu *Wa-aq-ru-um* alam zabar *ú-še-ri-bu*
8237	No date	Legal case concerning theft; YOS 14, 40 (C)
8238	No date	Disbursement of beer and flour to workshop and palace dependents; cf. NBC 8473
8239	No date	Ration list
8241	No date	List of field acreages
8242	No date	Receipt of barley
8244	No date	Ration list
8245	No date	Ration list
8246	No date	List of sheep
8247	Lost?	Fragmentary account of sheep and oxen (ledger)
8248	Lost?	Fragmentary account of copper implements (ledger)
8249	No date	Account of barley
8250	Lost?	Division of property; sealed
8251	No date	Ration list—barley
8252	No date	Ration list—barley; list of PNs
8253	SIID.LA.07.01.19	Record concerning skins; YOS 14, 293 (C)
8254	No date	Payments of silver to various individuals
8255	xx.06.—	Guarantee of debt
8256	Lost?	Hire of team of oxen; sealed
8257	No date?	List of property of various types
8258	IPE2.ŠA.B.—.—	Receipt of barley; sealed; YOS 14, 55 (C)
8260	No date	Sale of real property
8261	No date	List of quantities of silver, large cattle, and barley
8262	IPE2.ŠA.H.—.—	Loan of silver; sealed; YOS 14, 6 (C)
8263	IPE2.ŠA.H.05.20	Hire of person; sealed; YOS 14, 48 (C)

NBC	Date	Description
8264	No date	Loan of barley; YOS 14, 57 (C)
8265	SUEL.LA.28.01.—?	Disbursement of small cattle
8266	No date	Ration list
8267	—.11.01	Ration list—fodder; ITIKi-is-ki-sum; YOS 14, 56 (C)
8268	No date	Ration list
8269	No date	Ration list—dates
8270	SAIL.BA.27.04.09	Receipt of bran; sealed
8271	DATA.EŠ.02.—.—	Loan (ḫubuttātum) of barley; YOS 14, 2 (C)
8272	IPE2.ŠA.03.—.—	Loan of silver; YOS 14, 63 (C)
8273	SAIL.BA.26.12.03	Loan of barley; sealed
8274	IPAD.EŠ.D.—.—	Loan (ḫubuttātum) of wheat; YOS 14, 10 (C)
8275	—.06.—	Loan of silver; iti dÚ-gu-lá; YOS 14, 64 (C)
8276	—.09.23	Disbursement(?) of silver
8277	Illegible	Record concerning hides
8278	No date	Ration list—barley
8279	Lost	Loan of barley; YOS 14, 36 (C)
8280	IPE2.ŠA.09.—.—	Loan of barley; YOS 14, 45 (C)
8281	HADU.ŠA.B.—.—	Loan of silver; YOS 14, 62 (C)
8282	No date	Sale of field; YOS 14, 58 (C)
8283	SAIL.BA.22.11.10	Loan of barley; sealed
8285	No date	List of quantities of wool
8286	No date	Ration list
8287	IPE2.ŠA.08.—.—	Harvest labor contract; sealed; YOS 14, 9 (C)
8288	—.—.05	Loan (ḫubuttātum) of bricks; day in text; YOS 14, 44 (C)
8289	IPAD2.ŠA.A.—.—	Ration list—oil; mu urudualam kù-sig$_{17}$ Ši-ma-ḫa-tu
8290	IPE2.ŠA.07.—.—	Loan (ḫubuttātum) of barley; YOS 14, 3 (C)

NBC	Date	Description
8291	UN.ŠA.M.—.—	Loan of silver and barley; YOS 14, 37 (C)
8292	Lost?	Ration list—barley
8293	UN.ŠL.H.—.—	Loan of silver; YOS 14, 53 (C)
8294	SAIL.BA.26.11.05	Loan of silver to be repaid in ewes(?)
8296	No date	Loan of silver; sealed; YOS 14, 66 (C)
8297	IŠIR.IS.13.—.—	Disbursement of bags to various individuals; BIN 9, 408 (C)
8298	No date	List of workers; sealed
8299	xx.xx.17	List of workers; BIN 10, 309 (C)
8300	No date	Contract concerning barley
8301	SIID.LA.07.09.01	Ration list—barley
8302	Lost?	Ration list—barley
8303	Lost	Ration list—barley
8304	Lost	List of workers
8305	ENBA.IS.B.06.—	Sale of field; sealed
8306	xx.11.—	Adoption; sealed
8307	No date	List of PNs and numerals
8308	RISI.LA.38.01.27	Receipt of quantities of barley
8309	UN.UN.L.—.—	Sale of girl; sealed; mu bàd gar-ra-[x(?)-]BU-um x-[...]
8310	RISI.LA.30.??.16	Delivery of sheep; sealed; iti-23 ki-5
8311	—.09.08	Promissory note—barley
8312	—.01.09	Disbursement of oil
8313	—.02.08	Statement of arrears in barley
8314	No date	Assumption of losses in silver
8411	IŠIR.IS.23.07.—	Receipt of hides and skins; BIN 9, 61 (C)
8412	ŠUIL.IS.01.09.18	Disbursement of bag; BIN 9, 418 (C)

NBC	Date	Description
8413	IŠIR.IS.18.—.—	Tag for tablet container; BIN 9, 503 (C)
8414	IŠIR.IS.33.12D.—	Delivery of felt; BIN 10, 85 (C)
8415	IŠIR.IS.25.02.—	Receipt of hides and skins; BIN 9, 57 (C)
8416	IŠIR.IS.23.01.—	Disbursement of leather; BIN 9, 185 (C)
8417	IŠIR.IS.16.05.07	Disbursement of glue; BIN 9, 157 (C)
8418	IŠIR.IS.16.05.05	Disbursement of bags; BIN 9, 296 (C)
8419	IŠIR.IS.21.06.—	Receipt of hides and skins; BIN 9, 14 (C)
8420	—.10.08	Disbursement of bags; BIN 9, 295 (C)
8421	IŠIR.IS.16.08.08	Disbursement of bags and leather; BIN 9, 297 (C)
8422	No date	Loan of silver
8423	IŠIR.IS.25.07.25	Disbursement of bags; BIN 9, 298 (C)
8424	IŠIR.IS.19.02.05	Disbursement of doors, bags, and leather; BIN 9, 344 (C)
8425	ŠUIL.IS.01.10.—	Receipt of bitumen; BIN 10, 52 (C)
8427	IŠIR.IS.16.12.25	Disbursement of bags and leather; BIN 9, 299 (C)
8428	IŠIR.IS.09.09.—	Receipt of cover for bed; BIN 10, 74 (C)
8429	No date	Receipt of unspecified commodity
8430	—.12.—	List of baskets of/for baked goods
8431	IŠIR.IS.14.12.25	Disbursement of bags; BIN 9, 300 (C)
8432	IŠIR.IS.22.02.—	Receipt of hides; BIN 9, 26 (C)
8433	IŠIR.IS.22.02.—	Delivery of pomegranate products; BIN 10, 25 (C)
8434	IŠIR.IS.17.03.21	Disbursement of bag and accessories; BIN 9, 225 (C)
8435	IŠIR.IS.20.10.25	Receipt of wool; BIN 10, 21 (C)
8436	IŠIR.IS.12.08.24	Disbursement of bags and reed objects; BIN 9, 387 (C)
8437	IŠIR.IS.11.05.—	Disbursement of leather bags; sealed; BIN 9, 118 (C)
8438	IŠIR.IS.20.09.—	Disbursement of garment; sealed; BIN 9, 510 (C)
8439	IŠIR.IS.22.02.—	Disbursement of skins; BIN 10, 26 (C)

NBC	Date	Description
8440	IŠIR.IS.19.06.27	Disbursement of bags, leather, and wooden containers; sealed; BIN 9, 398 (C)
8441	IŠIR.IS.27.06.—	Receipt of bitumen; BIN 10, 41 (C)
8442	IŠIR.IS.11.06.—	Disbursement of wool; BIN 10, 101 (C)
8443	IŠIR.IS.13.08.27	List of workers; BIN 10, 252 (C)
8444	IŠIR.IS.13.07.08	List of workers; BIN 10, 251 (C)
8445	IŠIR.IS.09.04.16	List of workers; BIN 10, 230 (C)
8446	No date	Disbursement of reeds and other materials
8447	IŠIR.IS.27.02.09	Disbursement of bags and bowls; BIN 9, 409 (C)
8448	IŠIR.IS.27.04.05	Disbursement of bags and bowls; BIN 9, 411 (C)
8449	No date	List of receptacles
8450	—.03.—	Disbursement of foodstuff
8451	IŠIR.IS.26.09.05	Disbursement of oil and leather; sealed; BIN 9, 373 (C)
8452	IŠIR.IS.08.06.13	List of workers; BIN 9, 522 (C)
8453	No date	Disbursement of barley flour and beer
8454	IŠIR.IS.09.07.10	List of workers; BIN 10, 231 (C)
8455	IŠIR.IS.19.xx.—?	Disbursement of chair, chariot, and harness equipment; sealed; BIN 9, 430 (C)
8457	xx.10.—	Sale of real property; sealed
8458	IŠIR.IS.15.04.21	Disbursement of sandals, bags, and woolen garments; BIN 9, 326 (C)
8459	IŠIR.IS.21.12.21	Disbursement of reed containers, leather, and bags; sealed; BIN 9, 401 (C)
8460	IŠIR.IS.11.04.15	List of workers; BIN 9, 508 (C)
8461	IŠIR.IS.20.xx.22?	Disbursement of leather products; BIN 9, 233 (C)
8462	xx.05.—?	Disbursement of leather products; BIN 10, 195 (C)
8463	IŠIR.IS.08.07.08	List of workers; BIN 10, 227 (C)

NBC	Date	Description
8465	IŠIR.IS.20.07.06	Disbursement of boots and reed containers; BIN 9, 428 (C)
8466	IŠIR.IS.08.08.—	Disbursement of sieves; sealed; BIN 10, 98 (C)
8467	IŠIR.IS.23.08.05	Disbursement of skins, bags, and musical instruments; sealed; BIN 9, 365 (C)
8468	—.01.24	Disbursement of vessels; BIN 10, 173 (C)
8469	IŠIR.IS.19.02.30	Disbursement of chairs and sandals; BIN 9, 432 (C)
8470	IŠIR.IS.14.07.23	Disbursement of sandals, bags, and woolen clothing; BIN 9, 327 (C)
8471	No date	Disbursement of reed objects and bags; BIN 9, 450 (C)
8472	IŠIR.IS.25.02.—	Disbursement of oil and hides; BIN 9, 375 (C)
8473	No date	Disbursement of flour and beer; cf. NBC 8238
8474	IŠIR.IS.26.12.14	Disbursement of bags and leather; BIN 9, 301 (C)
8475	IŠIR.IS.08.05.15	List of workers; BIN 10, 225 (C)
8476	No date	Ration list—barley
8477	IŠIR.IS.25.08.—	Disbursement of furniture; BIN 9, 499 (C)
8478	IŠIR.IS.07.08.25	List of workers; BIN 10, 218 (C)
8479	IŠIR.IS.19.07.—	Receipt of leather; BIN 9, 103 (C)
8480	IŠIR.IS.33.11.24	Disbursement of bags and leather; BIN 9, 226 (C)
8481	—.07.—	Disbursement of containers, sandals, boots, and other objects; BIN 9, 431 (C)
8482	IŠIR.IS.19.06.—	Receipt of wool and skins; BIN 9, 128 (C)
8483	IŠIR.IS.19.09.22	Disbursement of leather, shoes, and bags; sealed; BIN 9, 384 (C)
8484	IŠIR.IS.25.04.30	Receipt of sesame oil; BIN 10, 38 (C)
8485	IŠIR.IS.23.06.07	Disbursement of bags, leather, and musical instruments; BIN 9, 402 (C)
8486	IŠIR.IS.06.01.xx	Disbursement of musical instruments and reed objects; BIN 10, 87 (C)

NBC	Date	Description
8487	IŠIR.IS.33.09.—	Delivery of reeds and wood; BIN 9, 531 (C)
8488	IŠIR.IS.26.12.—	Receipt of skins; BIN 9, 40 (C)
8489	IŠIR.IS.14.11.—	Receipt of wool; BIN 10, 9 (C)
8490	IŠIR.IS.19.03.24	Disbursement of glue and leather; BIN 9, 177 (C)
8491	No date	Ration list
8492	IŠIR.IS.08.04.03	List of workers; BIN 10, 222 (C)
8493	No date	List of persons under authority of others; cf. NBC 9781
8494	HARA.BA.24.10.25	Contract of uncertain character
8496	—.12D.30	Receipt of thread; BIN 10, 54 (C)
8497	IŠIR.IS.09.05.—	Receipt of textile; BIN 10, 73 (C)
8498	IŠIR.IS.13.08.—	Disbursement of leather covers; BIN 9, 333 (C)
8499	IŠIR.IS.15.04.25	List of workers; BIN 10, 267 (C)
8500	—.06.28	List of workers; BIN 10, 311 (C)
8501	—.02.13	Disbursement of leather; BIN 9, 190 (C)
8502	IŠIR.IS.18.12D.—	Receipt of hides and gypsum; BIN 9, 79 (C)
8503	IŠIR.IS.15.02.10	Disbursement of wool; BIN 10, 66 (C)
8504	—.09.—	Disbursement of doors; BIN 10, 175 (C)
8506	No date	Receipt(?) of foodstuff
8508	—.06.29	List of workers; BIN 10, 312 (C)
8509	No date	Disbursement of barley flour
8510	xx.xx.11	Disbursement of leather; BIN 10, 192 (C)
8511	No date	Disbursement of barley for beer and flour
8512	No date	List of PNs?
8518	IŠIR.IS.16.06.10	Disbursement of glue; BIN 9, 165 (C)
8519	IŠIR.IS.10.01.xx	List of foodstuffs

NBC	Date	Description
8520	IŠIR.IS.15.01.18?	List of workers; BIN 10, 263 (C)
8521	—.07.06	Disbursement of glue and flour; BIN 10, 70 (C)
8522	IŠIR.IS.15.04.12	Disbursement of glue and bag; BIN 9, 309 (C)
8523	IŠIR.IS.13.12.—	Receipt of skins; BIN 9, 115 (C)
8524	—.06.17	Disbursement of hides and dead sheep
8525	No date	Disbursement of foodstuff
8526	Lost	Receipt of silver for sheep; sealed
8527	Lost	Disbursement of oil
8528	xx.07.21	Record of barley allotment for donkeys
8529	No date	List of witnesses to sale
8530	SAIL.BA.06.10.19	Memorandum concerning shipment of barley
8531	—.06.26	List of wooden objects
8532	SAIL.BA.07.10.24?	Record concerning barley; sealed
8533	SAIL.BA.08.12.20	Loan of barley; sealed
8534	??.01.—	Receipt of silver and barley; sealed; mu gibil
8535	No date	Letter to Marduk-muballiṭ from Ḫammurabi-liwwir concerning disbursement of barley; sealed
8536	Lost	Fragmentary administrative record of uncertain character; sealed
8537	No date	Memorandum concerning two persons
8538	SAIL.BA.07.06.07	Record of barley allotment for slaves
8539	SAIL.BA.08.06.02	Consignment of small cattle; sealed
8540	SAIL.BA.06.11.03	Record concerning barley
8541	No date	List of garments
8542	No date	Ration list—flour
8543	SAIL.BA.??.01.01	Disbursement of barley; sealed; mu gibil; RN in sealing

NBC	Date	Description
8544	No date	Memorandum concerning unspecified objects on hand for two months
8545	UN.EŠ.P.12D.05	Receipt of barley; sealed; ITI DIRI *Ki-in-kum*
8546	HARA.BA.42.10.—	Loan of barley; sealed
8547	RISI.LA.59.04.—	Account of sesame
8548	DATA.NE..03.12D.23	Receipt of barley; sealed; ITI DIRI *Ki-in-kum*; YOS 14, 73 (C)
8549	No date	Tablet and fragment of case—record concerning barley and another foodstuff
8550	No date	Delivery of barley; sealed
8551	SAIL.BA.07.09.10	Record concerning fodder for sheep
8552	SAIL.BA.07.08.24?	Record concerning barley for fodder; sealed
8553	SAIL.BA.07.08.22	Receipt of barley
8554	SAIL.BA.07.06.15	Receipt of milk; sealed
8555	HARA.BA.42.05.—	Loan of silver
8556	SAIL.BA.07.03.30	Receipt of barley; sealed; cf. NBC 8768
8557	Lost	Record concerning barley; sealed
8558	SAIL.BA.07.07.25	Fragmentary economic record of uncertain character; sealed
8559	SAIL.BA.07.01.25	Receipt of barley
8560	SAIL.BA.07.05.28	Hire of teams of oxen; sealed
8561	RISI.LA.14.—.—	Loan (šu-lá) of silver; sealed
8562	—.02.xx	Ration list; cf. NBC 8565
8563	SAIL.BA.08.01.14	Receipt of sickles; sealed
8564	SAIL.BA.06.02.22	Loan of barley; sealed
8565	—.08.xx	Ration list; cf. NBC 8562
8566	No date	Record concerning barley
8567	SAIL.BA.06.09.22	Record of fodder for one day; sealed

NBC	Date	Description
8568	SAIL.BA.07.06.11	Loan of barley; sealed
8569	—.01.15?	Disbursement of barley
8570	SAIL.BA.05.11.01	Loan of barley; sealed
8571	SAIL.BA.08.04.26	Loan of barley; sealed
8572	—.07.—	Account of small cattle
8573	RISI.LA.28.10.10	Ration list—barley
8574	—.01.03	Fragmentary receipt
8575	—.04.11	Record concerning bran for fattening; sealed
8576	—.xx.14	Ration list
8577	SAIL.BA.24.01.12	Promissory note—beer; sealed
8578	SAIL.BA.??.01.02	Disbursement of barley; sealed; mu gibil
8579	RISI.LA.48.05.07	Disbursement of small cattle
8580	RISI.LA.27.10.27	Delivery of barley; sealed
8581	—.07.26	Memorandum concerning hired men
8582	SAIL.BA.07.07.09	Agreement concerning payment of barley; sealed
8583	—.04.02	Ration list—barley
8584	SAIL.BA.22.12.10	Receipt of aromatics, porridge, etc.; sealed
8585	—.09.04	Memorandum concerning hired man
8586	No date	Memorandum concerning receipt of oil from four persons
8587	—.08.10	Promissory note—barley(?)
8588	SAIL.BA.07.10.07	Receipt of beer; sealed
8589	SAIL.BA.06.02.30	List of objects; sealed
8590	No date	List of numbers of slave-girls and their owners
8591	RISI.LA.38.01.—	Receipt of quantities of barley
8592	No date	Memorandum concerning oil

NBC	Date	Description
8593	SUEL.LA.23.09.—	Sale of orchard; sealed; YOS 14, 263 (C)
8594	No date	Ration list—beer
8595	No date	List of PNs
8596	RISI.LA.58.03.—	Herding contract for equids; sealed
8597	No date	Receipt of wooden beams
8601	SAIL.BA.19.08.15	Hire of person; sealed
8602	Lost	Disbursement
8603	DATA.ŠA.C.—.—	Tablet and case—loan of barley; sealed; YOS 14, 22 (C); ENES 768
8604	NASI.ŠA.I.—.—	Tablet and case—loan of barley; sealed; YOS 14, 16 (C); ENES 767
8605	IRIM.IS.E.—.—	Tablet and portion of case—sale of field; sealed; YOS 14, 319 (C)
8606	HARA.BA.32.03.15+	List of field acreages; sealed
8607	No date?	Account of foodstuff (ledger)
8609	RISI.LA.30+.10.—	Record concerning barley
8610	SAIL.BA.07.07.01	Ration list—barley; sealed
8611	No date	List of PNs
8612	WASI.LA.04.06.14?	Receipt of wooden objects
8613	—.—.xx	List of quantities of silver
8614	No date	List of PNs and numbers of workers(?)
8615	No date	Receipt of barley
8616	DADU.ŠA.C.—.—	Tablet and portion of case—loan of barley; sealed; YOS 14, 17 (C)
8619	RISI.LA.59.03.08	Account of barley
8620	RISI.LA.47.02.22	Rental of field; sealed
8621	BUSI.IS.E.12.—	Division of inheritance; sealed; YOS 14, 320 (C)
8622	ZAMB.IS.A.04.—	Division of inheritance; sealed; YOS 14, 322 (C)

NBC	Date	Description
8623	No date	Sale of orchard
8627	RISI.LA.48.04.01	Account of barley
8628	No date	List of PNs
8629	No date	Payment
8630	No date	Oath concerning restitution of grain from field; fingernail impressions
8631	HARA.BA.38.05.—?	Ration list
8632	No date	List of PNs and quantities of barley
8633	—.02.—	Disbursement of barley to various categories of worker
8634	—.09.25	Disbursement of seed (ledger)
8635	xx.07.xx	Nursing contract
8636	DAIL.IS.05.12D.—	Sale of uncultivated field; sealed; YOS 14, 329 (C)
8638	No date	Disbursement of large quantity of silver
8639	No date	List of witnesses
8640	RISI.LA.59.02.—	Disbursement of barley
8641	RISI.LA.47.03.24	Account of barley
8642	SAIL.BA.22.10.14	Receipt of silver; sealed
8643	RISI.LA.03.03.10?	Ration list—barley
8644	xx.02.xx	Record concerning barley for harvest workers
8645	SUEL.LA.02.02.08	Tag—delivery of bran for fodder; sealed
8646	—.—.22	Receipt of small cattle
8647	SAIL.BA.07.07.17	Disbursement of flour; sealed
8649	RISI.LA.57.06.20	Hire of slave-girl; sealed
8650	HARA.BA.42.04.—	Loan of barley; sealed
8651	SAIL.BA.xx.12.22+	Disbursement of barley; sealed
8652	No date	Disbursement of barley

NBC	Date	Description
8653	No date	Ration list—barley
8654	No date	List of PNs
8655	No date	Tablet and portion of case—loan of barley
8656	RISI.LA.26.07.06	Rental of field
8657	SAIL.BA.08.06.16	Tablet and case—record concerning bran
8658	—.05.27	Ration list—barley (ledger)
8659	RISI.LA.39.04.—	Account of silver(?)
8660	No date	Ration list
8661	RISI.LA.32+.xx.26	Ration list—barley flour
8662	SAIL.BA.08.xx.30	Ration list
8663	SAIL.BA.07.10.10	Disbursement of *naḫramu*-garments
8664	No date	Account of barley; YOS 14, 41 (C)
8665	No date	Letter to Sîn-[...], Adad-[...], Šamaš-[...], Sîn-[...], An-na-da(?), and the accountants from Sumu-Emutbalim concerning large quantities of wool
8666	IŠDA.IS.C.01.—	List of quantities of silver paid as tax (gun); YOS 14, 314 (C)
8667	LIIŠ.IS.B.02.08	Disbursement of beer and other foodstuffs
8668	No date	Disbursement of silver?
8669	Lost?	Record concerning reeds; sealed
8671	SUAB.BA.01.11.—	Sale of slave-girls; sealed; YOS 14, 128 (C)
8672	No date	Fragment of case—letter to "my father"; sealed
8673	No date	Door sealing—seal impression only
8674	xx.11.xx	Fragment of case—record concerning field acreages; sealed
8674A	Lost	Fragment of case—contract of uncertain character; sealed

NBC	Date	Description
8675	Lost	Fragments of cases—miscellaneous economic records—loan of barley(?), loan(?) of silver, list of witnesses; sealed
8676	RISI.LA.59.09.—	Ration list—barley
8677	No date	List of workers/soldiers
8679	Lost	Sale of real property
8681	No date	Legal case concerning slave-girl
8682	Lost?	Fragmentary cadastre
8683	RISI.LA.59.08.29	Account of barley
8684	IPE2.ŠA.10.07.30	Fragmentary record concerning barley for fodder and rations; [mu] erin$_2$ Šu-bir$_4$ ḫé-an-na ^{giš}tukul; ^{iti}Ki-nu-nu
8685	Lost	Fragmentary list of votive objects, chiefly gold rings
8686	No date?	Fragmentary record of lambs for *sattukku* offerings
8687	No date	List of numerals and PNs
8688	IŠDA.IS.O.09.—	Fragmentary record of votive offerings of copper vessels; YOS 14, 316 (C)
8689	RISI.LA.59.02.—	Disbursement of barley for two months (ledger)
8690	No date	List of numerals and PNs
8691	Lost?	Economic record of uncertain character
8692	SAIL.BA.04.08.16	Promissory note—silver; sealed
8693	SAIL.BA.07.06.20?	Record concerning slave; sealed
8694	RISI.LA.07.08.03	Account of barley; [mu abu]l-la-a 2-a-bi [Maš-gán-]šabra^{ki} mu-un-dù-a
8695	No date	Ration list—barley
8696	No date	Tablet and portion of case—letter to Lu-Ninurta, Balmunamḫe, Ipqu-Irra, Iddin-Sîn, ZI-mu-x-x, and Sîn-meme from Rīm-Sîn concerning fortifications; sealed
8697	HARA.BA.40.03.05	Rental of field; sealed

NBC	Date	Description
8698	SAIL.BA.07.03.01	Rental of field; sealed
8699	RISI.LA.30.04.15	Record concerning shipping between(?) Larsa and Nippur; mu-ús-sa uru^{ki} Du-un-nu-um^{ki} mu-dib-ba
8700	xx.—.—	Disbursement of bitumen and other materials; mu-ús-sa [...]
8702	Lost	Hire of teams of oxen; sealed
8703	Lost	Record concerning sheep; sealed
8704	HARA.BA.41.04.—	Receipt of small cattle
8705	RISI.LA.26.07.—?	Rental of field
8706	xx.01.—	Record concerning small cattle; sealed
8707	No date	Disbursement of silver
8708	Illegible	Account of silver
8709	—.07.—	Disbursement of wool
8710	RISI.LA.01.08.—?	Partnership for cultivation of field; sealed
8712	—.04.16	Fragmentary ration list?
8713	SAIL.BA.07.08.01	Tablet and portion of case—receipt of barley from various households
8714	No date?	List of PNs and quantities of silver
8715	NASI.ŠA.F.—.—	Loan of barley; YOS 14, 14 (C)
8717	SAIL.BA.07.08.19	Disbursement of barley; sealed
8718	SAIL.BA.07.07.14	Disbursement of barley; sealed
8719	SAIL.BA.07.09.03	Receipt of two spades; sealed
8720	SAIL.BA.07.11.xx	Disbursement of barley; sealed
8721	No date?	Record of large quantities of bricks and beams
8722	SAIL.BA.06.09.22	Record concerning barley; sealed
8723	SAIL.BA.06.06.18	Loan of silver; sealed
8724	SAIL.BA.07.09.25	Receipt of fodder; sealed

NBC	Date	Description
8725	SAIL.BA.07.04.21	Record concerning barley; sealed
8726	SAIL.BA.07.05.22	Hire of team of oxen; sealed
8727	No date	List of witnesses
8728	SAIL.BA.06.10.17	Record concerning barley
8729	SAIL.BA.06.04.06?	Receipt of barley; sealed
8730	SAIL.BA.08.07.03	Receipt of shoes
8731	SAIL.BA.07.10.01	Record concerning barley; sealed
8732	SAIL.BA.07.02.24	Disbursement of barley; sealed
8733	RISI.LA.21.06.15	Receipt of barley
8735	SAIL.BA.06.08.01	Receipt of barley
8736	xx.11.10+	Disbursement of barley
8737	SAIL.BA.06.11.18	Record concerning fodder; sealed
8738	SAIL.BA.04.05.12	Receipt of barley; sealed
8739	SAIL.BA.07.07.21	Disbursement of wooden tablet(?); sealed
8740	SAIL.BA.07.07.09	Disbursement of barley; sealed
8741	SAIL.BA.06.12.30	Disbursement of barley; sealed
8742	SAIL.BA.07.10.28	Disbursement of barley; sealed
8743	SAIL.BA.07.11.30	Loan of silver; sealed
8744	SAIL.BA.07.05.17	Loan of barley; sealed
8745	SAIL.BA.07.10.22	Fragmentary economic record of uncertain character
8746	No date	List of PNs and quantities of flour
8747	SAIL.BA.06.04.28	Receipt of silver
8748	No date	Disbursement of barley
8749	SAIL.BA.06.12.20	Record concerning fodder
8750	SAIL.BA.07.08.22	Receipt of beer; sealed
8751	SAIL.BA.07.04.04	Disbursement of barley; sealed

NBC	Date	Description
8752	SAIL.BA.07.09.02	Record concerning barley for fodder; sealed
8753	SAIL.BA.07.07.20	Record concerning barley for fodder; sealed
8754	SAIL.BA.07.08.18?	Disbursement of barley; sealed
8755	Lost	Fragmentary disbursement of oil
8756	SAIL.BA.xx.04.14	Fragmentary promissory note—barley; sealed
8757	SAIL.BA.07.09.07	Record concerning barley for fodder; sealed
8758	SAIL.BA.07.07.20	Record concerning barley for fodder; sealed
8759	SAIL.BA.07.09.08	Record concerning barley for fodder; sealed
8760	SAIL.BA.06.12.25	Disbursement of barley; sealed
8761	SAIL.BA.06.07.06?	Record concerning barley for fodder
8762	SAIL.BA.07.07.02	Disbursement of barley for fodder; sealed
8763	SAIL.BA.07.07.01	Receipt of silver
8764	SAIL.BA.06.10.15	Record concerning feed for geese
8765	SAIL.BA.07.07.18	Disbursement of barley; sealed
8766	SAIL.BA.07.10.04	Disbursement of barley for fodder; sealed
8767	SAIL.BA.06.06.17?	Record concerning barley; sealed
8768	SAIL.BA.07.12.20	Loan of silver; sealed; cf. NBC 8556
8769	SAIL.BA.06.12.26	Record concerning barley; sealed
8770	SAIL.BA.07.07.14?	Disbursement of barley; sealed
8771	—.06D.16	Memorandum concerning bran
8772	No date	Record concerning headbands(?)
8773	—.11.26	Record concerning fodder
8774	SAIL.BA.07.xx.24?	Record concerning barley; sealed
8775	SAIL.BA.07.11.30	Receipt of beer; sealed
8776	—.10.24	Record concerning barley for fodder; sealed
8777	Illegible	List of PNs

NBC	Date	Description
8778	SAIL.BA.07.10.—	Record concerning barley for fodder; sealed
8779	SAIL.BA.07.07.09	Receipt of beer; sealed
8780	SAIL.BA.07.08.25	Record concerning barley
8781	SAIL.BA.07.10.06	Record concerning barley for fodder; sealed
8782	SAIL.BA.27.12.24?	Receipt of beer
8783	SAIL.BA.07.08.28	Record concerning fodder
8784	No date	Disbursement of silver
8785	SAIL.BA.07.10.05	Receipt of beer
8786	SAIL.BA.07.08.08	Receipt of beer; sealed
8787	SAIL.BA.07.07.18	Disbursement of barley; sealed
8788	SAIL.BA.07.04.04	Receipt of barley; sealed
8789	UN.UN.AU.07.—	Record concerning flour; ITI*Ki-nu-nu* mu É-gal-la-tum^{ki} ba-gul
8790	—.08.12	Tag—receipt of oil; sealed
8791	SAIL.BA.07.07.07	Record concerning barley; sealed
8792	SAIL.BA.07.09.—	Record concerning barley for fodder; sealed
8793	SAIL.BA.07.10.16	Disbursement of barley for fodder; sealed
8794	—.05.—	Receipt of oil; ITI*Zi-ib-nim*
8795	SAIL.BA.07.10.17	Receipt of beer; sealed
8796	SAIL.BA.07.10.19	Receipt of beer; sealed
8797	SAIL.BA.07.09.25	Record concerning barley for fodder; sealed
8798	SAIL.BA.07.06.01	Receipt of beer; sealed
8799	RISI.LA.38.03.20?	Record concerning barley for *naptanum*; cf. NBC 8811, 8813, 8816-8818, 8821-8823, 9235, 9237-9240, 9412-9416, 9418, 9433, 9454, 9615, 9629, 9638, 9641-9643, 9645-9647, 9700, 9708
8800	—.12.10	Record concerning flour; cf. NBC 8802
8801	SAIL.BA.23.11.23	Loan of silver; sealed

NBC	Date	Description
8802	—.12.20	Record concerning flour; cf. NBC 8800
8803	RISI.LA.50.05.16	Receipt of sheep; sealed; cf. NBC 8808
8804	SAIL.BA.28.04.12?	Record concerning bran; sealed
8805	RISI.LA.25.09.04?	Delivery of fine oil; sealed
8806	RISI.LA.37.12.27	Record concerning barley; sealed
8807	No date	Economic record of uncertain character
8808	Illegible	Receipt of ram; sealed; cf. NBC 8803
8809	SAIL.BA.07.10.—	Record concerning barley for fodder; sealed
8810	No date	Record concerning large quantities of oil
8811	—.02.23	Record concerning barley for *naptanum*; sealed; cf. NBC 8799
8812	RISI.LA.37.09.30	Receipt of barley
8813	—.02.30?	Record concerning barley for *naptanum*; sealed; cf. NBC 8799
8814	SAIL.BA.07.07.21?	Record concerning barley for fodder; sealed
8815	SAIL.BA.28.01.14	Hire of workers; sealed
8816	RISI.LA.38.05.18	Account of barley for *naptanum*; sealed; cf. NBC 8799
8817	RISI.LA.38.03.30?	Record concerning barley for *naptanum*; sealed; cf. NBC 8799
8818	RISI.LA.38.12D.xx	Record concerning flour; sealed; cf. NBC 8799
8819	SAIL.BA.08.08.12?	Receipt of barley; sealed
8820	Lost	Record concerning barley
8821	RISI.LA.38.04.30?	Record concerning dates; sealed; cf. NBC 8799
8822	RISI.LA.38.10.03?	Record concerning barley for *naptanum*; cf. NBC 8799
8823	RISI.LA.38.02.27?	Record concerning barley and dates for *naptanum*; sealed; cf. NBC 8799
8824	SAIL.BA.07.07.11	Record concerning barley for fodder; sealed
8825	SAIL.BA.06.10.10	Disbursement of barley

NBC	Date	Description
8826	SAIL.BA.07.07.05	Record concerning transport of oxen
8827	SAIL.BA.07.04.03	Disbursement of barley for fodder; sealed
8828	—.07.01	Receipt of silver
8829	SAIL.BA.07.10.—	Disbursement of barley for fodder; sealed
8830	SAIL.BA.07.07.07	Record concerning barley for fodder; sealed
8831	SAIL.BA.05.08.10	Receipt of silver
8832	SAIL.BA.xx.xx.xx	Record concerning fodder; sealed
8833	SAIL.BA.07.10.15?	Disbursement of barley for fodder; sealed
8834	SAIL.BA.07.04.13	Receipt of barley for fodder; sealed
8835	SAIL.BA.07.10.08	Record concerning barley for fodder; sealed
8836	SAIL.BA.06.09.28	Memorandum concerning receipt of foodstuff
8837	No date	Record concerning barley and silver
8838	SAIL.BA.07.xx.01?	Record concerning barley for fodder; sealed
8839	SAIL.BA.06.12.26	Record concerning barley for fodder; sealed
8840	—.10.25	Receipt of wool
8841	SAIL.BA.07.04.13	Disbursement of barley for fodder; sealed
8842	SAIL.BA.07.07.21	Record concerning barley for fodder; sealed
8843	SAIL.BA.07.09.10	Record concerning barley for fodder; sealed
8844	SAIL.BA.07.09.24?	Record concerning barley for fodder; sealed
8845	SAIL.BA.07.01.16	Receipt of barley for fodder; sealed
8846	SAIL.BA.07.06.xx	Record concerning barley for fodder; sealed
8847	—.11.01	Disbursement of barley
8848	SAIL.BA.06.10.06	Record concerning barley for fodder
8849	SAIL.BA.07.06.08	Loan of silver; sealed
8850	SAIL.BA.07.07.19	Disbursement of barley for fodder; sealed
8851	IŠIR.IS.20.07.—?	Receipt of hides and skins; BIN 9, 17 (C)

NBC	Date	Description
8852	IŠIR.IS.14.07.xx	List of workers; BIN 10, 260 (C)
8853	IŠIR.IS.23.05.05	Receipt of alum, madder, and wool; BIN 9, 105 (C)
8854	—.12.21	Delivery of thread; BIN 9, 142 (C)
8855	IŠIR.IS.28.09.22	Disbursement of leather and woolen cloth; BIN 9, 265 (C)
8856	IŠIR.IS.16.01.07	Receipt of hides; BIN 9, 78 (C)
8857	IŠIR.IS.13.09.—	Receipt of hides and skins; BIN 9, 53 (C)
8858	—.06.—	Disbursement of bags; BIN 9, 223 (C)
8862	ŠUIL.IS.02.12.—	Record concerning large cattle
8863	IŠDA.IS.A.04.—?	Letter order to the accountants concerning slave-girl; sealed; Hallo, BiOr 26, 1969, p. 175, no. 389 (T, Tr)
8864	No date	Loan of barley; sealed
8865	SAIL.BA.06.11.26	Receipt of fodder for oxen and sheep
8866	SAIL.BA.07.10.12	Disbursement of barley for fodder; sealed
8867	SAIL.BA.07.08.28	Disbursement of barley to *ḫazannum* and for fodder; sealed
8868	SAIL.BA.07.08.01?	Record concerning barley for fodder; sealed
8869	SAIL.BA.07.07.08	Receipt of barley
8870	SAIL.BA.07.07.23	Receipt of flour; sealed
8871	SAIL.BA.07.01.16	Record concerning barley for fodder; sealed
8872	SAIL.BA.??.04.02	Disbursement of barley for fodder; sealed; mu gibil
8873	SAIL.BA.07.10.21?	Disbursement of barley for fodder; sealed
8874	SAIL.BA.05.11.13?	Loan of silver; sealed
8875	SAIL.BA.07.04.15?	Receipt of barley; sealed
8876	??.11.21	Consignment of small cattle; mu é ^{d}EN.ZU(!) ba-<dù>
8877	SAIL.BA.06.10.05	Record concerning barley and flour
8878	SAIL.BA.xx.xx.xx	Record concerning barley for fodder; sealed
8879	SAIL.BA.07.10.xx	Record concerning barley for fodder; sealed

NBC	Date	Description
8880	SAIL.BA.07.07.xx	Disbursement of barley; sealed
8881	SUEL.LA.02.01.13	Tag—delivery of bran for fodder; sealed; cf. NBC 8883
8882	No date	Disbursement of barley
8883	SUEL.LA.02.02.09	Tag—delivery of bran for fodder; sealed; cf. NBC 8881
8884	xx.05.—	Account of barley?
8885	SAIL.BA.21.04.21	Receipt of barley; sealed
8886	xx.12.20?	List of PNs; sealed
8887	—.09.16	List of workers; BIN 10, 286 (C)
8888	IŠIR.IS.20.05.18	List of workers; BIN 10, 273 (C)
8889	Lost	Account of small cattle; sealed
8890	Lost?	Record concerning uncertain commodity
8891	RISI.LA.37.12D.08	Receipt of barley; sealed
8893	Illegible	Record concerning barley
8894	RISI.LA.57.05.xx	Receipt of barley
8895	No date	List of persons and replacements
8896	—.05.25	Fragmentary list of PNs
8897	—.07.02?	Disbursement of barley; sealed
8898	HARA.BA.31.03.14?	Receipt of barley in repayment of debt; sealed
8899	AMDI.BA.30.01.09	Receipt of silver as partial payment of *ilku*; sealed; YOS 13, 366 (C)
8906	—.07.25	List of workers; BIN 10, 278 (C)
8907	IŠIR.IS.20.06.26	Disbursement of chairs and sandals; BIN 9, 440 (C)
8908	SAIL.BA.07.11.14?	Record concerning flour; sealed
8909	SAIL.BA.07.09.02	Disbursement of barley; sealed
8910	SAIL.BA.07.02.22	Record concerning barley for fodder; sealed

NBC	Date	Description
8911	SAIL.BA.07.09.20?	Record concerning barley for fodder; sealed
8912	SAIL.BA.07.09.02	Record concerning barley for fodder; sealed
8913	SAIL.BA.06.03.20	Receipt of axes; sealed
8933	Lost	Cultivation contract?
8934	IŠIR.IS.21.03.24	Disbursement of bags and reed containers; BIN 9, 391 (C)
8935	RISI.LA.55.10.—	Division of inheritance; sealed; dupl. TIM 4, 4; O'Callaghan, JCS 8, 1954, pp. 137-43 (C, T, Tr)
8936	RISI.LA.10.03.—?	Ration list—barley
8937	RISI.LA.47.08.01	Tablet and case—statement of debt in barley after accounting; sealed
8938	IŠIR.IS.08.—.—	Disbursement of leather, glue, reed containers, and furniture; BIN 9, 491 (C)
8939	—.11.26	List of workers; BIN 10, 300 (C)
8940	—.07.—	Disbursement of skins; BIN 9, 476 (C)
8941	xx.04.13+	Receipt of silver for purchase of barley; sealed
8942	SAIL.BA.08.05.xx	Record concerning barley; sealed
8943	RISI.LA.57.01.18	Receipt of large quantity of wool from many persons
8944	—.xx.06	List of workers; BIN 10, 308 (C)
8945	—.08.03	List of workers; BIN 10, 282 (C)
8946	IŠIR.IS.07.10.08	List of workers; BIN 10, 221 (C)
8947	No date	Ration list—bran
8948	—.12D.—	Account of hides
8949	No date	Letter?
8950	No date	Ration list—barley
8952	IŠIR.IS.xx.08.—	Receipt of beds; BIN 10, 53 (C)
8953	—.11.01	List of workers; BIN 10, 295 (C)

NBC	Date	Description
8954	IŠIR.IS.14.12D.24	Disbursement of doors and their materials, and hide; BIN 9, 477 (C)
8962	—.05.30	Disbursement of barley
8963	RISI.LA.16.08.28	List of workers
8964	RISI.LA.59.11.—	Receipt of dates
8965	RISI.LA.18.12D.—	Contract of uncertain character
8966	RISI.LA.16.08.30	Disbursement of tools
8967	RISI.LA.54+.07.—	Receipt of barley
8968	No date	Account of copper
8969	No date	Ration list
8970	xx.08.—	Division of inheritance; sealed
8971	No date	List of PNs and numbers of hides(?)
8972	RISI.LA.53.09.—	Consignment of large cattle; sealed; cf. NBC 8992
8973	RISI.LA.30.??.24	Administrative record of uncertain character; sealed; iti-32
8974	RISI.LA.13.10.19	Receipt of barley
8975	xx.09.10	Receipt of wool
8976	xx.08.21	Record concerning skins
8977	RISI.LA.16.06.—	Record concerning reed baskets
8978	RISI.LA.59.08.17	Receipt of grain
8979	RISI.LA.47.12.—	Receipt of large quantities of wool
8980	No date	Delivery of small cattle; sealed; cf. NBC 8972
8981	RISI.LA.47.10.13	Receipt of barley and dates
8982	—.09.20+	Record concerning barley
8984	RISI.LA.45.03.17	Tablet and fragment of case—receipt of barley; sealed
8985	RISI.LA.24.08.30?	Receipt of silver; sealed
8986	RISI.LA.45.01.10	Receipt of small cattle; sealed

NBC	Date	Description
8987	RISI.LA.16.07.xx	Receipt of silver; sealed
8988	RISI.LA.16.01.xx?	Receipt of wool
8990	RISI.LA.57.01.10	Account of small cattle and wool
8991	No date	Letter to Balītum from Ṣilli-Šamaš concerning slaves
8992	RISI.LA.51.10.09	Tablet and case—consignment of large cattle; sealed; cf. NBC 8972
8993	xx.06.—	Disbursement of garments(?); mu íd x [...]
8994	RISI.LA.54.02.20	Account of wool
8995	RISI.LA.56.04.16	Account of small cattle
8996	RISI.LA.56.04.15	Receipt of small cattle; sealed
8997	RISI.LA.44.—.—	Account of sesame; date in text
8998	RISI.LA.43+.01.—	Receipt of wool; sealed
8999	Lost	Delivery of small cattle; sealed; cf. NBC 9006
9000	RISI.LA.16.06.24	Disbursement of wheat
9001	No date	Disbursement of barley
9002	No date	Disbursement of barley
9003	RISI.LA.31.07.06?	Disbursement of barley
9004	RISI.LA.16.03.—	Record concerning small cattle
9005	RISI.LA.57.01.11	Receipt of wool
9006	RISI.LA.31+.??.25	Delivery of small cattle; sealed; iti-6 ki-5; cf. NBC 8999
9007	xx.02.—	Loan (šu-lá) of silver
9008	RISI.LA.48.01.24	Delivery of garments
9009	RISI.LA.50.11.—	List of persons given as substitutes; sealed
9010	No date	Ration list—barley; list of PNs and quantities of silver
9011	RISI.LA.54.02.20	Disbursement of silver
9012	No date	Disbursement of silver and wool in exchange for rams

NBC	Date	Description
9013	RISI.LA.46.08.—	Account of silver
9014	No date	Letter to "the man" from Sîn-mudammiq concerning large quantities of barley
9015	No date	Ration list
9016	RISI.LA.59.08.01	Account of large quantities of barley
9017	RISI.LA.58.02.29	Account of barley for two months
9018	RISI.LA.—.??.24	Account of barley; iti-9
9019	No date	Letter from Ipquša concerning exchange of fields
9020	RISI.LA.47.12.—	Account of small cattle (ledger)
9021	No date	Account of small cattle (ledger); cf. NBC 9020
9022	RISI.LA.16.01.12	Receipt of copper tools
9023	No date	Fragmentary disbursement of silver
9024	RISI.LA.53.—.—	Account of silver by month
9025	No date	Letter
9026	RISI.LA.58.08.08	Fragmentary account of barley
9027	RISI.LA.57.03.—	Account of barley
9028	No date	Letter to Sîn-ēriš, Nūr-ilišu, and Ubar-[...] concerning work
9030	—.10.15	Account of barley and sesame
9031	No date	Letter from Samsuiluna concerning agricultural workers
9032	RISI.LA.57.01.11	Account of small cattle (ledger)
9033	Lost	Fragmentary account of barley
9036	No date	List of PNs and quantities of silver
9037	RISI.LA.07.07.12+	Account of barley
9038	Lost	Record concerning land for sustenance of soldiers
9039	RISI.LA.47.12.—	Tablet and case—account of sesame; sealed

NBC	Date	Description
9040	RISI.LA.—.??.17	Account of barley; iti-9
9041	RISI.LA.54.02.17	Account of wool
9042	xx.07.25	Record concerning foodstuff
9043	No date	List of field acreages and quantities of barley for various purposes
9045	RISI.LA.48.01.—	Disbursements of barley
9046	RISI.LA.53.12.30	Account of silver
9047	No date	Fragmentary economic record of uncertain character; cf. NBC 5515
9048	Lost?	Tablet and portion of case—disbursement of sheep for various purposes
9049	No date	List of small field acreages
9049A	Lost	Fragmentary list of PNs
9050	SUEL.LA.14.03.—	Record of bricks for irrigation construction; YNER 4, no. 99 (C, T)
9051	—.—.21	Tag—disbursement of barley for fodder and seed; cf. NBC 9052-55, 9059
9052	—.—.11	Tag—disbursement of barley for fodder and seed; cf. NBC 9051
9053	—.—.xx	Tag—disbursement of barley for fodder and seed; cf. NBC 9051
9054	—.09.01	Tag—disbursement of barley for fodder and seed; cf. NBC 9051
9055	—.—.14	Tag—disbursement of barley for fodder and seed; cf. NBC 9051
9056	RISI.LA.57.01.15	Loan (šu-lá) of silver; sealed
9057	RISI.LA.16.05.05?	Disbursement of spades
9058	No date	Receipt of silver
9059	—.—.13	Tag—disbursement of barley for fodder and seed; cf. NBC 9051

NBC	Date	Description
9060	Illegible	Fragmentary economic record of uncertain character
9061	—.08.28	Receipt of beer
9062	xx.xx.10	Economic record of uncertain character; sealed
9063	RISI.LA.31.05.—	Receipt of sheep, wool, and silver
9064	RISI.LA.16.08.30	Delivery of spades
9065	RISI.LA.30.05.—	Loan of sesame to be repaid in silver
9066	RISI.LA.16.10.—	Economic record of uncertain character
9067	—.05.25	List of numerals and PNs
9068	RISI.LA.31.xx.30	Delivery of large and small cattle; sealed
9069	RISI.LA.47.01.20	Disbursement of barley
9070	SUEL.LA.01.10.17	Tag—delivery of bran for fodder; sealed; cf. NBC 8881
9071	RISI.LA.31+.03.—	Disbursement of silver
9072	UN.LA.A.03.—?	Delivery?; mu ^{urudu}alam níg-gul-ta é-^{d}Utu-šè
9073	WASI.LA.10.07.—	Contract for delivery of bricks; sealed
9074	RISI.LA.59.04.—	Account of barley
9075	RISI.LA.53+.xx.—	Account of barley
9076	RISI.LA.58.06.—	Disbursement of barley
9077	—.05.24	Fragmentary list
9078	Lost?	Fragmentary list of numerals and PNs
9079	RISI.LA.47.11.16	Consignment of small cattle; sealed
9080	RISI.LA.49+.04.30	Disbursement of barley (ledger)
9081	RISI.LA.59.11.—	Disbursement of barley
9082	WASI.LA.10.04.—	Receipt of improved residential property in exchange; sealed
9083	RISI.LA.54.09.—	Consignment of large cattle; cf. NBC 8972
9084	SUEL.LA.14.—.—	Record concerning bricks; YNER 4, no. 113 (C, T)

NBC	Date	Description
9086	RISI.LA.31.??.30?	Disbursement; sealed; iti-29 ki-4
9087	RISI.LA.47.12.20	Disbursement of barley
9088	RISI.LA.59.12.—	Receipt of dates; sealed
9089	RISI.LA.57.04.xx	Fragmentary account of sesame
9090	No date	Letter to Ea-rīm-ilī and Bettetum(?) from Apil-Sîn concerning payment of barley
9091	RISI.LA.56.04.15	Deliveries of barley
9092	RISI.LA.48.03.xx?	Deliveries of barley; sealed
9093	RISI.LA.59.07.13	Disbursement of wool rations
9094	Lost	Disbursement of barley(?) over several months (ledger)
9095	No date	Account of silver
9096	SUEL.LA.06.07.14	Tag—record of workers; sealed; cf. NBC 5432
9151	NASI.ŠA.I.—.—	Loan of barley; YOS 14, 19 (C)
9152	NASI.ŠA.J.—.—	Tablet and portion of case—loans of barley; YOS 14, 21 (C)
9153	No date	Loan of barley; YOS 14, 71 (C)
9154	No date	Loan (ḫubuttātum) of barley; YOS 14, 23 (C)
9155	No date	Loan of silver; mentions ITISa-ḫa-ra-tim in text; YOS 14, 25 (C)
9156	No date	Loan of barley; YOS 14, 24 (C)
9157	No date	Loan (ḫubuttātum) of silver; YOS 14, 68 (C)
9158	IPAD.EŠ.D.—.—	Loan (ḫubuttātum) of barley and silver; YOS 14, 11 (C)
9159	NASI.ŠA.F.—.—	Loan of barley; YOS 14, 13 (C)
9160	NASI.ŠA.I.—.—	Loan of barley; YOS 14, 12 (C)
9161	NASI.ŠA.I.—.—	Loan of barley and silver; YOS 14, 18 (C)
9162	IQTI.ŠA.01.—.—	Loan of barley and silver; YOS 14, 15 (C)
9164	xx.12D.—?	Disbursement of barley; YOS 14, 251 (C)

NBC	Date	Description
9166	GUNG.LA.08.09.—	Delivery of small cattle
9167	IŠIR.IS.12.11.—	Receipt of boats; sealed; ^{iti}ezem-me-ki-gál
9169	No date	List of witnesses to oath promising payment within five days; YOS 14, 46 (C)
9171	IŠDA.IS.O.11.—	Loan of barley and beer?; sealed
9174	GUNG.LA.07.05.—	Tag—delivery of reeds(?); sealed
9175	SIIQ.LA.01.04.—	Disbursement of foodstuff
9177	IŠIR.IS.06.10.—	Disbursement of skins and bitumen; BIN 10, 93 (C)
9178	IŠIR.IS.12.09.—	Disbursement of gold
9179	LIIŠ.IS.B.06.—?	Record concerning tax on orchards
9180	IDDA.IS.02.08.—	Receipt of barley; sealed
9181	IDDA.IS.E.01.—	Receipt of bran; sealed; mu-ús-sa ^{d}I-din-^{d}Da-gan lugal-e ^{d}Šu-nir-gal ^{d}Nin-in-si-na mu-na-dím
9182	RISI.LA.09.07.—	Loan of barley; sealed
9183	No date	Letter to ^{d}ZA.MÙŠ.GAL-rabat from Busatum
9184	SUEL.LA.08.02.—	Disbursement of cow and caprid; mu ka-íd-da^{ki} ba-ḫul
9185	SIER.LA.01.04.15?	Disbursement of barley flour for *naptanum*
9186	RISI.LA.37.02.04	Receipt of barley
9187	SIID.LA.05.11.20	Disbursement of foodstuff
9191	IPE2.ŠA.B.—.—	Loan of barley; mu ^{giš}gigir kù-sig$_{17}$ *ana* é [...] *Ibāl-pī-el ušēri*[*b*]
9192	SIID.LA.07.11.—	Delivery of persons
9193	IPE2.ŠA.08.08.01	Receipt of barley for fodder; YOS 14, 80 (C)
9194	—.01.21	Disbursement of rations; ^{iti}bara$_2$-za-gar
9195	NUAD.LA.D.09.—?	Tag—delivery of ingredient for beer; sealed; or GUNG.LA.07 or ABSA.LA.11?: mu-ús-sa en ^{d}Utu; cf. NBC 9400

NBC	Date	Description
9196	NUAD.LA.D.09.—?	Tag—delivery of ingredient for beer; sealed; or GUNG.LA.07 or ABSA.LA.11?: mu-ús-sa en ᵈUtu; cf. NBC 9400
9197	ENBA.IS.01.12D.—	Sale of field; sealed
9198	UN.IS.A.03.—	Sale of field of rushes; sealed; mu *Na-aḫ-ma-tum* en ᵈNin-urta ba-ḫun-gá
9200	SAIL.BA.27.12D.19	Consignment of small cattle
9201	SAIL.BA.28.07.09	Disbursement of barley(?); mu *Ya-di-a-bu-um*
9202	SAIL.BA.24.02.20	Delivery of sheep for Šamaš; sealed
9203	No date	Payment of debt to Šamaš
9204	No date	Record of travel provisions for five persons; sealed
9205	??.05.06+	Receipt; sealed; mu íd x x x x x mu-un-ba-al
9206	IPE2.ŠA.10.—.—	Promissory note—barley; sealed; YOS 14, 77 (C)
9207	IPAD2.ŠA.A.05.27	Disbursement of flour; mu alam kù-sig$_{17}$ *Ši-ma-ḫa-tu* ⁱᵗⁱ*A-bi-i*
9208	SAIL.BA.06.09.—?	Loan of silver; mu alam ᵈUtu ᵈAmar-Utu
9209	??.—.—	Loan of barley; mu bàd Da-du-x *ša* KA 2 x; YOS 14, 74 (C)
9210	No date	Memorandum concerning barley; YOS 13, 413 (C)
9211	No date	Memorandum concerning silver; YOS 13, 459 (C)
9213	SUEL.LA.02.01.16?	Tag—delivery of bran for fodder; sealed; cf. NBC 8881
9216	—.06.18	Exchange of sheep
9217	WASI.LA.11.12.01	Disbursement of sheep
9218	SIER.LA.01.12D.25?	Disbursement of barley flour for *naptanum*
9222	SAIL.BA.xx.08.—	Division of inheritance; sealed
9224	IŠIR.IS.15.10.—	Delivery; sealed; BIN 10, 123 (C)
9225	SAIL.BA.28.01.16	Receipt of vessels and equipment
9226	SAIL.BA.27.09.xx	Loan of silver and barley; sealed

NBC	Date	Description
9227	IŠIR.IS.13.09.21	Disbursement?; sealed; BIN 10, 111 (C)
9228	RISI.LA.22+.04.—	Fragmentary receipt of garments; [mu ...] ᵈEn-líl ᵈEn-ki-ga-ta [...]
9229	IŠIR.IS.26.12D.—	Contract of uncertain character; sealed
9230	Lost?	Ration list
9231	—.02.28?	Ration list
9232	No date	List of PNs and quantities of barley
9233	No date	List of PNs and numbers of sheep(?)
9234	RISI.LA.18.09.xx	Loan (šu-lá) of barley; sealed
9235	RISI.LA.—.03.08	Record concerning barley for *naptanum*; sealed; cf. NBC 8799
9236	RISI.LA.—.12D.25	Record concerning barley for *naptanum*; sealed; cf. NBC 8799
9237	RISI.LA.—.02.09?	Record concerning barley for *naptanum*; cf. NBC 8799
9238	RISI.LA.38.04.xx	Record concerning barley for *naptanum*; sealed; cf. NBC 8799
9239	RISI.LA.—.10.13	Record concerning barley and dates for *naptanum*; sealed; cf. NBC 8799
9240	RISI.LA.36.07.xx	Record concerning barley and dates for *naptanum*; sealed; cf. NBC 8799
9263	RISI.LA.39.10.05	Unopened case—sale of improved residential property; sealed
9264	SAIL.BA.27.12D.21	Exchange of fields; sealed
9265	NUAD.LA.I.xx.—	Loan of silver; sealed; mu bàd gal Ararmaᵏⁱ ba-dù
9266	No date	Loan(?) (šu-lá) of barley; sealed
9267	NUAD.LA.I.01.—	Tag—record concerning large cattle; sealed; mu bàd gal Ararmaᵏⁱ ba-dù; Beckman, NABU 1988/13 (C, T); ENES 758
9269	UN.UN.AW.—.—	Loan (*ḫubuttātum*) of barley; mu é A-ba-tum
9270	SAIL.BA.07.—.—	Rental of field; sealed

NBC	Date	Description
9272	—.01.17	Disbursement of hide
9273	—.05.13	Account of barley for *naptanum*
9274	—.01.03?	Account of barley for workers
9275	RISI.LA.—.—.—	Record concerning votive offering for Inanna and Nana; RN in oath
9276	No date	Adoption
9277	RISI.LA.31.12.xx	Account of barley for months *Kislimu* through *Addaru*
9278	No date	List of PNs and quantities of silver(?)
9279	SIID.LA.07.03.xx	Account of wheat
9280	ITŠA.KI.C.12.—	Loan of silver and barley; sealed; mu ti-lim-da kù-babbar mu-na-dù
9281	No date	Ration list—barley
9282	IŠIR.IS.22.12.—	Receipt of oil; BIN 10, 32 (C)
9283	—.07.18?	Loan of barley; sealed; ^{iti}du$_6$-kù mu-18-kam (for u$_4$-18-kam?)
9284	RISI.LA.22.12.—	Loan (šu-lá) of silver
9285	—.12.09?	Delivery of persons(?)
9286	No date	Record concerning hides
9288	—.07.06	Disbursement of barley
9290	—.09.11	Disbursement of incense burners
9291	xx.09.—	Receipt; sealed
9292	No date	Loan of silver
9293	No date	Receipt of barley from various individuals
9294	No date	Loan of silver
9295	??.08.20	Loan of silver to be repaid in dates; sealed; mu *Sa-am-si*-^{d}x lugal
9296	xx.xx.22	Record concerning barley; sealed
9297	SAIL.BA.24.03.20	Loan of silver for five days; sealed

NBC	Date	Description
9299	Lost	List of PNs and numerals
9300	SAIL.BA.25.05.21?	Tag—disbursement of sheep; sealed
9301	xx.02.12	Receipt of barley
9302	Lost?	Loan of barley
9303	No date	Ration list
9304	No date	Ration list
9305	No date	List of workers
9306	—.11.—	Receipt of silver
9307	RISI.LA.32.11.xx	Deliveries of barley; sealed
9308	No date?	Ration list—barley
9309	—.05.16	Receipt of small cattle
9310	No date	Record concerning wooden objects and textiles
9311	RISI.LA.43.11.01?	Loan of silver; sealed
9312	No date?	List of quantities of foodstuffs
9313	No date	Record concerning groups of ten persons
9314	No date	Disbursement of barley
9315	SAIL.BA.19.10.02?	Receipt of wool; sealed
9316	??.06.—	Record concerning produce of field; mu é-maḫ(?) Inanna(?) ᵈA-x
9317	No date?	List of PNs and quantities of silver(?)
9318	No date	Disbursement of barley flour
9319	No date	List of witnesses
9320	—.??.—	Disbursement of flour; ᴵᵀᴵSa-ḫa-ra-[tum]
9321	No date	List of PNs
9322	RISI.LA.32.12.—	Receipt of small cattle; sealed
9323	xx.09.01	Disbursement of barley?

NBC	Date	Description
9325	RISI.LA.07.06.—	Account of barley(?)
9326	SUEL.LA.16.06.—	Record concerning wool
9327	SUEL.LA.16.07.—	List of PNs and numbers of workers
9384	No date	Account of barley
9385	Lost	Adoption; sealed; cf. NBC 9806
9386	No date	List of PNs
9387	No date	Fragmentary account of foodstuffs (ledger)
9387A	—.06.—	Fragmentary account of foodstuffs for temple of Nintinugga for months of *Simanu* through *Elūlu*
9388	RISI.LA.25.xx.—?	Sale of orchard; sealed; note also RN in oath
9389	SIIQ.LA.02.04.19	Receipt of barley for distribution for three months
9390	No date	List of PNs and quantities of foodstuff
9391	RISI.LA.47.06.—	Tablet and fragment of case—agreement concerning produce of orchard; sealed
9392	RISI.LA.18.02.02	Vow of silver
9393	DAIL.IS.04.01.—	Sale of improved residential property
9394	No date	Disbursement of foodstuff
9395	RISI.LA.47.08.10	Receipt of barley; sealed
9396	xx.07.—	Transfer of orchard; mu ugnim(?) x x x ^{ki}(?)
9397	SIIQ.LA.04.09.17	Receipt of silver; cf. NBC 9398
9398	SIIQ.LA.—.08.02	Receipt of barley; reign from comparison to NBC 9397
9399	RISI.LA.59.01.—	Receipt of foodstuff
9400	UN.UN.W.02.—	Tag—delivery of ingredient for beer; sealed; mu íd Amar-^{d}EN.ZU ba-ba-al; cf. NBC 9195-9196, 10171, 10356, 10358
9401	No date	Receipt of textiles and other commodities, with silver equivalents
9402	No date	List of numerals and PNs

NBC	Date	Description
9403	RISI.LA.59.06.01	Receipt of objects of copper and other materials
9404	No date	Receipt of bricks
9405	No date	Record concerning barley
9406	No date	Record concerning barley
9407	SAIL.BA.27.10.14	Delivery of bundles of straw; sealed
9408	No date	Bulla—cylinder seal impression only
9409	No date	List of PNs
9410	—.11.04	Disbursement of barley flour
9411	—.05.20	Tablet and fragment of case—receipt of barley; sealed; ^{ITI}A-bi
9412	RISI.LA.38.04.04	Record concerning barley for *naptanum*; sealed; cf. NBC 8799
9413	RISI.LA.38.11.29	Record concerning barley for *naptanum*; sealed; cf. NBC 8799
9414	RISI.LA.38.03.24	Record concerning barley and barley flour for *naptanum* sealed; cf. NBC 8799
9415	RISI.LA.32+.03.08	Record concerning barley and flour for *naptanum*; sealed; cf. NBC 8799
9416	RISI.LA.37.xx.01?	Record concerning barley for *naptanum*; sealed; cf. NBC 8799
9417	RISI.LA.36.12.27	Receipt of barley
9418	RISI.LA.xx.xx.17	Record concerning barley for *naptanum*; sealed; cf. NBC 8799
9419	No date	Record concerning shirts
9420	—.02.05	Economic record of uncertain character; sealed
9421	No date	Payment of bran
9422	RISI.LA.50.08.—	Record concerning dead cattle; sealed
9423	RISI.LA.37.12D.17?	Receipt of barley; sealed
9424	No date	Seal impression only

NBC	Date	Description
9425	xx.11.14	Record concerning foodstuff
9426	RISI.LA.10.03.24	Receipt; sealed; mu bàd gal *Iš-ku-un*-dUTU mu-dù-a
9427	No date	Receipt of lambs
9428	ŠUIL.IS.05.12D.—	Receipt of silver; sealed
9429	HARA.BA.01.02.—	Tag—receipt of foodstuff; sealed
9430	SAIL.BA.05.08.26	Receipt of garments; sealed
9431	—.01.23	Disbursement of flour
9432	Lost	Receipt of goat; sealed
9433	RISI.LA.32+.xx.26	Record concerning barley, dates, and other foodstuffs for *naptanum*; sealed; cf. NBC 8799
9434	No date	Receipt of silver
9435	—.06.26	Exchange of sheep
9436	No date	Loan of silver for business venture; cf. NBC 5515
9440	No date	List of PNs
9441	xx.07.04	Rental of field(?); sealed
9443	Lost	Record concerning payment
9444	No date	Delivery of foodstuffs
9445	SUEL.LA.16.12D.—	Account of barley
9446	No date	Disbursement of barley
9449	SUEL.LA.17.02.—	Disbursement of foodstuff
9450	xx.07.14	Disbursement of foodstuff
9451	—.—.01	Disbursement of silver and barley
9452	No date	Fragmentary adoption; cf. NBC 5515
9453	—.02.11	Disbursement of silver
9454	RISI.LA.32+.xx.24	Record concerning barley(?) and dates for *naptanum*; sealed; cf. NBC 8799
9456	—.06.28	Receipt of barley flour; sealed

NBC	Date	Description
9457	—.06.21	Delivery of sheep
9458	No date	Record concerning foodstuffs
9459	No date	List of quantities of spades
9460	No date	Payment of silver as price of sickle
9461	—.03.04	Disbursement of wool
9462	IŠIR.IS.11.07.14?	List of workers; BIN 10, 243 (C)
9463	No date	List of PNs
9464	No date	Economic record of uncertain character
9465	—.04.—	Record concerning beams
9466	RISI.LA.38.06.xx	Disbursement
9467	SAIL.BA.27.08.10	Receipt of barley and silver
9468	RISI.LA.25.06.16	Receipt of barley; sealed
9469	SUEL.LA.17.01.12	Disbursement of barley
9470	—.06.18	Ration list
9471	RISI.LA.54.02.20	Unopened case—receipt of large quantities of silver in connection with wool; sealed
9472	No date	List of numerals and PNs
9473	No date?	Record of large numbers of workers and women
9474	SUEL.LA.01.11.27	Tag—delivery of fodder for oxen; sealed
9475	RISI.LA.07.12.—	Account of barley
9476	Lost	Fragmentary sale
9477	—.09.26	Disbursement of foodstuff
9478	SAIL.BA.28.05.xx	Receipt of silver; sealed
9479	RISI.LA.48.10.16	Economic record of uncertain character
9480	—.xx.22	Record concerning small cattle
9481	—.07.13?	Disbursement of foodstuff

NBC	Date	Description
9482	xx.08.04?	Receipt of silver and barley
9483	Lost?	Economic record of uncertain character
9484	No date	List of PNs
9485	No date	Account of barley
9486	RISI.LA.39.07.25	Disbursement of barley
9487	Lost	Tablet and portion of case—receipt of barley and dates; sealed
9488	RISI.LA.50.05.20?	Receipt of small cattle; sealed
9489	RISI.LA.36.12.03	Delivery of textiles
9490	SAIL.BA.24.03.—	Record concerning barley; sealed
9491	No date	Disbursement of barley
9492	—.xx.19	Disbursement of foodstuff
9493	No date	Disbursement of silver
9494	—.07.13	Contract of uncertain character; sealed
9495	SUEL.LA.17.02.—	Disbursement of foodstuff
9496	SUEL.LA.16.12.xx	List of small field acreages and of numbers of workers
9497	RISI.LA.07.12.28	Account of barley
9498	No date	Disbursement of foodstuff
9499	RISI.LA.49.09.—	Tablet and case—loan (šu-lá) of barley; sealed; mu ki-ús(!)-sa-20-kam Ì-si-in-na^{ki} ba-an-dab$_5$
9550	No date	List of PNs
9551	No date	List of PNs and numerals
9552	No date	Memorandum concerning cattle(?)
9553	xx.03.15+	Record concerning foodstuffs; mu ug[nim ...]
9554	No date	List of workers
9555	RISI.LA.57.03.22	Receipt of small cattle
9556	SUEL.LA.16.07.—	Fragmentary list of workers; cf. NBC 5504

NBC	Date	Description
9557	—.08.—	Fragmentary disbursement of barley
9558	No date	Disbursement?
9559	RISI.LA.52.09.17	Record concerning small cattle; sealed
9561	SAIL.BA.27.10.20	Tablet and fragment of case—loan of silver; sealed
9562	SUEL.LA.18.01.16	Disbursement of barley
9563	RISI.LA.58.02.29	Account of barley
9564	RISI.LA.49.01.26	Account of dates
9565	SUEL.LA.19.07.—?	Disbursement of wool; mu-ús-sa-4-bi
9567	—.11.27	Record concerning foodstuffs for *naptanum*; sealed
9568	No date	Record of presentation of substitute for service; fingernail impressions
9569	RISI.LA.45.04.01	Receipt of barley; sealed
9570	RISI.LA.49.01.30	Receipt of small cattle; sealed
9571	No date	Record concerning barley and wool, with silver equivalents
9572	SAIL.BA.22.02.21	Receipt of barley; sealed
9573	SUEL.LA.02.02.21	Tag—delivery of bran for fodder; sealed
9574	RISI2.LA.03.05.05	Rental of house; sealed
9575	SUEL.LA.01.11.11	Tag—delivery of bran for fodder; sealed
9576	HARA.BA.01.03.—?	Rental of field
9577	—.08.14	Record concerning hired men; sealed; date in text
9578	Lost	Receipt of dates; sealed
9579	No date	List of PNs
9580	SUEL.LA.01.10.22	Tag—delivery of bran for fodder; sealed
9581	SAIL.BA.01.11.06	Hire of harvest labor; sealed
9582	SUEL.LA.01.11.21	Tag—delivery of bran for fodder; sealed
9583	SAIL.BA.22.11.10	Loan of barley; sealed

NBC	Date	Description
9584	SAIL.BA.11.08.02?	Rental of threshing floor(?); sealed
9585	RISI.LA.08.08.04	Disbursement of barley
9586	RISI.LA.06.04.—	Receipt of barley
9587	RISI.LA.25.10.14	Disbursement; sealed
9588	RISI.LA.xx.xx.xx	Fragmentary sale of orchard; sealed; date lost, but RN in oath
9589	RISI.LA.08.01.xx	Delivery of small cattle
9590	RISI.LA.59.03.13	Receipt of silver; sealed
9591	LIIŠ.IS.B.xx.xx	Receipt of vessels
9592	??.xx.xx	Hire of person; mu ^{giš}gu<-za> maḫ(!?)
9593	RISI.LA.49.05.09	Record concerning sheep for *naptanum*
9594	RISI.LA.07.12D.12	Record concerning wool
9595	No date	Record of numbers of workers
9596	RISI.LA.37.12.xx?	Receipt
9597	—.09.08	Disbursement of foodstuff
9598	No date	Fragmentary record of workers
9599	RISI.LA.32+.07.08	Record concerning production of shirts
9600	—.06.26	Record concerning foodstuff for *naptanum*
9601	SUEL.LA.16.12D.—	Fragmentary disbursement of barley
9602	RISI.LA.53.10.02	Receipt of barley
9603	—.12.02	Disbursement of barley; ^{iti}*Ki-in-ki*
9604	Lost	Disbursement of lambs
9605	SAIL.BA.16.12.30	Disbursement of oil and dates
9606	—.06.23	Receipt of garments
9607	xx.02.—	Record of foodstuff; sealed
9608	RISI.LA.38.07.—	Record concerning soldiers and foodstuff; sealed

NBC	Date	Description
9609	RISI.LA.58.06.—	Receipt of barley flour as allotment for hired men; sealed
9610	SUEL.LA.01.11.01	Tag—delivery of bran for fodder; sealed
9611	No date	Record concerning foodstuff
9612	No date?	List of workers
9613	—.09.02	Fragmentary ration list
9614	xx.01.07	Loan of barley; sealed
9615	RISI.LA.38.04.03	Record concerning barley for *naptanum*; sealed; cf. NBC 8799
9616	??.12.24	Disbursement?; mu ma-da ba-an-ḫul
9617	SAIL.BA.25.04.26	Delivery of barley; sealed
9618	RISI.LA.53.03.—	Receipt of silver
9619	Lost	Fragmentary loan of silver
9620	No date	Tag—seal impressions only
9621	SAIL.BA.05.06.—	Loan (*ḫubuttātum*) of barley; sealed
9622	No date	Hire of harvest labor
9623	No date	Tag—seal impressions only; sealed
9624	RISI.LA.48.07.—?	Receipt of small cattle; sealed
9625	SAIL.BA.05.06.20?	Receipt of barley; sealed
9626	RISI.LA.48.05.24+	Consignment of sheep; sealed
9627	RISI.LA.48.08.30	Receipt of small cattle; sealed
9628	SAIL.BA.22.11.01	Receipt of silver
9629	RISI.LA.37.01.15	Record concerning barley and dates for *naptanum*; sealed; cf. NBC 8799
9630	No date	Disbursement of asphalt and bitumen for reed mats
9631	RISI.LA.58.07.26	Receipt of small cattle; sealed
9632	SAIL.BA.19.06.06	Disbursement of wool; sealed

NBC	Date	Description
9633	—.05.14	Tag—record concerning small cattle
9634	RISI.LA.41+.06.15	Record concerning dead small cattle; sealed
9636	—.12D.12?	Receipt of sesame
9637	RISI.LA.47.10.08	Receipt of small cattle; sealed
9638	RISI.LA.38.04.23	Record concerning barley for *naptanum*; sealed; cf. NBC 8799
9639	RISI.LA.38.04.01?	Disbursement of dates; sealed
9640	RISI.LA.50.12.20	Record concerning goat; sealed
9641	RISI.LA.38.05.28	Record concerning foodstuff for *naptanum*; sealed; cf. NBC 8799
9642	RISI.LA.38.03.24	Record concerning barley(?) for *naptanum*; sealed; cf. NBC 8799
9643	RISI.LA.32+.05.01	Record concerning foodstuff for *naptanum*; sealed; cf. NBC 8799
9644	RISI.LA.37.10.29	Receipt of barley
9645	RISI.LA.37.12.14	Record concerning barley for *naptanum*; sealed; cf. NBC 8799
9646	RISI.LA.38.05.17	Record concerning foodstuff for *naptanum*; sealed; cf. NBC 8799
9647	RISI.LA.37.12.24	Record concerning barley for *naptanum*; sealed; cf. NBC 8799
9648	—.12.10	Record concerning foodstuffs for two days; ᵐKi-in-ki-im
9649	SIIQ.LA.01.11.15	Receipt of cow as votive offering
9650	IŠDA.IS.—.—.—	Record concerning foodstuffs; sealed; RN in sealing
9651	No date	List of PNs and quantities of silver
9652	No date	Receipt of silver and other valuable goods
9653	—.12.—	Ration list—barley; ᵐKi-in-kum
9654	SAIL.BA.21.02.06	Record concerning consumption of bran

NBC	Date	Description
9655	SAIL.BA.27.08.01	Loan of silver; sealed
9656	No date	List of PNs
9657	xx.xx.—	Promissory note—silver
9658	No date	Disbursement of silver
9659	SUEL.LA.01.11.15	Tag—delivery of bran for fodder; sealed
9660	—.09.17	Record concerning barley
9661	No date?	Record concerning foodstuff for *naptanum*
9662	No date	List of quantities of wool
9663	Lost	Disbursement of barley
9664	RISI.LA.25.09.14	Receipt of bitter garlic; sealed
9665	—.03.24	Receipt of barley
9666	—.02.14	Receipt of barley
9667	Lost	Receipt of silver; sealed
9668	No date	Economic record of uncertain character
9669	SAIL.BA.13.11.10	Fragmentary loan of silver; sealed
9670	No date	Ration list—oil
9671	—.12.20	Disbursement of foodstuffs for two days; ITI*Ki-in-kum*
9672	SAIL.BA.11.04.12	Agreement concerning delivery of dates
9673	No date	Record concerning barley flour
9674	RISI.LA.55.12.30?	Promissory note; sealed
9675	RISI.LA.31.12.—	Record concerning shearing of wool
9676	SAIL.BA.05.05.20?	Record concerning bran(?); sealed
9677	No date	List of reed objects
9678	—.08.14	Receipt of large cattle; sealed
9679	HARA.BA.16.—.—	Receipt of bran and beer; sealed
9680	Lost	Receipt

NBC	Date	Description
9682	SAIL.BA.23.11.13	Receipt of silver; sealed
9683	—.06.15	Record concerning barley for *naptanum*; cf. NBC 9661
9684	—.07.22	Promissory note—oil; sealed
9685	—.10.15	Disbursement of barley
9686	—.05.03	Record concerning wooden beams
9687	SUEL.LA.01.12D.—	Tag—delivery of bran for fodder; sealed
9689	—.03.—	Promissory note
9690	SAIL.BA.24.08.29?	Receipt of foodstuffs
9691	—.04.22	Economic record of uncertain character; sealed
9692	SAIL.BA.28.05.23?	Receipt of beer; sealed
9693	RISI.LA.??.xx.20	Receipt of sheep; sealed
9694	RISI.LA.36.02.19	Record concerning barley for *naptanum*; sealed
9695	No date	List of PNs
9696	SAIL.BA.19.07.29	Receipt of *naḫramu* garments; sealed
9697	RISI.LA.36.11.02	Record concerning dates and other foodstuffs; sealed
9698	—.02.07	Ration list—barley
9699	SAIL.BA.xx.02.22?	Loan of silver; sealed
9700	RISI.LA.37.02.20?	Record concerning foodstuffs for *naptanum*; sealed; cf. NBC 8799
9701	No date	Receipt of barley
9702	RISI.LA.32+.12.15	Disbursement of high-quality dates
9703	RISI.LA.45.03.xx	Receipt; sealed
9704	RISI.LA.37.01.12	Receipt of foodstuff
9705	RISI.LA.48.10.30	Receipt of dead ewes(?); sealed; cf. NBC 9711
9706	RISI.LA.35.03.03?	Record concerning barley; sealed
9707	—.12.06	Disbursement of barley; ITI*Ki-in-ki-im*; cf. NBC 9671

NBC	Date	Description
9708	RISI.LA.37.02.16?	Record concerning barley and dates for *naptanum*; sealed; cf. NBC 8799
9709	SAIL.BA.15.10.25	Receipt of oil and silver; sealed
9710	—.12.14	Disbursement of foodstuffs; ITI*Ki-in-kum*; cf. NBC 9671
9711	RISI.LA.48.09.20	Receipt of dead sheep; sealed; cf. NBC 9705
9712	No date	Ration list
9713	No date	List of quantities of silver(?)
9714	—.06.15	Receipt of quantities of silver
9715	—.09.16	Record concerning foodstuff
9716	Illegible	Tag—disbursement?; sealed
9717	??.03.xx	Loan of silver for purchase of ewes, to be repaid in barley; sealed
9718	—.01.—	Receipt of reed baskets and other objects; sealed
9719	—.12.18	Disbursement of foodstuffs; ITI*Ki-in-kum*; cf. NBC 9671
9720	—.07.09	Disbursement of barley; sealed
9721	—.08.10	Receipt of barley
9722	SAIL.BA.xx.xx.xx	Loan of copper for 15 days
9723	Lost	Fragment of case—loan of barley; sealed
9723A	xx.xx.28	Fragment of case—economic record of uncertain character— only list of witnesses preserved; sealed
9724	xx.01.01	Fragmentary loan of silver; sealed
9725	xx.07.—	Disbursement of barley
9726	SAIL.BA.22.xx.xx	Loan of barley; sealed
9727	Lost	Fragments of case—loan; sealed
9728	WASI.LA.03.03.—	Account of foodstuff
9729	RISI.LA.45.10.—	Sale of temple office; sealed

NBC	Date	Description
9730	SAIL.BA.22.01.20	Dowry?; sealed
9732	xx.12.xx	Fragment of case—contract concerning textiles and cattle; sealed
9733	No date	Record concerning supplies of silver
9734	Lost	Fragmentary hire of boat
9735	SAIL.BA.15.10.20?	Hire of harvest labor; sealed
9736	SAIL.BA.22.01.28?	Tag—hire of workers; sealed
9737	SAIL.BA.11.12.xx?	Loan of bricks; sealed
9739	—.11.22	Account of foodstuff (ledger); cf. NBC 9740
9740	—.—.14	Account of foodstuff (ledger); cf. NBC 9739
9741	No date	Disbursement of unspecified commodity (ledger)
9742	SAIL.BA.27.xx.xx	Rental of field; sealed
9743	No date	Tablet and portion of case—loan (ḫubuttātum) of silver and barley; sealed
9744	SAIL.BA.14.08.10	Receipt of barley; sealed
9745	No date	Receipt of barley
9746	xx.05.14	Hire of plow oxen; sealed
9747	SAIL.BA.27.08.21	Receipt of reed baskets; sealed
9748	No date	Loan of silver
9749	SAIL.BA.07.03.08	Promissory note—barley
9750	No date	Ration list
9752	No date	Ration list
9753	NASI.ŠA.I.—.—	Tablet and fragments of case—loans of barley; sealed; mu alam kù-[sig$_{17}$] ša Na-ra-am-30 [a-na é] ᵈTišpak [i-ru-bu-]ú
9754	No date	Loans of barley to several persons
9755	RISI.LA.39.—.—	Contract of uncertain character; sealed

NBC	Date	Description
9756	SAIL.BA.xx.06.xx	List of persons responsible for é-da-da offering for various days; sealed
9757	No date	Ration list; list of quantities of silver
9759	No date	Ration list
9760	No date?	Disbursement of silver
9761	NASI.ŠA.xx.—.—	Loans of barley to several persons; [m]u *Na-ra-am*-30 [...] x x x [...]
9762	NASI.ŠA.I.12.14	Tablet and portion of case—loan of silver; sealed; ITI*Ki-in-kum*; YOS 14, 350 (C); ENES 766
9764	No date	Letter to ÍD.GAL-dayyān from Šimat-antala
9765	RISI.LA.01.04.24	Guarantee of person?; sealed
9766	RISI.LA.01.04.24	Guarantee of person; sealed
9767	SAIL.BA.01.02.25	Guarantee of person; sealed
9768	RISI2.LA.03.10.10	Guarantee of person; sealed
9769	RISI2.LA.03.10.20	Rental of house; sealed
9771	RISI2.LA.03.03.16	Legal case concerning house; sealed
9772	SAIL.BA.07.12.30	Agreement for repair of house; sealed
9773	No date	List of field acreages
9774	No date	Ration list
9775	No date	List of PNs and quantities of silver(?)
9776	xx.01.30	Record of barley offerings to deities (ledger)
9777	SAIL.BA.xx.03.07	Sale of temple office; sealed
9778	No date?	Disbursement of unspecified commodity (ledger)
9779	SAIL.BA.25.05.08	Transfer of debt; sealed
9780	SUEL.LA.29.10.—	Sale of real property
9781	No date	List of persons under authority of others; cf. NBC 8493
9782	Lost	Fragmentary account of barley over several months

NBC	Date	Description
9783	WASI.LA.06.03.05?	Account of barley
9784	No date	Ration list
9785	Lost	Sale of field; sealed
9786	SAIL.BA.06.02.—?	Ration list—barley; mu ^{urudu}alam sub(?)-sub(?)-bi(!?) ^{d}lama-kù-sig$_{17}$-didli-bi(!?)-ta(!?)
9787	RISI.LA.—.06.04	Agreement concerning work for deity; sealed; RN in oath
9788	RISI.LA.35.04.—	Legal case concerning house; sealed
9789	SAIL.BA.05.01.—?	Sale of empty lot; sealed; mu gu-za nesag(!?)-gá; RN in oath
9790	RISI.LA.01.11.30	Guarantee of persons in connection with military campaign; sealed
9791	RISI2.LA.03.10.01	Account of barley over several months; sealed
9792	RISI.LA.39.06.—	Sale of improved residential property; sealed
9793	SIMA.IS.B.xx.—	Fragmentary division of property?; sealed
9793A	Lost	Fragmentary sale of temple office
9794	Lost	Fragmentary disbursement of barley
9794A	SUEL.LA.16.07.24	Fragmentary disbursement of bricks
9795	SAIL.BA.24.12.01?	Loan of silver for purchase of barley, to be repaid in barley; sealed
9796	No date	List of PNs and quantities of barley
9797	No date	Record of large quantities of building materials
9798	No date	Delivery of barley; sealed
9799	RISI.LA.55.08.—?	Loan (šu-lá) of barley; sealed
9800	SIIQ.LA.04.04.25	Gift of wooden objects; sealed
9801	SIIQ.LA.04.11.13	Receipt of wool; cf. NBC 9802
9802	SIIQ.LA.02.04.04	Receipt of wool; cf. NBC 9801
9803	No date	Ration list—beer

NBC	Date	Description
9804	Lost?	Account of rations for gangs of workers listed by overseer
9805	No date	List of workers by gangs
9806	RISI.LA.32+.07.—	Adoption; sealed; cf. NBC 9385
9807	DADU.ŠA.B.—.—	Adoption; sealed
9808	DAIL.IS.13.—.—	Division of inheritance; sealed
9809	No date	Ration list
9810	SAIL.BA.25.09.10	Receipt of barley and silver from several persons
9811	No date?	Account of barley (ledger)
9812	SAIL.BA.06.10.—	Legal case concerning field; sealed
9813	SAIL.BA.28.04.06	Receipt of barley from several persons
9817	Lost	Fragment of case—loan of barley; sealed
9821	No date	Tag—seal impressions only; sealed
9824	Illegible	Four case fragments of economic records, including witness list
9826	NUAD.LA.B.09.—	Tablet and case—loan of wool to be repaid in silver; sealed
9827	Lost	Fragment of case—loan of barley; sealed
9828	Lost	Fragments of case—loan of barley; sealed
9829	NASI.ŠA.I.—.—	Tablet and portion of case—loan of barley
9831	—.03.07	Record concerning sowing of field; sealed; date in text
9832	SAIL.BA.28.04.06?	Loan of barley
9833	SAIL.BA.25.12.28	Disbursement?; sealed
9834	SAIL.BA.26.12.—	Fragmentary record concerning foodstuff
9836	No date	List of PNs and quantities of foodstuff
9837	No date	Account of barley
9839	URDU.IS.01.—.—	List of field acreages

NBC	Date	Description
9840	—.03.22	Record concerning barley
9841	—.12.—	Disbursement of silver; sealed; $^{iti}du_6$-kù *adi* ^{iti}še-kin-ku$_5$
9842	RISI.LA.03.07.—	Loan (šu-lá) of silver; sealed
9844	No date	Account(?) of silver
9845	No date	Disbursement of foodstuff
9846	—.11.04	Account of barley
9847	SUEL.LA.xx.07.—	Sale of field; sealed
9848	No date	List of slaves
9849	—.01.19	List of garments
9850	No date	Statement of debt in silver after settling of accounts
9851	DAIL.IS.A.03.—	Sale of improved residential property
9852	Lost	Legal case; sealed
9855	UBAY.KI.01.04.—	Tablet and portion of case—loan of silver; sealed; $^{iti\,d}$Dumu-zi mu ^{giš}gu-za *Ú-ba-a-a iṣ-ba-tu$_4$*
9856	RISI.LA.20.12.—	Tablet and fragments of case—loan (šu-lá) of barley; sealed
9857	No date	Memorandum concerning disbursement(?) of unspecified commodity
9858	No date	List of PNs
9859	—.12.—	Disbursement of barley
9861	xx.12D.—	Sale of field; sealed
9862	No date	Disbursement of barley
9863	SIID.LA.07.04.15	Guarantee of person
9864	GUNG.LA.14.02.01	Disbursement of silver
9865	SIID.LA.07.04.13	Disbursement of barley(?)
9866	—.10.—	Loan of barley
9868	SIID.LA.07.10.17	Receipt of foodstuff from various persons

NBC	Date	Description
9869	No date	Memorandum concerning disbursement of barley
9870	—.03.30	Disbursement of barley
9871	No date	Letter to [...]-Adad from [...]-ilišu
9872	—.01.15	Disbursement of barley
9873	No date	Ration list—barley
9874	SIER.LA.01.09.—?	Receipt of wool(?)
9875	RISI.LA.01.07.18	Loan of silver; sealed
9876	No date	List of PNs
9877	SIID.LA.07.07.02	Record concerning surplus barley
9878	—.05.04	Receipt of silver as price of fugitive
9879	—.05.03?	Receipt of silver
9880	RISI.LA.24.05.—	Tablet and fragments of case—loan (šu-lá) of silver; sealed
9881	IŠIR.IS.24.05.—?	Disbursement of glue
9882	—.02.01	Tag—label for records of payments of silver
9883	xx.03.13	Economic record of uncertain character; sealed
9884	Lost	Account of barley
9885	SAIL.BA.28.03.02	Receipt of foodstuffs for festival of Ilabrat; sealed
9886	GUNG.LA.26.05.14?	Tag—record of fine beer for *naptanum*; sealed; mu ᵘʳᵘᵈᵘalam kù-babbar é ᵈNanna mu-gub
9887	RISI.LA.30.09.—	Loan of barley
9888	No date	List of persons
9889	No date	List of witnesses to oath
9890	xx.10.10+	Tag—receipt
9891	—.02.10	Receipt of silver
9892	RISI.LA.30+.xx.14	Delivery of ox for *naptanum* of king; sealed
9893	URDU.IS.C.03.—	Loan of silver

NBC	Date	Description
9894	—.04.—	Loan of silver; sealed
9895	SIER.LA.01.04.26?	Receipt of shirt
9896	No date	Disbursement of foodstuff
9897	SIID.LA.07.xx.20?	Fragmentary economic record of uncertain character
9898	Lost	Fragmentary economic record of uncertain character
9899	SAIL.BA.20.11.—	Receipt of fugitive slaves
9900	—.06.24	Record concerning sheep
9901	No date?	Fragmentary list of property
9902	—.02.02	Tag—record of workers; sealed; cf. NBC 9912, 9915
9903	—.09.04	Memorandum concerning bran
9904	—.05.25	Receipt of silver(?); cf. NBC 7997, 9920
9905	SIID.LA.07.06.21	Record concerning bronze
9906	SIER.LA.01.11.—?	Loan of barley
9907	No date	Agreement to provide payments of wool, barley flour, barley, and oil to parent; sealed
9908	—.07.01	Receipt of silver for barley
9909	—.10.—	Receipt(?) of silver
9911	IŠIR.IS.32.xx.xx?	Disbursement of vessels
9912	—.02.03	Tag—record of workers; sealed; cf. NBC 9902
9913	??.04.07	Loan of silver; mu gibil gal(?)
9914	—.02.10	Record concerning silver and silver rings
9915	—.02.01	Tag—record of workers; sealed; cf. NBC 9902
9916	xx.04.09	Ration list—barley flour
9917	No date	Loan of barley
9918	RISI.LA.??.12.—	Loan (šu-lá) of silver to be repaid in barley; mu ᵈRīm-Sîn [lugal(?)] mu-ús-sa íd x
9919	SIER.LA.01.05.—	Disbursement of silver; mu-ús-<sa> Maš-gán-šabra(!)

NBC	Date	Description
9920	SIER.LA.01.05.—	Disbursement of silver; cf. NBC 7997, 9904
9921	SIER.LA.01.04.01	Disbursement of silver
9922	Lost	Disbursement of foodstuff
9923	No date	Record concerning barley; cf. NBC 9924
9924	No date	Record concerning small cattle; cf. NBC 9923
9931	IŠIR.IS.19.05.27	Disbursement of leather and leather products; sealed; BIN 10, 128 (C)
9932	IŠIR.IS.03.05.14?	Disbursement?; BIN 10, 194 (C)
9938	IŠIR.IS.24.01.—	Delivery of silver by several persons; or IŠIR.IS.33?
9944	No date	Letter to Šū-Ninin and Irrišum; sealed
9952	IDDA.IS.02.12.—	Disbursement of barley for months *Tašrītu* through *Addaru* [mu ^{d}*I*]-*din*-^{d}*Da-gan* lugal-e [*Ma-tum-*]*ni-a-tum* dumu-munus-ni [lugal] An-ša-an^{ki}-ke$_4$ ba-an-tuk
9973	DAIL.IS.B.01.16	Delivery; sealed
9975	SAIL.BA.28.02.25	Record concerning baskets and other objects of reed; sealed
9976	UN.UN.AX.11.15	Economic record of uncertain character; sealed; mu-ús-sa Uri$_2$^{ki} ba-dab$_5$
9978	IDDA.IS.02.07.—	Record of replacement of cow; sealed; [mu ^{d}]*I-din-*^{d}*Da-gan* [lugal-]e *Ma-tum-ni-a-tum* [dumu-munus-ni] lugal An-ša-an^{ki}-ke$_4$ ba-an-tuk
9984	IŠIR.IS.33.06.—	Delivery of cloth; sealed
9995	IŠIR.IS.13.06.—	Account of oil; BIN 10, 83 (C)
10007	IŠIR.IS.11.01.—	Record concerning foodstuff; sealed
10008	ŠUIL.IS.08.xx.—	Receipt of barley to fatten oxen; sealed
10011	IDDA.IS.03.02.—	Disbursement of barley flour; sealed; [mu-ús-sa] ^{d}*I-din-*^{d}*Da-gan* [lugal-e *Ma-tum-ni-*]*a-tum* dumu-munus-a-ni [An-š]a-an^{ki}-šè ba-an-tuk-a
10051	SAIL.BA.19.11.07	Receipt of wool; sealed

NBC	Date	Description
10054	??.12.26	Receipt of foodstuffs; [mu al]am gibil KA x šà(?) erin$_2$(?) KUM DA
10057	HARA.BA.33.06.01	Record concerning cultivation of allotment field; sealed; ^{iti}kin-ne-^{d}Inanna u$_4$-1-kam [mu] íd-da gi-gi Ḫa-am-mu-ra-bi-nu-ḫu-uš-ni-ši i-ba-al
10058	SAIL.BA.xx.01.15	Payment of dates for three years; sealed
10062	xx.10.—	Receipt of dates; [mu ...] x x x mu-un-ba-al
10065	RISI.LA.—.—.—	Receipt of small cattle from various persons; iti-21 ki-6 u$_4$-8-kam,
10066	SIMU.BA.13.08.—	Marriage contract
10067	SAIL.BA.27.01.07	Consignment of small cattle; sealed
10068	RISI.LA.31.??.26	Record concerning fattening barn; sealed; iti-2 ki-4
10069	IŠIR.IS.27.04.11	Disbursement of bags and bowls; BIN 10, 160 (C)
10070	RISI.LA.31.??.30	Account of small cattle; sealed; iti-30 ki-5
10072	RISI.LA.35.12.—	Sale of field; sealed
10073	IŠIR.IS.25.xx.06	Disbursement of bags and leather; BIN 10, 159 (C)
10075	IŠIR.IS.13.02.—	Disbursement of musical instruments and reed containers; BIN 10, 104 (C)
10076	SUEL.LA.01.01.06	Disbursement of reed mats and baskets; BIN 10, 166 (C)
10077	RISI.LA.42.06.—	Agreement concerning produce of orchard; sealed
10078	RISI.LA.31.??.30	Delivery of dead small cattle; sealed; iti-27 ki-5
10079	No date	Ration list—barley
10080	RISI.LA.31.??.17	Delivery of sheep; sealed; iti-26 ki-2
10081	RISI.LA.31+.xx.24	Delivery of large and small cattle; sealed; text mentions iti-7(?) ki-5; cf. NBC 10082
10082	RISI.LA.31+.??.05	Delivery of small cattle; sealed; iti-26 ki-6; cf. NBC 10081
10084	SAIL.BA.13.xx.xx	Division of inheritance; sealed
10085	Lost	Fragmentary sale of temple office; sealed

NBC	Date	Description
10086	Lost	Rental of field
10087	HARA.BA.03.04.06	Loan of barley
10088	—.12.—	Disbursement of small cattle to various deities
10089	No date	Sale; cf. NBC 5515
10090	ABSA.LA.10.08.—	Sale of slave; sealed
10091	No date	Ration list
10092	IPE2.ŠA.—.02.02	Record concerning large number of small cattle; sealed; RN in seal inscription; ᵐE-lu-nu
10093	HARA.BA.xx.09.—	Sale of field; sealed
10095	Lost?	Disbursement of barley
10096	SAIL.BA.12.12.20	Sale of improved residential property; sealed
10097	SUEL.LA.28.12D.xx	Record concerning small cattle
10098	No date	List of numerals and PNs
10099	Lost?	Adoption; sealed
10101	Lost?	Record of boats in quay of Isin
10102	No date	List of numerals and PNs
10103	NASI.EŠ.11.12.19?	Receipt(?) of wool; ᵐKi-in-kum mu 2 alam ù(?) kù-sig$_{17}$
10104	—.02.—	Tag—delivery?; sealed
10105	No date	Record of harvest labor; sealed
10106	No date	Receipt(?) of silver
10107	SAIL.BA.xx.01.14	Disbursement of barley; sealed
10108	IŠIR.IS.07.06.—	Economic record of uncertain character; sealed; mu nin ᵈNin-urta mu-un-íl
10110	No date	List of numerals and PNs
10113	SAIL.BA.21.07.10	Promissory note—sesame; sealed
10114	No date	Tag—seal impression only; sealed

NBC	Date	Description
10115	xx.—.—	Promissory note—barley
10116	No date	Disbursement of barley and flour
10118	SIIQ.LA.02.03.03	Receipt of barley; mu ᵈNu-muš-da ᵈNam-bi-ra-at ᵈLugal-a-pi-ak šà Ka-zal-lu
10119	No date?	Record of tax payments?
10120	BUSI.IS.F.08.11	Tag—record concerning dead sheep; sealed; mu bàd gal-gal min-a-bi mu-dù
10122	No date	Loan of silver
10123	No date	Tag—delivery(?) of sesame; sealed; cf. NBC 10180
10126	SAIL.BA.28.—.—	Record concerning barley for fodder; mu *Ya-di-a-bu*
10127	RISI.LA.01.12.—	Loan of barley; sealed
10128	ABSA.LA.03.12.—	Loan of barley; sealed; mu alam kù-babbar é ᵈNanna-ka <i->ni-in-ku₄-ra; cf. NBC 10131
10130	ABSA.LA.04.12.—	Record concerning small cattle
10131	ABSA.LA.03.12.—	Loan of barley; sealed; mu alam kù-babbar é ᵈNanna-ka; cf. NBC 10128
10132	ABSA.LA.04.03.—	Loan of silver
10133	No date	Economic record of uncertain character
10134	ABSA.LA.02.11.—	Loan of barley; sealed
10135	GUNG.LA.17.11.—	Disbursement of barley; mu ⁱᵈ*Im-gur*-ᵈEN.ZU gal-lí-tum ba-ba-al; cf. NBC 10128 and NBC 10131
10136	Lost?	Loan of silver to several persons
10138	—.02.01	Disbursement of barley
10139	—.01.28	Memorandum concerning flour rations; ⁱᵗⁱbara₂-za-gar
10140	SAIL.BA.19.05.20	Loan of millstone
10141	SAIL.BA.26.06.30	Disbursement of cult furnishing; sealed
10142	SAIL.BA.23.02.15	Tag—hire of harvest labor; sealed
10144	SAIL.BA.20.11.25	Record concerning debt of barley; sealed

NBC	Date	Description
10145	No date	List of numerals and PNs
10146	No date	Memorandum concerning disbursement of barley by storehouse; sealed
10147	SAIL.BA.06.xx.27	Receipt of reed mats; sealed
10149	—.04.23	Disbursement of foodstuff
10150	SAIL.BA.26.06.05	Record concerning consigned sheep; sealed; cf. NBC 10188
10151	LIIŠ.IS.A.xx.xx	Record concerning object of silver; sealed
10152	Illegible	Disbursement
10156	SIMU.BA.03.04.—	Memorandum concerning debts(?); sealed
10158	No date	List of persons
10159	Illegible	Loan of barley
10160	SAIL.BA.28.05.01	Delivery of bran; sealed; cf. NBC 10175
10163	No date	Ration list—barley
10164	No date	Loan of silver with interest to be paid in dates
10165	SAIL.BA.26.04.13	Loan(?) of silver; sealed
10166	No date	Disbursement of barley
10168	No date	Receipt; sealed
10169	SAIL.BA.25.05.30	Tag—disbursement of sheep; sealed; cf. NBC 10172
10170	No date	Tag—seal impression only
10171	UN.UN.W.02.—	Tag—receipt of ingredient for beer; sealed; mu íd Amar-^{d}EN.ZU-na saḫar-ḫi-ya(sic) ba-ba-al-la; cf. NBC 9400
10172	SAIL.BA.xx.07.03	Disbursement of sheep; sealed; date lost; reign from other texts in archive, month and day in text; cf. NBC 10169
10173	Lost	Sale of field
10175	SAIL.BA.28.05.01	Delivery of bran; sealed; cf. NBC 10160
10176	xx.04.21	Disbursement of barley; sealed

NBC	Date	Description
10177	No date	Memorandum concerning boxes of silver
10179	IPE2.ŠA.B.02.19	Tag—record of harvest labor; sealed; $^{iti}E\text{-}lu\text{-}nim$ mu gu$_4$-apin kù-sig$_{17}$
10180	No date	Tag—delivery(?) of sesame; sealed; cf. NBC 10123
10181	—.xx.15	Economic record of uncertain character
10182	No date	Ration list
10183	No date	Record of harvest labor
10184	No date	Record concerning barley(?)
10185	Lost?	Fragmentary ration list
10186	—.02.—	Ration list—barley
10187	xx.06.01	Record concerning flour(?)
10188	SAIL.BA.25.12.03?	Record concerning consigned sheep; sealed; cf. NBC 10150
10189	SAIL.BA.26.02.09	Disbursement of sheep; sealed; cf. NBC 10169
10190	xx.07.—	Loan of silver
10229	HARA.BA.39.01.18	Record concerning implements (ledger)
10230	HARA.BA.35.06.20	Record concerning dates; sealed; cf. NBC 10231
10231	HARA.BA.39.06.—	Agreement concerning produce of orchard; sealed; cf. NBC 10230
10331	xx.12.27	Record concerning barley
10332	RISI.LA.58.12.30	Fragmentary receipt of barley allotment(?); sealed
10333	—.04.—	Receipt of barley
10334	No date	Disbursement
10335	RISI.LA.20.03.08	Disbursement of reed baskets
10336	No date	List of PNs and quantities of foodstuff
10337	SUEL.LA.16.08.—	Tag—delivery of bran for oxen fodder; sealed; cf. NBC 10409
10338	No date	Account of silver (ledger)

NBC	Date	Description
10341	No date	Fragment of case—letter; sealed
10342	xx.xx.xx	Loan of silver; sealed
10344	SIIQ.LA.04.02.26	Account of barley
10345	SABI.BA.07.09.—	Record concerning debts connected with partnership; sealed; mu erin$_2$ Ararma^{ki}-ma
10347	ENBA.IS.N.03.—	Exchange(?) of improved residential property; sealed mu ^{d}En-líl-ba-ni lugal-e Nin-men-^{d}KA-x-kù(?) nin-dingir ^{d}Iškur ba-íl
10348	ABSA.LA.02.11.—	Loan of barley; sealed; mu íd *Im-gur-^{d}Inanna* Zaba[lam^{ki}]
10349	URDU.IS.01.12.—?	Sale of field; sealed; [mu ...]x-ga lugal
10350	Lost?	Fragmentary account of barley
10351	SAIL.BA.17.xx.xx	Rental of field; sealed
10352	Lost	Fragment of case—contract of uncertain character—only list of witnesses preserved; sealed
10353	HARA.BA.31.09.—	Tag—receipt of bitumen; cf. NBC 10379
10355	HARA.BA.36.08.14	Receipt of beer; sealed; mu u$_6$-nir ki-tuš maḫ
10356	UN.UN.W.02.—	Tag—delivery of ingredient for beer; sealed; mu íd Amar-^{d}EN.ZU ba-ba-al; cf. NBC 9400
10357	No date	Memorandum concerning silver
10358	ABSA.LA.10.01.—	Tag—delivery of ingredient for beer; sealed; mu-ús-sa en ^{d}Utu; cf. NBC 9400
10360	ENBA.IS.L.05.—	Fragmentary sale of field; Sigrist and Cohen, Or 45, 1976, pp. 421-23 (C, T, Tr)
10361	—.11.12	Account of foodstuff (ledger)
10362	NASI.ŠA.F.—.—	Tablet and case—loan of barley; sealed; mu *mu-uš-ḫu-ši-im i-na* ká ḫuš-ḫi-a gub-ba
10363	SAIL.BA.27.xx.xx	Hire of teams of oxen; sealed
10365	No date?	Ration list(?)
10366	xx.xx.xx	Ration list—barley

NBC	Date	Description
10367	IDDA.IS.05.12.—	Loan of barley(?)
10368	Lost?	Loan (šu-lá) of barley
10369	No date	List of numerals and PNs
10370	RISI.LA.33.04.—	Receipt of garments; sealed; mu-ús-sa ki-4-bi
10371	No date	Ration list—barley
10372	—.03.xx	Ration list
10373	SIIQ.LA.04.02.13	Tag—receipt of cattle; sealed
10374	No date?	Rental of field; sealed
10376	Lost	Rental of boats
10377	—.11.12	Disbursement of foodstuff
10378	SAIL.BA.18.06.26	Tag—receipt of barley
10379	HARA.BA.31.08.12	Tag—receipt of bitumen; cf. NBC 10353
10380	—.10.—	Receipt
10382	RISI.LA.50.01.09	Record concerning foodstuff
10383	—.12.20	Disbursement of barley; sealed
10385	RISI.LA.23.12.—	Tablet and portion of case—loan (šu-lá) of silver; sealed
10386	RISI.LA.xx.xx.xx	Fragmentary division of inheritance; sealed; date lost, but RN in oath
10387	No date	Ration list—barley
10388	No date?	Fragmentary list of PNs and quantities of unclear commodity
10389	RISI.LA.31+.10.—	Rental of boat; sealed
10390	Lost?	Ration list—oil
10391	No date	Adoption
10392	Lost	Sale of house
10393	WASI.LA.10.11.—	Sale of house; sealed

NBC	Date	Description
10394	HARA.BA.33.05.18	Tablet and case—agreement concerning produce of orchard; sealed
10395		Numerous fragmentary economic records
10396	SUEL.LA.26.06.—?	Disbursement of silver; mu-ús-sa-ús-sa-4-bi
10397	No date	List of numerals and PNs; cf. NBC 10400
10398	RISI.LA.26.12.05?	Division(?) of property; sealed
10399	No date	Disbursement of foodstuff and wool
10400	No date	List of numerals and PNs; cf. NBC 10397
10401	No date	List of soldiers/workers; fingernail impressions
10403	—.—.07	List of numerals and PNs
10404	SUEL.LA.16.03.—	List of field acreages
10405	SUEL.LA.16.12.04	Record of manufacture of bricks
10406	No date	List of quantities of silver and PNs
10407	SUEL.LA.06.07.11	Tag—record of workers; sealed
10408	No date	Letter to Nūr-Sîn from Išar-kubi
10409	SUEL.LA.16.11.04	Tag—delivery of bran for sheep fodder; sealed; cf. NBC 10337
10411	Lost?	Ration list
10412	No date?	Fragmentary inventory of wooden objects, including measures of various capacities
10413	No date	Fragmentary list of quantities of silver
10415	No date?	Fragmentary account?
10416	No date?	Bulla—list of PNs and quantities of silver(?)
10417	RISI.LA.49.10.—	Disbursement of lambs; sealed
10419	Lost	Fragmentary sale; sealed
10420	Lost?	Delivery of barley
10421	xx.xx.—	Fragmentary economic record of uncertain character

NBC	Date	Description
10422	Lost	Promissory note—silver
10433	Lost	Fragmentary economic record of uncertain character
10434	Lost	Fragmentary loan of silver
10435	Lost?	Fragmentary ration list
10436		Numerous fragmentary economic records
10438	—.10.—	List of PNs and quantities of barley; ᴵᵀᴵ*Ma-mi-tim*
10439	No date	Letter to Šamaš-ēriš from Šamaš-kīma-ilī
10440	RISI.LA.29.08.—	Fragmentary account?
10441	RISI.LA.53.01.—	Receipt of silver from several persons; sealed
10442	RISI.LA.58.01.—	Disbursement of foodstuff; cf. NBC 10444
10443	RISI.LA.53.07.—?	Receipt of cattle(?); ⁱᵗⁱdu$_6$-KUD
10444	Lost	Disbursement of foodstuff; cf. NBC 10442
10445	RISI.LA.59.11.30	Disbursement of barley for months *Araḫsamna* through *Šabaṭu*
10446	RISI.LA.31+.01.01	Disbursement of barley
10447	RISI.LA.29.07.02	Account of barley
10448	WASI.LA.10.04.—	Exchange of real property; sealed
10449	Lost?	Fragmentary disbursement of barley
10450	No date	List of quantities of sesame and barley issued to individuals, with names of responsible officials
10451	RISI.LA.57.12.11	Disbursement of wool
10452	No date	Receipt of wool
10453	RISI.LA.59.02.—	Ration list—barley and dates (ledger)
10454	RISI.LA.31+.xx.06	Fragmentary record concerning large and small cattle; sealed
10455	No date	Ration list—barley (ledger)
10456	RISI.LA.60.03.—	Account of sesame and oil for months *Ayyaru* and *Simanu*

NBC	Date	Description
10457	SAIL.BA.18.xx.30	Receipt of reed mats; sealed
10458	RISI.LA.59.06.—	Disbursement of oil for months *Du'ūzu* through *Elūlu*
10459	WASI.LA.11.06.—	Legal case concerning orchard; sealed
10460	RISI.LA.22.12.—?	Sale of orchard; sealed; mu íd sikil-la ba-ba-al
10461	UN.UN.AY.—.—	Sale of slave; sealed; mu *A-ši-ma-nu-um* ba-ši-du$_8$
10462	No date	List of personnel; cf. NBC 10490
10463	RISI.LA.48.02.29	Account of barley
10464	—.10.02	Disbursement of barley over eight days (ledger); zag ^{iti}gan-gan-è ud-25<-kam> en-na ^{iti}ab-è ud-2-kam
10465	RISI.LA.53.01.30	Receipt of wool; sealed
10466	RISI.LA.31.??.16	Delivery of sheep; sealed; iti-6 ki-4
10467	RISI.LA.31+.xx.—	Disbursement of sesame
10468	RISI.LA.59.08.16	List of PNs and quantities of gold, with silver equivalents
10469	No date	Disbursement of barley
10470	No date	Ration list
10471	RISI.LA.47.01.—?	Record concerning small cattle; sealed
10472	RISI.LA.31.09.xx	Economic record of uncertain character
10476	—.11.03	Receipt of barley
10477	—.02.20?	Receipt of barley
10478	No date	Record concerning workers(?); sealed
10479	RISI.LA.59.01.—	Account of foodstuff
10480	Lost	Disbursement of barley
10481	RISI.LA.40.01.20	Tablet and portion of case—loan of silver; sealed
10482	HARA.BA.40.03.15	Record of plowed fields (ledger)
10483	RISI.LA.34.10.—	Sale of real property; sealed
10485	Lost	Tag—seal impression only

NBC	Date	Description
10486	No date	Record of fields, their owners, and quantities of grain for various days (ledger)
10487	RISI.LA.47.11.—	Account of barley
10488	RISI.LA.16.04.23	Disbursement(?)
10490	No date	List of personnel—living, dead, fugitive, and supplementary; cf. NBC 10462
10491	RISI.LA.59.06.—	Disbursement of dates for offering to dead
10493	No date	Fragmentary ration list—dates
10494	SIIQ.LA.02.05.04	List of days and PNs
10495	No date?	Record concerning cultivation of field
10496	RISI.LA.58.12.30	Disbursement of sesame
10497	UN.LA.B.02.05	Disbursement of barley; mu alam gub(?) ù 3 ^{giš}gu-za kù-sig$_{17}$ <<ù>> é ^{d}En-líl é ^{d}Utu ù é ^{d}Nanna-šè(?) i-ni-in-ku$_4$-re
10498	No date	Record concerning garments (ledger)
10499	Lost?	Fragmentary account of sesame
10500	HARA.BA.33.04.—	Tablet and case—loan (šu-lá) of silver; sealed
10501	No date	List of PNs or titles and numbers of ox hides
10502	RISI.LA.16.04.xx	List of numbers of dead sheep
10503	RISI.LA.59.03.—	Account of barley
10504	RISI.LA.24.04.—?	Ration list
10506	No date	Letter to "my father" from Šumi-abum
10508	RISI.LA.13.12.30	Account of silver; sealed
10509	RISI.LA.16.12.—	Tablet and portion of case—list of witnesses; sealed; dupl. NBC 10510
10510	RISI.LA.16.12.—	Tablet and fragments of case—list of witnesses; sealed; dupl. NBC 10509
10511	—.07.01	Ration list—barley for fodder
10512	RISI.LA.60.01.—	Ration list—barley and dates

NBC	Date	Description
10513	RISI.LA.31.xx.xx	Disbursement of cattle for days 8, 15, 23, and 24; sealed; cf. NBC 10082
10514	No date	Letter
10515	No date	List of numerals and PNs
10516	RISI.LA.54.02.20	Record concerning sesame, barley, dates, and wool; sealed
10517	No date	Record of payments of barley and expenses in silver for various goods and persons
10518	xx.xx.xx	Sale of orchard; sealed
10519	SAIL.BA.01.01.05?	Loan of silver for six days; sealed
10520	SUEL.LA.02.02.21	Tag—delivery of bran for sheep fodder; sealed; mu alam kù-babbar *Su-mu-el* lugal; cf. NBC 8881
10521	No date	Tag—seal impression only
10523	RISI.LA.57.01.11	Record of tax on wool
10524	xx.11.25	Loan of silver; sealed
10525	SIIQ.LA.02.07.25	Receipt of wool for garments
10526	RISI.LA.47.04.—	Receipt of barley, wool, sesame, and dates
10527	xx.01.01	Loan of silver; sealed
10528	RISI.LA.31+.11.—	Ration list—barley
10535	No date	Record concerning date production; = 6NT 426
10612	No date?	Fragmentary list of numerals and PNs; = 6NT-753
10673	Lost?	Fragmentary account of uncertain commodity over several years; = 6NT-751
10675	Lost	Account of foodstuff (ledger); = 6NT 824
10682	No date?	Account of foodstuffs (ledger); = 6NT 749
10715	Lost	Fragmentary administrative record of uncertain character; = 6NT 973
10731	No date	Record concerning cattle; = 6NT-961
10777	Lost	Fragmentary account; = 6NT-868

NBC	Date	Description
10809	No date	Disbursement of foodstuff; record of work assignments
10820	RISI.LA.48.04.—	Disbursement of barley over one month
10828	No date	Disbursement of foodstuff for deities (ledger)
10831	No date	List of PNs
10837	No date	Ration list—barley
10840	RISI.LA.48.10.14	Account of barley
10893	xx.xx.xx	Promissory note—silver; sealed
10913	SAIL.BA.01.01.02	Loan of silver to be repaid in barley; sealed
10916	Lost?	List of field acreages? (ledger); cf. NBC 8161
10918	No date	List of workers with patronymics
10919	No date	Letter to [...]-lum from Arabutum concerning cultivation of field
11124	SIID.LA.07.05.27	Fragmentary record of *sattukku* offerings in Ešumeša; = 4NT 78; BiMes 11, no. 191
11125	SUEL.LA.28.08.22	Fragmentary record of *sattukku* offerings in Ešumeša; = 4NT 80; BiMes 11, no. 45
11126	IRIM.IS.D.06.14	Fragmentary record of *sattukku* offerings in Ešumeša; = 4NT 82; BiMes 11, no. 62
11127	Illegible	Fragmentary record of *sattukku* offerings in Ešumeša; = 4NT 226; BiMes 11, no. 163
11128	Lost	Fragmentary record of *sattukku* offerings in Ešumeša; = 4NT 242; BiMes 11, no. 222
11129	Lost	Fragmentary record of *sattukku* offerings in Ešumeša; = 4NT 243; BiMes 11, no. 214
11130	Lost	Fragmentary record of *sattukku* offerings in Ešumeša; = 4NT 244; BiMes 11, p. 128, no. 318 (T)
11131	Lost	Fragmentary record of *sattukku* offerings in Ešumeša; = 4NT 245; BiMes 11, no. 75
11132	Lost	Fragmentary record of *sattukku* offerings in Ešumeša; = 4NT 247; BiMes 11, no. 392

NBC	Date	Description
11133	Lost	Fragmentary record of *sattukku* offerings in Ešumeša; = 4NT 87; BiMes 11, no. 49
11134	Lost	Record of *sattukku* offerings in Ešumeša; = 4NT 88; BiMes 11, no. 216
11135	Lost	Fragmentary record of *sattukku* offerings in Ešumeša; = 4NT 92; BiMes 11, no. 83
11136	Lost	Fragmentary record of *sattukku* offerings in Ešumeša; = 4NT 94; BiMes 11, no. 154
11137	xx.xx.24	Record of *sattukku* offerings in Ešumeša; = 4NT 96; BiMes 11, no. 128
11138	Lost	Fragmentary record of *sattukku* offerings in Ešumeša; = 4NT 97; BiMes 11, no. 97
11139	Lost	Fragmentary record of *sattukku* offerings in Ešumeša; = 4NT 98; BiMes 11, no. 153
11140	Lost	Fragmentary record of *sattukku* offerings in Ešumeša; = 4NT 100; BiMes 11, no. 212
11141	Lost	Fragmentary record of *sattukku* offerings in Ešumeša; = 4NT 102; BiMes 11, no. 205
11142	SIER.LA.xx.08.08	Fragmentary record of *sattukku* offerings in Ešumeša; = 4NT 225; BiMes 11, 103f, no. 196 (T)
11143	Lost	Record of *sattukku* offerings in Ešumeša; = 4NT 228; BiMes 11, no. 213
11144	Lost	Record of *sattukku* offerings in Ešumeša; = 4NT 240; BiMes 11, no. 211
11145	Lost	Fragmentary record of *sattukku* offerings in Ešumeša; = 4NT 84; BiMes 11, no. 126
11146	Lost	Fragmentary record of *sattukku* offerings in Ešumeša; = 4NT 86; BiMes 11, no. 158
11147	SUEL.LA.25.06.16	Fragmentary record of *sattukku* offerings in Ešumeša; = 4NT 227; BiMes 11, no. 31
11148	RISI.LA.28.06.27	Record of *sattukku* offerings in Ešumeša; = 4NT 229; BiMes 11, no. 307
11149	Lost	Fragmentary record of *sattukku* offerings in Ešumeša; = 4NT 246; BiMes 11, no. 210

NBC	Date	Description
11150	Lost	Fragmentary record of *sattukku* offerings in Ešumeša; = 4NT 248; BiMes 11, no. 370
11151	Lost	Fragmentary record of *sattukku* offerings in Ešumeša; = 4NT 249; BiMes 11, no. 245
11152	Lost	Fragmentary record of *sattukku* offerings in Ešumeša; = 4NT 250; BiMes 11, no. 76
11153	Lost	Fragmentary record of *sattukku* offerings in Ešumeša; = 4NT 251; BiMes 11, no. 341
11154	Lost	Fragmentary record of *sattukku* offerings in Ešumeša; = 4NT 252; BiMes 11, no. 342
11155	Lost	Fragmentary record of *sattukku* offerings in Ešumeša; = 4NT 253; BiMes 11, no. 343
11156	RISI.LA.28.09.20	Record of *sattukku* offerings in Ešumeša; = 4NT 254; BiMes 11, no. 308
11157	RISI.LA.28.06.04	Record of *sattukku* offerings in Ešumeša; = 4NT 255; BiMes 11, no. 306
11158	—.02.09	Record of *sattukku* offerings in Ešumeša; = 4NT 256; BiMes 11, no. 311
11159	Lost	Record of *sattukku* offerings in Ešumeša; = 4NT 257; BiMes 11, no. 310
11160	xx.xx.02	Record of *sattukku* offerings in Ešumeša; = 4NT 258; BiMes 11, p. 119, no. 312 (T)
11161	Lost	Fragmentary record of *sattukku* offerings in Ešumeša; = 4NT 103; BiMes 11, no. 85
11162	Lost	Fragmentary record of *sattukku* offerings in Ešumeša; = 4NT 104; BiMes 11, no. 131
11163	Lost	Fragmentary record of *sattukku* offerings in Ešumeša; = 4NT 105; BiMes 11, no. 206
11164	Lost	Fragmentary record of *sattukku* offerings in Ešumeša; = 4NT 106; BiMes 11, no. 20
11165	Lost	Fragmentary record of *sattukku* offerings in Ešumeša; = 4NT 107; BiMes 11, no. 50
11166	Lost	Fragmentary record of *sattukku* offerings in Ešumeša; = 4NT 108; BiMes 11, no. 390

NBC	Date	Description
11167	Lost	Fragmentary record of *sattukku* offerings in Ešumeša; = 4NT 109; BiMes 11, no. 181
11168	Lost	Fragmentary record of *sattukku* offerings in Ešumeša; = 4NT 110; BiMes 11, no. 414
11169	Lost	Fragmentary record of *sattukku* offerings in Ešumeša; = 4NT 111a; BiMes 11, no. 135
11170	Lost	Fragmentary record of *sattukku* offerings in Ešumeša; = 4NT 112; BiMes 11, no. 217
11171	Lost	Fragmentary record of *sattukku* offerings in Ešumeša; = 4NT 113; BiMes 11, no. 378
11172	ENBA.IS.I.xx.xx	Fragmentary record of *sattukku* offerings in Ešumeša; = 4NT 114; BiMes 11, no. 121
11173	Lost	Fragmentary record of *sattukku* offerings in Ešumeša; = 4NT 115; BiMes 11, no. 129
11174	LIEN.IS.01.05.—	Fragmentary record of *sattukku* offerings in Ešumeša; = 4NT 81; BiMes 11, no. 2
11175	Lost	Fragmentary record of *sattukku* offerings in Ešumeša; = 4NT 91; BiMes 11, no. 111
11176	Lost	Fragmentary record of *sattukku* offerings in Ešumeša; = 4NT 95; BiMes 11, no. 155
11177	Lost	Record of *sattukku* offerings in Ešumeša; = 4NT 93; BiMes 11, 133, no. 328 (T)
11178	Lost	Fragmentary record of *sattukku* offerings in Ešumeša; = 4NT 89; BiMes 11, no. 265
11179	Lost	Fragmentary record of *sattukku* offerings in Ešumeša; = 4NT 85; BiMes 11, no. 106
11180	Lost	Fragmentary record of *sattukku* offerings in Ešumeša; = 4NT 241; BiMes 11, no. 72
11181	Lost	Record of *sattukku* offerings in Ešumeša; = 4NT 173; BiMes 11, no. 74
11182	SIIQ.LA.01.xx.01	Record of *sattukku* offerings in Ešumeša; = 4NT 99; BiMes 11, no. 209
11183		Fragments including record of *sattukku* offerings in Ešumeša; =4NT 258A; BiMes 11, no. 300

NBC	Date	Description
11184		Fragments including record of *sattukku* offerings in Ešumeša; = 4NT 115A; BiMes 11, no. 187
11185		Includes record of *sattukku* offerings in Ešumeša; = 4NT 227A
11186	Lost	Record of *sattukku* offerings in Ešumeša; = 4NT 79; BiMes 11, no. 166
11187	Lost	Record of *sattukku* offerings in Ešumeša; = 4NT 90; BiMes 11, no. 127
11188	ENBA.IS.L.08.10	Record of *sattukku* offerings in Ešumeša; = 4NT 77; BiMes 11, no. 157
11189	xx.xx.25	Fragmentary record of *sattukku* offerings in Ešumeša; = 4NT 101; BiMes 11, no. 152
11190	ENBA.IS.L.03.08?	Record of *sattukku* offerings in Ešumeša; = 4NT 83; BiMes 11, no. 156
11203	SIIQ.LA.05.02.12	Record of *sattukku* offerings in Ešumeša; = 5NT 91; BiMes 11, p. 112, no. 227 (C)
11204	Lost	Record of *sattukku* offerings in Ešumeša; = 5NT 102; BiMes 11, no. 112
11205	Lost	Record of *sattukku* offerings in Ešumeša; = 5NT 104; BiMes 11, no. 120
11206	xx.xx.16?	Fragmentary record of *sattukku* offerings in Ešumeša; = 5NT 108; BiMes 11, no. 239
11207	LIEN.IS.01.04.20	Fragmentary record of *sattukku* offerings in Ešumeša; = 5NT 109; BiMes 11, p. 45, no. 3 (C)
11208	Lost	Fragmentary record of *sattukku* offerings in Ešumeša; = 5NT 132; BiMes 11, no. 119
11209	Lost	Fragmentary record of *sattukku* offerings in Ešumeša; = 5NT 117; BiMes 11, no. 179
11210	Lost	Fragmentary record of *sattukku* offerings in Ešumeša; = 5NT 121; BiMes 11, no. 340
11211	Lost	Fragmentary record of *sattukku* offerings in Ešumeša; = 5NT 111; BiMes 11, no. 114
11212	ENBA.IS.xx.xx.20	Fragmentary record of *sattukku* offerings in Ešumeša; = 5NT 134; BiMes 11, no. 175

NBC	Date	Description
11213	Lost	Fragmentary record of *sattukku* offerings in Ešumeša; = 5NT 137; BiMes 11, no. 270
11214	Lost	Fragmentary record of *sattukku* offerings in Ešumeša; = 5NT 142; BiMes 11, no. 122
11215	Lost	Fragmentary record of *sattukku* offerings in Ešumeša; = 5NT 146; BiMes 11, no. 99
11216	Lost	Fragmentary record of *sattukku* offerings in Ešumeša; = 5NT 149; BiMes 11, no. 285
11217	Lost	Fragmentary record of *sattukku* offerings in Ešumeša; = 5NT 158; BiMes 11, no. 113
11218	Illegible	Record of *sattukku* offerings in Ešumeša; = 5NT 160; BiMes 11, no. 105
11219	SIIQ.LA.02.04.26	Fragmentary record of *sattukku* offerings in Ešumeša; = 5NT 164; BiMes 11, no. 272
11220	ENBA.IS.I.08.07	Fragmentary record of *sattukku* offerings in Ešumeša; = 5NT 166; BiMes 11, no. 94
11221	Lost	Fragmentary record of *sattukku* offerings in Ešumeša; = 5NT 168; BiMes 11, no. 269
11222	Lost	Fragmentary record of *sattukku* offerings in Ešumeša; = 5NT 174; BiMes 11, no. 375
11223	Lost	Fragmentary record of *sattukku* offerings in Ešumeša; = 5NT 184; BiMes 11, no. 395
11224	Lost	Fragmentary record of *sattukku* offerings in Ešumeša; = 5NT 186; BiMes 11, no. 93
11225	Lost	Fragmentary record of *sattukku* offerings in Ešumeša; = 5NT 190; BiMes 11, no. 379
11226	Lost	Fragmentary record of *sattukku* offerings in Ešumeša; = 5NT 192; BiMes 11, no. 247
11227	Lost	Fragmentary record of *sattukku* offerings in Ešumeša; = 5NT 197; BiMes 11, no. 329
11228	Lost	Fragmentary record of *sattukku* offerings in Ešumeša; = 5NT 199; BiMes 11, no. 185
11229	Lost	Fragmentary record of *sattukku* offerings in Ešumeša; = 5NT 202; BiMes 11, no. 248

NBC	Date	Description
11230	Lost	Fragmentary record of *sattukku* offerings in Ešumeša; = 5NT 207; BiMes 11, no. 5
11231	Lost	Fragmentary record of *sattukku* offerings in Ešumeša; = 5NT 211; BiMes 11, no. 159
11232	Lost	Fragmentary record of *sattukku* offerings in Ešumeša; = 5NT 223; BiMes 11, no. 338
11233	Lost	Fragmentary record of *sattukku* offerings in Ešumeša; = 5NT 224; BiMes 11, no. 194
11234	Lost	Fragmentary record of *sattukku* offerings in Ešumeša; = 5NT 234; BiMes 11, no. 339
11235	Lost	Fragmentary record of *sattukku* offerings in Ešumeša; = 5NT 236; BiMes 11, no. 374
11236	Lost	Fragmentary record of *sattukku* offerings in Ešumeša; = 5NT 330; BiMes 11, no. 330
11237	xx.xx.16	Fragmentary record of *sattukku* offerings in Ešumeša; = 5NT 241; BiMes 11, no. 373
11238	Lost	Fragmentary record of *sattukku* offerings in Ešumeša; = 5NT 242; BiMes 11, p. 134, no. 337 (T)
11239	Lost	Fragmentary record of *sattukku* offerings in Ešumeša; = 5NT 244; BiMes 11, no. 340
11240	Lost	Fragmentary record of *sattukku* offerings in Ešumeša; = 5NT 247; BiMes 11, no. 266
11241	SIID.LA.07.xx.15	Fragmentary record of *sattukku* offerings in Ešumeša; = 5NT 250; BiMes 11, no. 192
11242	Lost	Fragmentary record of *sattukku* offerings in Ešumeša; = 5NT 255; BiMes 11, no. 335
11243	Lost	Fragmentary record of *sattukku* offerings in Ešumeša; = 5NT 260; BiMes 11, no. 336
11244	Lost	Fragmentary record of *sattukku* offerings in Ešumeša; = 5NT 264; BiMes 11, no. 133
11245	SIIQ.LA.03.xx.26	Fragmentary record of *sattukku* offerings in Ešumeša; = 5NT 265; BiMes 11, no. 229
11246	Lost	Fragmentary record of *sattukku* offerings in Ešumeša; = 5NT 272; BiMes 11, no. 372

NBC	Date	Description
11247	Lost	Record of *sattukku* offerings in Ešumeša; = 5NT 278; BiMes 11, no. 219
11248	Lost	Record of *sattukku* offerings in Ešumeša; = 5NT 279; BiMes 11, no. 165
11249	ENBA.IS.H.xx.xx	Fragmentary record of *sattukku* offerings in Ešumeša; = 5NT 280; BiMes 11, no. 66
11250	Lost	Fragmentary record of *sattukku* offerings in Ešumeša; = 5NT 286; BiMes 11, no. 208
11251	WASI.LA.09.xx.10	Fragmentary record of *sattukku* offerings in Ešumeša—date only preserved; = 5NT 289; BiMes 11, no. 303
11252	Lost	Fragmentary record of *sattukku* offerings in Ešumeša; = 5NT 291; BiMes 11, no. 6
11253	Lost	Fragmentary record of *sattukku* offerings in Ešumeša; = 5NT 292; BiMes 11, no. 246
11254	Lost	Fragmentary record of *sattukku* offerings in Ešumeša; = 5NT 294; BiMes 11, no. 278
11255	Lost	Fragmentary record of *sattukku* offerings in Ešumeša; = 5NT 295; BiMes 11, no. 281
11256	Lost	Fragmentary record of *sattukku* offerings in Ešumeša; = 5NT 296; BiMes 11, no. 125
11257	Lost	Fragmentary record of *sattukku* offerings in Ešumeša; = 5NT 305; BiMes 11, no. 382
11258	Lost	Fragmentary record of *sattukku* offerings in Ešumeša; = 5NT 307; BiMes 11, no. 377
11259	Lost	Fragmentary record of *sattukku* offerings in Ešumeša; = 5NT 308; BiMes 11, no. 276
11260	Lost	Fragmentary record of *sattukku* offerings in Ešumeša; = 5NT 310; BiMes 11, no. 375
11261	Lost	Fragmentary record of *sattukku* offerings in Ešumeša; = 5NT 317; BiMes 11, no. 115
11262	Lost	Fragmentary record of *sattukku* offerings in Ešumeša; = 5NT 318; BiMes 11, no. 223

NBC	Date	Description
11263	SUEL.LA.23.xx.xx	Fragmentary record of *sattukku* offerings in Ešumeša; = 5NT 324; BiMes 11, p. 54, no. 46 (T)
11264	SUEL.LA.24.xx.05	Fragmentary record of *sattukku* offerings in Ešumeša; = 5NT 332; BiMes 11, p. 49, no. 12 (C)
11265	Lost	Fragmentary record of *sattukku* offerings in Ešumeša; = 5NT 343; BiMes 11, no. 51
11266	Lost	Fragmentary record of *sattukku* offerings in Ešumeša; = 5NT 346; BiMes 11, no. 36
11267	Lost	Fragmentary record of *sattukku* offerings in Ešumeša; = 5NT 353; BiMes 11, no. 53
11268	Lost	Record of *sattukku* offerings in Ešumeša; = 5NT 357; BiMes 11, p. 53, n. 19, no. 22 (T)
11269	SUEL.LA.24.05.28	Record of *sattukku* offerings in Ešumeša; = 5NT 359; BiMes 11, no. 15
11270	Lost	Record of *sattukku* offerings in Ešumeša; = 5NT 362; BiMes 11, no. 21
11271	Lost	Fragmentary record of *sattukku* offerings in Ešumeša; = 5NT 364; BiMes 11, pp. 24-25, no. 317 (C)
11272	Lost	Fragmentary record of *sattukku* offerings in Ešumeša; = 5NT 364b; BiMes 11, no. 319
11273	Lost	Fragmentary record of *sattukku* offerings in Ešumeša; = 5NT 366; BiMes 11, no. 320
11274	Lost	Fragmentary record of *sattukku* offerings in Ešumeša; = 5NT 369; BiMes 11, no. 412
11275	Lost	Fragmentary record of *sattukku* offerings in Ešumeša; = 5NT 378; BiMes 11, p. 130, no. 324 (T)
11276	Lost	Record of *sattukku* offerings in Ešumeša; = 5NT 381
11277	ENBA.IS.L.04.08	Fragmentary record of *sattukku* offerings in Ešumeša; = 5NT 136; BiMes 11, no. 136
11278	Lost	Fragmentary record of *sattukku* offerings in Ešumeša; = 5NT 384; BiMes 11, no. 184
11279	Lost	Record of *sattukku* offerings in Ešumeša; = 5NT 386; BiMes 11, no. 102

NBC	Date	Description
11280	Lost	Fragmentary record of *sattukku* offerings in Ešumeša; = 5NT 390; BiMes 11, no. 333
11281	xx.xx.04	Fragmentary record of *sattukku* offerings in Ešumeša; = 5NT 395; BiMes 11, no. 207
11282	SUEL.LA.25.02.23	Record of *sattukku* offerings in Ešumeša; = 5NT 403; BiMes 11, no. 34
11283	Lost	Record of *sattukku* offerings in Ešumeša; = 5NT 409; BiMes 11, no. 321
11284	Lost	Fragmentary record of *sattukku* offerings in Ešumeša; = 5NT 413; BiMes 11, no. 315
11285	LIEN.IS.E.09.02	Record of *sattukku* offerings in Ešumeša; sealed; = 5NT 418; Sigrist, RA 71, 1977, pp. 117-24 (C, T, Tr)
11316	Lost	Fragmentary record of *sattukku* offerings in Ešumeša; = 5NT 536; BiMes 11, no. 169
11317	Lost	Fragmentary record of *sattukku* offerings in Ešumeša; = 5NT 538; BiMes 11, 129, no. 325 (T)
11318	WASI.LA.04.02.26	Record of *sattukku* offerings in Ešumeša; = 5NT 546; BiMes 11, no. 302
11319	Lost	Fragmentary record of *sattukku* offerings in Ešumeša; = 5NT 548; BiMes 11, no. 160
11338	Lost	Fragmentary record of *sattukku* offerings in Ešumeša; = 5NT 642; BiMes 11, no. 334
11339	xx.xx.06	Fragmentary record of *sattukku* offerings in Ešumeša; = 5NT 643; BiMes 11, no. 388
11340	Lost	Fragmentary record of *sattukku* offerings in Ešumeša; = 5NT 645; BiMes 11, no. 60
11361	RISI.LA.53.07.—	Agreement concerning produce of orchard
11389	RISI.LA.01.05.24	Receipt of sheep
11390	xx.06.20	Rental of slave-girl; mu-ús-sa x x x
11406	RISI.LA.58.03.—	Disbursement of barley for one month
11407	Lost	Disbursement of barley
11415	RISI.LA.39.03.15?	Account of barley

NBC	Date	Description
11417	RISI2.LA.01.04.—	Receipt of large quantities of barley; sealed
11430	Lost	Fragmentary account of foodstuff (ledger)
11431	Lost?	Record concerning foodstuff; sealed
11454	AMDI.BA.06.04.20	Sale of cow and calf; sealed
11455	SIMU.BA.05.—.—	Loan of silver; mu-ús-sa x bara$_2$ maḫ(?) ^{d}Ši-da-da mu-na-dím
11460	HARA.BA.37.06.01	Unopened case—receipt of dates(?); sealed
11461	HARA.BA.42.08.03	Loan of barley; sealed
11464	RISI2.LA.03.09.01	Rental of field; sealed
11467	No date	Letter concerning activities of merchant
11471	No date	Letter to Ṣilli-Šamaš from Ali-ilī concerning sheep
11472	HARA.BA.39.09.—	Sale of slave; sealed
11474	HARA.BA.40.06.—	Partnership agreement for building house; sealed
11475	SAIL.BA.06.10.01	Loan of silver to purchase barley; sealed
11479	Lost?	Ration list
11480	No date?	Disbursement of rations to soldiers
11482	SIID.LA.07.06.—	Disbursement of silver
11483	NUAD.LA.E.11.20?	Account of silver; mu ^{id}Buranun-na ba-ba-al
11485	Lost?	Fragmentary list of PNs
11486	No date	Letter to Mannum-kī[ma-...] from Ea-gāmil
11489	No date	List of field acreages
11491	No date	Letter to Nipurītum and Ya-im-lik-DINGIR from Balili
11492	SIID.LA.07.08.xx	Ration list
11493	xx.12.—	Economic record of uncertain character
11494	Lost?	Fragmentary account of foodstuff
11501	No date	Fragmentary disbursement of foodstuff

NBC	Date	Description
11503	Lost	Fragmentary record concerning small cattle; cf. NBC 11557
11504	HARA.BA.41.02.20	Transfer of large cattle
11505	No date	Disbursement of barley
11506	RISI.LA.50.08.28	Legal case concerning broken betrothal
11507	No date	Letter to Marduk-muballiṭ from Aḫī-lūmur concerning transaction in barley
11508	No date	List of quantities of unspecified commodity as éš-gàr
11509	—.11.01	Record of quantities of earth excavated (ledger); cf. YBC 1898
11511	ABEŠ.BA.02.09.06	Receipt of barley rations; mu *A-bi-e-šu-uḫ* lugal-e ^{d}EN.ZU dingir sag-dù-ga-ni
11512	No date	Unaddressed letter(?)
11514	—.09.—?	Tag—record concerning malt; sealed; ^{iti}gan(?)-gan(?)-gar
11515	WASI.LA.11.09.—	Promissory note—silver; sealed
11516	RISI.LA.47.12.—	Receipt of barley; sealed
11519	RISI.LA.xx.xx.xx	Tablet and fragments of case—sale of real property?; sealed; date lost; RN in oath
11520	RISI.LA.—.??.11	Account of barley; iti-9 ki-2
11521	RISI.LA.49.05.—	Account of barley
11524	—.xx.08	Disbursement of barley
11555	RISI.LA.53.12.30	Account of silver
11556	No date	Letter to Irra-gāmil
11557	xx.02.26	Record concerning small cattle and wool; cf. NBC 11503
11558	Lost	Fragmentary disbursement(?)
11559	—.xx.02	Disbursement of foodstuff
11560	Lost?	Account of foodstuff (ledger)

NBC	Date	Description
11561	RISI.LA.58.03.30	Record concerning barley
11562	Lost?	Fragmentary ration list?
11565	RISI.LA.30.06.xx	Disbursement
11566	—.10.xx	Record concerning foodstuff
11567	Lost	Ration list
11583	Lost	List of field acreages?
11584	RISI.LA.47.01.—	Disbursement of barley for one month
11587	xx.06.—	Receipt of quantities of uncertain commodity; sealed; mu ugn[im ...]
11593	Lost	Fragmentary list of quantities of barley(?) and PNs with patronymics

INDICES

ISIN

Išbi-Irra

IŠIR.IS.03.05.14?	9932
IŠIR.IS.04.11.—	6423
IŠIR.IS.05.08.—	5665
IŠIR.IS.06.01.xx	8486
IŠIR.IS.06.03.—	5631, 7571
IŠIR.IS.06.06.—	6386
IŠIR.IS.06.08.—	6436
IŠIR.IS.06.10.—	6422, 9177
IŠIR.IS.06.—.—	7078
IŠIR.IS.07.01.—	6367
IŠIR.IS.07.05.—	7463
IŠIR.IS.07.06.16	7180
IŠIR.IS.07.06.16?	7177
IŠIR.IS.07.06.30	8169
IŠIR.IS.07.06.—	10108
IŠIR.IS.07.06.—?	7183
IŠIR.IS.07.07.01	7203
IŠIR.IS.07.07.04	5643
IŠIR.IS.07.07.06	6442
IŠIR.IS.07.07.21	7484
IŠIR.IS.07.07.24	6390
IŠIR.IS.07.07.26	7217
IŠIR.IS.07.07.xx	7168
IŠIR.IS.07.08.14	7653
IŠIR.IS.07.08.17	7388
IŠIR.IS.07.08.25	8478
IŠIR.IS.07.08.—	6355
IŠIR.IS.07.09.22	7475
IŠIR.IS.07.10.04	7483
IŠIR.IS.07.10.08	8946
IŠIR.IS.07.10.09	7570
IŠIR.IS.07.10.12	7436
IŠIR.IS.07.—.—	6441, 7454
IŠIR.IS.08.04.03	8492
IŠIR.IS.08.05.09	6414
IŠIR.IS.08.05.10	6393
IŠIR.IS.08.05.15	8475
IŠIR.IS.08.06.13	8452
IŠIR.IS.08.07.01	7266
IŠIR.IS.08.07.08	8463
IŠIR.IS.08.08.—	8466
IŠIR.IS.08.11.—	7599
IŠIR.IS.08.12.—	7201, 7499
IŠIR.IS.08.12D.08	5651
IŠIR.IS.08.12D.12	7136
IŠIR.IS.08.??.—	7745
IŠIR.IS.08.—.—	5655, 8938
IŠIR.IS.09.04.16	8445
IŠIR.IS.09.04.—	7673
IŠIR.IS.09.05.02	7441
IŠIR.IS.09.05.14	7083
IŠIR.IS.09.05.—	8497
IŠIR.IS.09.06.10	7565
IŠIR.IS.09.07.10	8454
IŠIR.IS.09.07.18	7658
IŠIR.IS.09.07.25	7670
IŠIR.IS.09.08.23	6428
IŠIR.IS.09.08.—	6453
IŠIR.IS.09.09.26	5688
IŠIR.IS.09.09.—	8428
IŠIR.IS.09.10.26	6439
IŠIR.IS.09.10.—	5620
IŠIR.IS.09.11.14	7175
IŠIR.IS.09.11.—	5653
IŠIR.IS.10.01.xx	8519
IŠIR.IS.10.02.06	6445
IŠIR.IS.10.03.04+	7269
IŠIR.IS.10.03.—	7165
IŠIR.IS.10.05.06	7556
IŠIR.IS.10.05.30	8139
IŠIR.IS.10.06.26	6387
IŠIR.IS.10.07.28	6364
IŠIR.IS.10.08.04	7357
IŠIR.IS.10.08.21	7268
IŠIR.IS.10.09.28	7597
IŠIR.IS.10.10.—	8126
IŠIR.IS.10.12D.—	7119
IŠIR.IS.10.—.15	7560
IŠIR.IS.11.01.—	7626, 10007
IŠIR.IS.11.02.—	7505
IŠIR.IS.11.03.—	7062, 7064, 7364
IŠIR.IS.11.04.15	8460
IŠIR.IS.11.05.23	7559
IŠIR.IS.11.05.—	7164, 8437
IŠIR.IS.11.06.—	7199, 8442
IŠIR.IS.11.07.14?	9462
IŠIR.IS.11.07.17	6450
IŠIR.IS.11.07.—	7412
IŠIR.IS.11.12.—	7584
IŠIR.IS.12.02.—	7367
IŠIR.IS.12.03.—	7128
IŠIR.IS.12.04.01?	7710
IŠIR.IS.12.04.27	7354
IŠIR.IS.12.04.—	5650, 7240
IŠIR.IS.12.06.—	7082, 7123, 7255
IŠIR.IS.12.07.27	7375
IŠIR.IS.12.07.—	7246
IŠIR.IS.12.08.24	8436
IŠIR.IS.12.08.—	7249
IŠIR.IS.12.09.—	6368, 7081, 9178
IŠIR.IS.12.10.26	7672
IŠIR.IS.12.10.29	7085
IŠIR.IS.12.10.—	5680, 7588, 7608
IŠIR.IS.12.11.24	7558
IŠIR.IS.12.11.—	9167
IŠIR.IS.12.12.06	7428
IŠIR.IS.12.12.10	5669
IŠIR.IS.12.12.—	7195
IŠIR.IS.13.01.08	7259
IŠIR.IS.13.01.12	7107
IŠIR.IS.13.01.22	7261
IŠIR.IS.13.01.—	7074, 8137
IŠIR.IS.13.02.08	7052
IŠIR.IS.13.02.10	5774, 7385
IŠIR.IS.13.02.11	5673
IŠIR.IS.13.02.—	10075
IŠIR.IS.13.03.19	7361
IŠIR.IS.13.03.20	7649
IŠIR.IS.13.04.02	7258
IŠIR.IS.13.04.11	5683
IŠIR.IS.13.04.23	5678
IŠIR.IS.13.04.—	6491
IŠIR.IS.13.05.10	5687
IŠIR.IS.13.05.11	5602
IŠIR.IS.13.05.14	6475

IŠIR.IS.13.05.17	7526	IŠIR.IS.14.03.16	5627	IŠIR.IS.15.04.28	7498
IŠIR.IS.13.05.20	7527	IŠIR.IS.14.03.—	7401	IŠIR.IS.15.05.—	7050
IŠIR.IS.13.05.24	6477	IŠIR.IS.14.04.06	7405, 7481	IŠIR.IS.15.06.28	7368
IŠIR.IS.13.05.30	7557	IŠIR.IS.14.06.03	6361, 7407	IŠIR.IS.15.07.—	6425, 7549
IŠIR.IS.13.05.—	7095	IŠIR.IS.14.06.10	6400	IŠIR.IS.15.09.20?	7550
IŠIR.IS.13.06.05	7521, 8025	IŠIR.IS.14.06.17	7461	IŠIR.IS.15.09.29	5623
IŠIR.IS.13.06.17	6374	IŠIR.IS.14.06.17+	7486	IŠIR.IS.15.10.07	7493
IŠIR.IS.13.06.19	7094	IŠIR.IS.14.06.22	7109	IŠIR.IS.15.10.11	7156
IŠIR.IS.13.06.27	7135	IŠIR.IS.14.06.28	7144	IŠIR.IS.15.10.—	5677, 9224
IŠIR.IS.13.06.—	7191, 9995	IŠIR.IS.14.07.03	6336	IŠIR.IS.15.12.—	7099, 7403
IŠIR.IS.13.07.08	8444	IŠIR.IS.14.07.06	5622	IŠIR.IS.15.—.—	5617, 6524,
IŠIR.IS.13.07.13	5675	IŠIR.IS.14.07.12	7389		7066, 7627
IŠIR.IS.13.07.—	6358	IŠIR.IS.14.07.21	7443	IŠIR.IS.16.01.07	7525, 8856
IŠIR.IS.13.08.27	8443	IŠIR.IS.14.07.22	5619	IŠIR.IS.16.01.09	5666
IŠIR.IS.13.08.—	5609, 5684,	IŠIR.IS.14.07.23	8470	IŠIR.IS.16.01.14	7222
	5686, 6476, 8498	IŠIR.IS.14.07.xx	8852	IŠIR.IS.16.01.15	7072
IŠIR.IS.13.09.14	7548	IŠIR.IS.14.08.22	7092	IŠIR.IS.16.01.17	7232
IŠIR.IS.13.09.21	9227	IŠIR.IS.14.09.22	5618	IŠIR.IS.16.01.18	7399
IŠIR.IS.13.09.—	7076, 7514,	IŠIR.IS.14.11.12	7214	IŠIR.IS.16.01.19	7101
	8857	IŠIR.IS.14.11.—	7126, 7639,	IŠIR.IS.16.01.20	7464
IŠIR.IS.13.10.02	7075		8489	IŠIR.IS.16.01.21	7098
IŠIR.IS.13.10.08	7251	IŠIR.IS.14.12.01	7434	IŠIR.IS.16.01.24+	7496
IŠIR.IS.13.10.13	5685	IŠIR.IS.14.12.18	6362	IŠIR.IS.16.01.25	7522
IŠIR.IS.13.10.20	7600	IŠIR.IS.14.12.25	8431	IŠIR.IS.16.01.26	7227
IŠIR.IS.13.11.02	7254	IŠIR.IS.14.12D.24	8954	IŠIR.IS.16.01.—	6363
IŠIR.IS.13.11.05	7719	IŠIR.IS.14.12D.—	6398	IŠIR.IS.16.04.01?	7714
IŠIR.IS.13.11.23	7413	IŠIR.IS.14.xx.09	6483	IŠIR.IS.16.04.—	6389, 7105,
IŠIR.IS.13.11.—	6461, 7643,	IŠIR.IS.15.01.13	7524		7115
	8136	IŠIR.IS.15.01.18?	8520	IŠIR.IS.16.05.05	8418
IŠIR.IS.13.12.06	7250	IŠIR.IS.15.01.19	5624	IŠIR.IS.16.05.07	8417
IŠIR.IS.13.12.18	7587	IŠIR.IS.15.01.20	7466	IŠIR.IS.16.05.19	7491
IŠIR.IS.13.12.—	8523	IŠIR.IS.15.02.03	7669	IŠIR.IS.16.05.22	7615
IŠIR.IS.13.12D.02	7158	IŠIR.IS.15.02.10	8503	IŠIR.IS.16.05.29	7356
IŠIR.IS.13.—.—	8297	IŠIR.IS.15.02.15	7355	IŠIR.IS.16.06.01	7630
IŠIR.IS.14.01.20	5625	IŠIR.IS.15.02.28	6369	IŠIR.IS.16.06.08	7409
IŠIR.IS.14.01.—	7257	IŠIR.IS.15.02.—	7149, 7430	IŠIR.IS.16.06.10	8518
IŠIR.IS.14.02.08	7104	IŠIR.IS.15.03.10+	7416	IŠIR.IS.16.06.13	7427
IŠIR.IS.14.02.10	7523	IŠIR.IS.15.03.16	5681	IŠIR.IS.16.06.16	7415
IŠIR.IS.14.02.12	7631	IŠIR.IS.15.03.—	7572	IŠIR.IS.16.06.28	5671
IŠIR.IS.14.02.24	7410	IŠIR.IS.15.04.12	8522	IŠIR.IS.16.06.—	6407
IŠIR.IS.14.02.—	7569	IŠIR.IS.15.04.21	8458	IŠIR.IS.16.07.13	7113
IŠIR.IS.14.03.04	6373	IŠIR.IS.15.04.23	7456	IŠIR.IS.16.07.15	7414
IŠIR.IS.14.03.05+	7622	IŠIR.IS.15.04.24	7224	IŠIR.IS.16.08.08	8421
IŠIR.IS.14.03.14	7221	IŠIR.IS.15.04.25	8499	IŠIR.IS.16.08.10	7426

IŠIR.IS.16.08.12	7060	IŠIR.IS.18.12D.—	8502	IŠIR.IS.20.01.—	5626
IŠIR.IS.16.08.14	7509	IŠIR.IS.18.xx.16	6482	IŠIR.IS.20.01.—	7376
IŠIR.IS.16.10.07	6446	IŠIR.IS.18.—.—	8413	IŠIR.IS.20.02.18	7383
IŠIR.IS.16.10.17	7381	IŠIR.IS.19.01.05	7581	IŠIR.IS.20.02.—	6469, 7451
IŠIR.IS.16.10.—?	7716	IŠIR.IS.19.01.08	7154, 7188	IŠIR.IS.20.03.—	7102, 7194
IŠIR.IS.16.11.22+	7378	IŠIR.IS.19.01.17	7207	IŠIR.IS.20.05.18	8888
IŠIR.IS.16.11.24	7520	IŠIR.IS.19.01.23	7473	IŠIR.IS.20.06.26	8907
IŠIR.IS.16.11.25	7377	IŠIR.IS.19.02.05	8424	IŠIR.IS.20.07.06	8465
IŠIR.IS.16.12.01	7589	IŠIR.IS.19.02.10	7211	IŠIR.IS.20.07.17	5679
IŠIR.IS.16.12.03	7068, 7373	IŠIR.IS.19.02.11	7181	IŠIR.IS.20.07.—	7063
IŠIR.IS.16.12.07	7369	IŠIR.IS.19.02.12	7370	IŠIR.IS.20.07.—?	8851
IŠIR.IS.16.12.17	7634	IŠIR.IS.19.02.17	6384, 6385	IŠIR.IS.20.09.—	8438
IŠIR.IS.16.12.21	7374	IŠIR.IS.19.02.30	8469	IŠIR.IS.20.10.25	8435
IŠIR.IS.16.12.22	7585	IŠIR.IS.19.02.—	7079, 7171	IŠIR.IS.20.12.16	7150
IŠIR.IS.16.12.25	8427	IŠIR.IS.19.03.05	5621	IŠIR.IS.20.xx.22?	8461
IŠIR.IS.16.12.26	7528	IŠIR.IS.19.03.08	7459	IŠIR.IS.21.03.24	8934
IŠIR.IS.16.12.—	5636, 5682	IŠIR.IS.19.03.24	8490	IŠIR.IS.21.03.—	7139
IŠIR.IS.16.12D.13	7071, 7503	IŠIR.IS.19.04.01?	7339	IŠIR.IS.21.04.04	5637
IŠIR.IS.16.12D.—	7365	IŠIR.IS.19.05.14	7151	IŠIR.IS.21.04.29	7196
IŠIR.IS.17.03.15	7420	IŠIR.IS.19.05.27	9931	IŠIR.IS.21.04.—	6357, 7676
IŠIR.IS.17.03.21	8434	IŠIR.IS.19.05.—	7231	IŠIR.IS.21.05.30	6505, 6513
IŠIR.IS.17.03.22	7073	IŠIR.IS.19.06.05	7596	IŠIR.IS.21.05.—	6410
IŠIR.IS.17.04.13	7238	IŠIR.IS.19.06.07	5645	IŠIR.IS.21.06.05	7114
IŠIR.IS.17.04.17	5663	IŠIR.IS.19.06.20	6412, 7582	IŠIR.IS.21.06.06	7121
IŠIR.IS.17.04.—	5676	IŠIR.IS.19.06.27	8440	IŠIR.IS.21.06.17	6408
IŠIR.IS.17.05.17	5654	IŠIR.IS.19.06.—	6360, 7056, 8482	IŠIR.IS.21.06.—	5656, 7228, 7515, 8419
IŠIR.IS.17.06.—	7070				
IŠIR.IS.17.09.05	6474	IŠIR.IS.19.07.16	7551	IŠIR.IS.21.07.22	7134
IŠIR.IS.17.09.08	6473	IŠIR.IS.19.07.30	8235	IŠIR.IS.21.07.26	7692
IŠIR.IS.17.09.25	7252	IŠIR.IS.19.07.—	8479	IŠIR.IS.21.07.—	6409
IŠIR.IS.17.11.18	7242	IŠIR.IS.19.08.—	6417, 7088	IŠIR.IS.21.09.26	6397
IŠIR.IS.17.12.12	7162	IŠIR.IS.19.09.08	7360	IŠIR.IS.21.09.—	7595
IŠIR.IS.17.12.—	5630	IŠIR.IS.19.09.21	7613	IŠIR.IS.21.10.25	7552
IŠIR.IS.17.12D.01	5670	IŠIR.IS.19.09.22	8483	IŠIR.IS.21.10.—	7067
IŠIR.IS.17.—.—	6444	IŠIR.IS.19.10.18	7540	IŠIR.IS.21.11.06	7209
IŠIR.IS.18.01.03	5629	IŠIR.IS.19.10.24	7133	IŠIR.IS.21.12.02	7561
IŠIR.IS.18.01.06	7632	IŠIR.IS.19.10.29	6405	IŠIR.IS.21.12.20	7166
IŠIR.IS.18.03.04	7478	IŠIR.IS.19.11.06	7130	IŠIR.IS.21.12.21	8459
IŠIR.IS.18.03.—	5628, 7402	IŠIR.IS.19.11.17	7423	IŠIR.IS.21.12.22	7394
IŠIR.IS.18.06.19	7641	IŠIR.IS.19.11.30	7253	IŠIR.IS.21.12D.12	7396
IŠIR.IS.18.06.26	7511	IŠIR.IS.19.11.—	6411, 7143	IŠIR.IS.21.12D.—	7080
IŠIR.IS.18.06.27	6394, 7160	IŠIR.IS.19.12.—	6404, 7644	IŠIR.IS.22.01.01	5667
IŠIR.IS.18.12.—	7069	IŠIR.IS.19.xx.—?	8455	IŠIR.IS.22.01.10	7397
IŠIR.IS.18.12D.08	7489	IŠIR.IS.19.—.—	7198	IŠIR.IS.22.01.13	7590

IŠIR.IS.22.01.29	6443	IŠIR.IS.23.07.04?	7379	IŠIR.IS.25.09.19	7140
IŠIR.IS.22.01.—	5648	IŠIR.IS.23.07.16	7142	IŠIR.IS.25.09.—	7500
IŠIR.IS.22.02.10	6424, 7125	IŠIR.IS.23.07.—	6522, 8411	IŠIR.IS.25.09.—?	7429
IŠIR.IS.22.02.13	7663	IŠIR.IS.23.08.05	8467	IŠIR.IS.25.10.25	7618
IŠIR.IS.22.02.—	5638, 7616, 8432, 8433, 8439	IŠIR.IS.23.09.—	6383, 7116	IŠIR.IS.25.11.29	7059
		IŠIR.IS.23.10.—	6378, 7054, 7153	IŠIR.IS.25.12.14?	6391
IŠIR.IS.22.03.11	6365			IŠIR.IS.25.12.—	6395, 7182, 7654
IŠIR.IS.22.03.12	6388, 6438	IŠIR.IS.23.11.—	6379		
IŠIR.IS.22.03.—	6452, 7256	IŠIR.IS.23.12.—	6371, 7131	IŠIR.IS.25.xx.06	10073
IŠIR.IS.22.04.14	7205	IŠIR.IS.24.01.—	7359, 9938	IŠIR.IS.25.xx.10	6426
IŠIR.IS.22.04.16	6370	IŠIR.IS.24.02.21	7547	IŠIR.IS.25.—.—	7089
IŠIR.IS.22.04.28	7406	IŠIR.IS.24.03.16	7633	IŠIR.IS.26.01.11	7440
IŠIR.IS.22.04.—	6470, 7120, 7519	IŠIR.IS.24.05.—?	9881	IŠIR.IS.26.01.29	7553
		IŠIR.IS.24.06.07	5632	IŠIR.IS.26.02.—	7210
IŠIR.IS.22.05.—	6479, 7043, 7077	IŠIR.IS.24.07.—	7111	IŠIR.IS.26.03.26	7668
		IŠIR.IS.24.08.06	7117	IŠIR.IS.26.05.28	6366
IŠIR.IS.22.06.08	6480	IŠIR.IS.24.08.—	7058	IŠIR.IS.26.07.13	7591
IŠIR.IS.22.06.—	7230	IŠIR.IS.24.08.—?	7421	IŠIR.IS.26.08.15	7264
IŠIR.IS.22.07.07	7482	IŠIR.IS.24.09.—	6401, 7096, 7100, 7141, 7619	IŠIR.IS.26.08.—	6399
IŠIR.IS.22.07.—	7045, 7047			IŠIR.IS.26.09.05	8451
IŠIR.IS.22.09.26	7190	IŠIR.IS.24.10.—	7087	IŠIR.IS.26.09.—	7395
IŠIR.IS.22.10.03	6454	IŠIR.IS.25.01.—	7386	IŠIR.IS.26.10.—	7372
IŠIR.IS.22.10.18	7609	IŠIR.IS.25.02.03	6447	IŠIR.IS.26.11.22	7384
IŠIR.IS.22.10.—	7049	IŠIR.IS.25.02.10	7485	IŠIR.IS.26.11.26	6402
IŠIR.IS.22.11.01	5633, 6463	IŠIR.IS.25.02.11	7218	IŠIR.IS.26.11.—	7566
IŠIR.IS.22.11.18	7065	IŠIR.IS.25.02.17	7541	IŠIR.IS.26.12.06	7358
IŠIR.IS.22.11.—	7086, 7122	IŠIR.IS.25.02.—	5642, 7091, 7103, 8415, 8472	IŠIR.IS.26.12.14	8474
IŠIR.IS.22.12.05	7418			IŠIR.IS.26.12.—	7363, 8488
IŠIR.IS.22.12.07	7417	IŠIR.IS.25.03.07	7197	IŠIR.IS.26.12D.—	9229
IŠIR.IS.22.12.20?	7425	IŠIR.IS.25.03.15	6435	IŠIR.IS.27.02.09	8447
IŠIR.IS.22.12.—	9282	IŠIR.IS.25.03.—	6403, 7267	IŠIR.IS.27.03.02	7542
IŠIR.IS.22.xx.xx	7568, 7598	IŠIR.IS.25.04.03	7055	IŠIR.IS.27.03.23	7667
IŠIR.IS.22.—.—	7578	IŠIR.IS.25.04.23	7593	IŠIR.IS.27.04.05	8448
IŠIR.IS.23.01.05+	7438	IŠIR.IS.25.04.24	6376	IŠIR.IS.27.04.11	10069
IŠIR.IS.23.01.27	7611	IŠIR.IS.25.04.30	8484	IŠIR.IS.27.06.—	8441
IŠIR.IS.23.01.—	8416	IŠIR.IS.25.05.26	7534	IŠIR.IS.27.07.—	7057, 7382
IŠIR.IS.23.03.15	6508	IŠIR.IS.25.06.—	6459	IŠIR.IS.27.10.—	8079
IŠIR.IS.23.03.—	6521, 7163	IŠIR.IS.25.07.04	7051	IŠIR.IS.27.11.—	7108
IŠIR.IS.23.04.06	5641	IŠIR.IS.25.07.25	8423	IŠIR.IS.28.01.—	6421
IŠIR.IS.23.04.26	7192	IŠIR.IS.25.07.—	6372, 7465	IŠIR.IS.28.02.20	7244
IŠIR.IS.23.04.—	5674, 7178	IŠIR.IS.25.08.13	7432	IŠIR.IS.28.03.25	7675
IŠIR.IS.23.05.05	8853	IŠIR.IS.25.08.—	5657, 6382, 8477	IŠIR.IS.28.04.01	7422
IŠIR.IS.23.06.07	8485			IŠIR.IS.28.04.02	7046
IŠIR.IS.23.06.—	7112, 7387	IŠIR.IS.25.09.09?	7129	IŠIR.IS.28.07.—	5608, 7053

IŠIR.IS.28.09.11	7127	IŠIR.IS.33.12D.27	7449	ŠUIL.IS.03.01.30	7650, 7664
IŠIR.IS.28.09.22	8855	IŠIR.IS.33.12D.30?	7564	ŠUIL.IS.03.03.01	7651
IŠIR.IS.28.12.—	5649	IŠIR.IS.33.12D.—	7602, 8414	ŠUIL.IS.03.03.10	7506
IŠIR.IS.28.—.—	7124	IŠIR.IS.xx.02.09	7444	ŠUIL.IS.03.03.24	7447
IŠIR.IS.29.05.—	7592	IŠIR.IS.xx.08.—	8952	ŠUIL.IS.03.03.29	7404
IŠIR.IS.30.02.—	5634, 6381, 7260, 7516	IŠIR.IS.xx.xx.xx	7235	ŠUIL.IS.03.04.16	7219
		### Šū-ilišu		ŠUIL.IS.03.04.16	7563, 7606
IŠIR.IS.31.02.12	7380	ŠUIL.IS.01.03.18	7533	ŠUIL.IS.03.04.18	7487
IŠIR.IS.32.04.—	7488	ŠUIL.IS.01.04.03	7202	ŠUIL.IS.03.05.05	7580
IŠIR.IS.32.11.—	7476	ŠUIL.IS.01.04.10	6472	ŠUIL.IS.03.05.13	7583
IŠIR.IS.32.12.—	7504	ŠUIL.IS.01.04.11	7573	ŠUIL.IS.03.05.24	7614
IŠIR.IS.32.xx.xx?	9911	ŠUIL.IS.01.04.—	7366	ŠUIL.IS.03.05.—	7390
IŠIR.IS.33.01.06	7097, 7517	ŠUIL.IS.01.06.16	7623	ŠUIL.IS.03.06.03	7532
IŠIR.IS.33.01.08	7445	ŠUIL.IS.01.06.—	7391	ŠUIL.IS.03.06.06	7152
IŠIR.IS.33.01.24	5603	ŠUIL.IS.01.07.17	7362	ŠUIL.IS.03.06.—	7469, 7470
IŠIR.IS.33.02.—	7237	ŠUIL.IS.01.07.—	7535	ŠUIL.IS.05.12D.—	9428
IŠIR.IS.33.03.05	6440	ŠUIL.IS.01.08.03	7586	ŠUIL.IS.08.xx.—	10008
IŠIR.IS.33.03.06	7647	ŠUIL.IS.01.08.—	7213	ŠUIL.IS.10.—.—	6817
IŠIR.IS.33.03.11	5647	ŠUIL.IS.01.09.11	5635	### Iddin-Dagan	
IŠIR.IS.33.03.—	7492	ŠUIL.IS.01.09.18	8412	IDDA.IS.02.07.—	9978
IŠIR.IS.33.04.02	7245	ŠUIL.IS.01.09.29	7147	IDDA.IS.02.08.—	9180
IŠIR.IS.33.04.18	7625	ŠUIL.IS.01.10.11	7176	IDDA.IS.02.12.—	6418, 9952
IŠIR.IS.33.04.—	7118	ŠUIL.IS.01.10.12	7612	IDDA.IS.03.02.—	10011
IŠIR.IS.33.05.04	7452, 7743	ŠUIL.IS.01.10.15	7458	IDDA.IS.05.12.—	10367
IŠIR.IS.33.05.10	7110, 7629	ŠUIL.IS.01.10.16	7531	IDDA.IS.09.02.—	6488
IŠIR.IS.33.05.12	7624	ŠUIL.IS.01.10.—	7607, 8425, 7239	IDDA.IS.09.12.—	6498
IŠIR.IS.33.05.18	7433			IDDA.IS.A.04.—	6431
IŠIR.IS.33.05.22	7234	ŠUIL.IS.01.11.14	7048	IDDA.IS.E.01.—	9181
IŠIR.IS.33.05.30	7393	ŠUIL.IS.02.02.14	7206	IDDA.IS.xx.02.—	6523
IŠIR.IS.33.06.10	7621	ŠUIL.IS.02.02.—	7371	### Išme-Dagan	
IŠIR.IS.33.06.—	9984	ŠUIL.IS.02.02.—?	7732	IŠDA.IS.A.04.—?	8863
IŠIR.IS.33.09.11	7518	ŠUIL.IS.02.03.23	7554	IŠDA.IS.C.01.—	8666
IŠIR.IS.33.09.30	7480	ŠUIL.IS.02.04.21	7455	IŠDA.IS.H.07.02	6499
IŠIR.IS.33.09.—	7468, 7471, 8487	ŠUIL.IS.02.06.21	5664	IŠDA.IS.I.09.14	6497
		ŠUIL.IS.02.07.—	7577	IŠDA.IS.N.07.01	6507
IŠIR.IS.33.10.—	7187, 7204, 7659	ŠUIL.IS.02.09.10	7392	IŠDA.IS.N.07.03	6416
		ŠUIL.IS.02.09.30	7576	IŠDA.IS.O.09.—	8688
IŠIR.IS.33.11.11	7495	ŠUIL.IS.02.09.—	7208	IŠDA.IS.O.11.—	9171
IŠIR.IS.33.11.15	7220	ŠUIL.IS.02.11.13	7233	IŠDA.IS.—.—.—	9650
IŠIR.IS.33.11.21	7446	ŠUIL.IS.02.12.—	8862	### Lipit-Ištar	
IŠIR.IS.33.11.24	8480	ŠUIL.IS.03.01.09	7579	LIIŠ.IS.01.—.—	6496
IŠIR.IS.33.12.30	7265	ŠUIL.IS.03.01.13	7645	LIIŠ.IS.A.05.30	6509
IŠIR.IS.33.12D.23	7507	ŠUIL.IS.03.01.22	7545		
IŠIR.IS.33.12D.25	6377				

LIIŠ.IS.A.11.14	6430	ITPI.IS.A.05.—	6760	ABSA.LA.04.12.—	10130
LIIŠ.IS.A.xx.xx	10151	**Urdukuga**		ABSA.LA.07.12D.—	5572
LIIŠ.IS.B.02.08	8667	URDU.IS.01.12.—?	10349	ABSA.LA.10.01.—	10358
LIIŠ.IS.B.02.—	6429	URDU.IS.01.—.—	9839	ABSA.LA.10.08.—	10090
LIIŠ.IS.B.06.—?	9179	URDU.IS.B.09.—	6506	ABSA.LA.10.12.—	5338, 5408
LIIŠ.IS.B.xx.xx	9591	URDU.IS.C.03.—	9893		5409, 5411, 5412

Ur-Ninurta

URNI.IS.G.—.—	7655	**Sîn-māgir**			5428, 5469, 5510
URNI.IS.J.09.—	7677	SIMA.IS.A.03.—	6451		5528, 6291, 6296
		SIMA.IS.B.xx.—	9793		6298, 6327, 6331,

Būr-Sîn

		Damiq-ilišu			6334
BUSI.IS.E.12.—	8621	DAIL.IS.01.03.—	5349	ABSA.LA.11.03.—	6727
BUSI.IS.F.08.11	10120	DAIL.IS.04.01.—	9393	ABSA.LA.11.12.—	6293

Lipit-Enlil

		DAIL.IS.05.12D.—	5314, 8636	**Sumu-el**	
LIEN.IS.01.04.20	11207	DAIL.IS.06.01.—	5318	SUEL.LA.01.01.06	10076
LIEN.IS.01.05.—	11174	DAIL.IS.13.03.—	5325	SUEL.LA.01.07.—	5503
LIEN.IS.B.04.10	5580	DAIL.IS.13.—.—	9808	SUEL.LA.01.10.17	9070
LIEN.IS.B.04.—	5577	DAIL.IS.A.01.—	6512	SUEL.LA.01.10.22	9580
LIEN.IS.E.09.02	11285	DAIL.IS.A.03.—	9851	SUEL.LA.01.11.01	9610

Irra-imittī

		DAIL.IS.A.04.—	5326	SUEL.LA.01.11.11	9575
IRIM.IS.D.06.14	11126	DAIL.IS.A.05.—	5459	SUEL.LA.01.11.15	9659
IRIM.IS.E.—.—	8605	DAIL.IS.A.11.—	5487	SUEL.LA.01.11.21	9582
		DAIL.IS.B.01.16	9973	SUEL.LA.01.11.27	9474
		DAIL.IS.C.03.—	5341	SUEL.LA.01.12D.—	9687

Enlil-bāni

ENBA.IS.01.12D.—	9197	**Dadbanaya**		SUEL.LA.02.01.13	8881
ENBA.IS.B.06.—	8305	DABA.IS.A.—.—	6493	SUEL.LA.02.01.16?	9213
ENBA.IS.C.12D.—	5513	**Unknown**		SUEL.LA.02.02.08	8645
ENBA.IS.D.12.29	7093	UN.IS.A.03.—	9198	SUEL.LA.02.02.09	8883
ENBA.IS.E.01.—	6338			SUEL.LA.02.02.21	9573, 10520
ENBA.IS.F.03.—	5352			SUEL.LA.03.05.—	5502
ENBA.IS.H.xx.xx	11249	**LARSA**		SUEL.LA.03.06.06	5433
ENBA.IS.I.08.07	11220	**Gungunum**		SUEL.LA.03.07.24	5445
ENBA.IS.I.xx.xx	11172	GUNG.LA.07.05.—	9174	SUEL.LA.03.08.01	5422
ENBA.IS.L.03.08?	11190	GUNG.LA.08.09.—	9166	SUEL.LA.04.05.10	5416
ENBA.IS.L.04.08	11277	GUNG.LA.14.02.01	9864	SUEL.LA.04.05.27	5518
ENBA.IS.L.05.—	10360	GUNG.LA.17.11.—	10135	SUEL.LA.04.06.02?	5431
ENBA.IS.L.08.10	11188	GUNG.LA.26.05.14?	9886	SUEL.LA.04.06.07	5441
ENBA.IS.N.03.—	10347	**Abī-sarē**		SUEL.LA.04.06.08	5520
ENBA.IS.xx.xx.20	11212	ABSA.LA.02.11.—	10134,	SUEL.LA.04.06.10	5434

Zambia

			10348	SUEL.LA.04.06.11	5438
ZAMB.IS.A.04.—	5322, 8622	ABSA.LA.03.12.—	10128,	SUEL.LA.04.06.19	5447

Itēr-pīša

			10131	SUEL.LA.04.06.20	5448
ITPI.IS.01.08.—	6510	ABSA.LA.04.03.—	10132	SUEL.LA.04.06.—	6281, 6292
				SUEL.LA.04.08.—	5500

SUEL.LA.04.11.xx	6800	SUEL.LA.14.12.12	9085	**Nūr-Adad**	
SUEL.LA.05.—.—	8032	SUEL.LA.14.12.15	5424	NUAD.LA.01.05.—	6796
SUEL.LA.06.06.28	5436	SUEL.LA.14.12.24	5426	NUAD.LA.B.06.—	7845
SUEL.LA.06.07.05	5442	SUEL.LA.14.12D.—	5529	NUAD.LA.B.09.—	5533, 9826
SUEL.LA.06.07.08	5418	SUEL.LA.14.—.—	9084	NUAD.LA.D.09.—?	9195, 9196
SUEL.LA.06.07.11	10407	SUEL.LA.15.02.—	5337	NUAD.LA.E.11.20?	11483
SUEL.LA.06.07.12	5444	SUEL.LA.15.04.17	5421	NUAD.LA.I.01.—	9267
SUEL.LA.06.07.14	9096	SUEL.LA.15.06.07	5425	NUAD.LA.I.04.—	6495
SUEL.LA.06.07.15	5437	SUEL.LA.15.08.—	5420, 5509	NUAD.LA.I.10.29	6494
SUEL.LA.06.07.19	5415	SUEL.LA.16.02.03	5523	NUAD.LA.I.xx.—	9265
SUEL.LA.06.07.22	5432	SUEL.LA.16.02.—	5512	**Sîn-iddinam**	
SUEL.LA.06.07.24	5446	SUEL.LA.16.03.—	10404	SIID.LA.05.11.20	9187
SUEL.LA.06.10.06	5440	SUEL.LA.16.06.—	9326	SIID.LA.06.05.19	6427
SUEL.LA.06.10.09	5417	SUEL.LA.16.07.24	9794A	SIID.LA.06.06.—	6766, 7722
SUEL.LA.07.06.29	5519	SUEL.LA.16.07.—	9327, 9556	SIID.LA.06.07.07	5644
SUEL.LA.08.02.—	9184	SUEL.LA.16.08.—	10337	SIID.LA.06.11.15	8014
SUEL.LA.09.06.—	5640	SUEL.LA.16.11.04	10409	SIID.LA.06.11.26	6432
SUEL.LA.10.12.—	5471	SUEL.LA.16.12.04	10405	SIID.LA.06.12.30	8005
SUEL.LA.12.08.—	5522	SUEL.LA.16.12.xx	9496	SIID.LA.07.01.01	6433
SUEL.LA.12.12.—	5330	SUEL.LA.16.12D.—	9445, 9601	SIID.LA.07.01.19	8253
SUEL.LA.12.—.—	5566	SUEL.LA.17.01.12	9469	SIID.LA.07.03.22	6801
SUEL.LA.12.—.—?	5477	SUEL.LA.17.02.—	9449, 9495	SIID.LA.07.03.xx	9279
SUEL.LA.13.08.—	6256	SUEL.LA.17.05.—	6323	SIID.LA.07.04.13	9865
SUEL.LA.13.09.—	5410	SUEL.LA.17.10.—	6322	SIID.LA.07.04.15	9863
SUEL.LA.13.12.—	6297	SUEL.LA.17.11.—	6300	SIID.LA.07.05.27	11124
SUEL.LA.13.12D.—	5501	SUEL.LA.18.01.16	9562	SIID.LA.07.06.18	7711
SUEL.LA.14.03.—	9050	SUEL.LA.19.07.—?	9565	SIID.LA.07.06.21	7911, 9905
SUEL.LA.14.04.08	5549	SUEL.LA.20.02.—	6770	SIID.LA.07.06.—	11482
SUEL.LA.14.05.29	5464	SUEL.LA.23.09.—	8593	SIID.LA.07.07.02	9877
SUEL.LA.14.05.—	5480, 6258	SUEL.LA.23.xx.xx	11263	SIID.LA.07.08.xx	11492
SUEL.LA.14.07.02	6339	SUEL.LA.24.05.28	11269	SIID.LA.07.09.01	8301
SUEL.LA.14.07.20	6352	SUEL.LA.24.12.—	6750	SIID.LA.07.09.23	7646
SUEL.LA.14.07.24	5521	SUEL.LA.24.xx.05	11264	SIID.LA.07.10.17	9868
SUEL.LA.14.07.—	5474, 5504, 5517	SUEL.LA.25.02.23	11282	SIID.LA.07.11.—	9192
SUEL.LA.14.08.13	6303	SUEL.LA.25.06.16	11147	SIID.LA.07.xx.15	11241
SUEL.LA.14.08.—	5419, 5547	SUEL.LA.26.06.—?	10396	SIID.LA.07.xx.20?	9897
SUEL.LA.14.09.—	5423, 5473, 5479	SUEL.LA.28.01.—?	8265	SIID.LA.07.—.—	8103
SUEL.LA.14.11.07	5462	SUEL.LA.28.07.—	8030	**Sîn-erībam**	
SUEL.LA.14.11.29	6283	SUEL.LA.28.08.22	11125	SIER.LA.01.02.—	6767
SUEL.LA.14.11.—	5506	SUEL.LA.28.12D.xx	10097	SIER.LA.01.04.01	9921
SUEL.LA.14.11.—?	6304	SUEL.LA.29.10.—	9780	SIER.LA.01.04.15?	9185
SUEL.LA.14.12.11?	5562	SUEL.LA.xx.07.—	9847	SIER.LA.01.04.26?	9895
				SIER.LA.01.05.—	9919, 9920

SIER.LA.01.06.21	6815	WASI.LA.09.xx.10	11251	RISI.LA.16.04.xx	10502
SIER.LA.01.06.26	6814	WASI.LA.10.04.—	9082, 10448	RISI.LA.16.05.05?	9057
SIER.LA.01.06.—	6808	WASI.LA.10.07.—	9073	RISI.LA.16.06.24	9000
SIER.LA.01.09.—?	9874	WASI.LA.10.11.—	10393	RISI.LA.16.06.—	8977
SIER.LA.01.10.27	6747	WASI.LA.11.06.—	10459	RISI.LA.16.07.xx	8987
SIER.LA.01.11.—?	9906	WASI.LA.11.09.—	11515	RISI.LA.16.08.28	8963
SIER.LA.01.12D.25?	9218	WASI.LA.11.12.01	9217	RISI.LA.16.08.30	8966, 9064
SIER.LA.01.12D.—	6805, 6810	WASI.LA.11.12.—	7695	RISI.LA.16.10.—	9066
	6813, 6816	**Rīm-Sîn**		RISI.LA.16.12.—	10509, 10510
	7729, 7847	RISI.LA.01.04.24	9765, 9766		
SIER.LA.02.01.14	6812	RISI.LA.01.05.24	11389	RISI.LA.17.11.—	7849
SIER.LA.xx.08.08	11142	RISI.LA.01.07.18	9875	RISI.LA.18.02.02	9392
Sîn-iqīšam		RISI.LA.01.08.—?	8710	RISI.LA.18.09.xx	9234
SIIQ.LA.01.04.—	9175	RISI.LA.01.11.30	9790	RISI.LA.18.10.—	6753
SIIQ.LA.01.11.15	9649	RISI.LA.01.12.—	10127	RISI.LA.18.12D.—	8965
SIIQ.LA.01.xx.01	11182	RISI.LA.03.03.10?	8643	RISI.LA.18.??.16	7274
SIIQ.LA.02.03.03	10118	RISI.LA.03.07.—	9842	RISI.LA.19.09.—	7313
SIIQ.LA.02.04.04	9802	RISI.LA.05.03.—?	5514	RISI.LA.19.11.20	6794
SIIQ.LA.02.04.19	9389	RISI.LA.06.04.—	9586	RISI.LA.20.03.08	10335
SIIQ.LA.02.04.19?	6834	RISI.LA.06.08.—	6746	RISI.LA.20.12.30	7301
SIIQ.LA.02.04.26	11219	RISI.LA.07.06.—	5460, 6341, 9325	RISI.LA.20.12.—	9856
SIIQ.LA.02.05.04	10494			RISI.LA.21.06.15	8733
SIIQ.LA.02.07.25	10525	RISI.LA.07.07.12+	9037	RISI.LA.22.03.—	8161
SIIQ.LA.03.xx.26	11245	RISI.LA.07.08.03	8694	RISI.LA.22.12.—	9284
SIIQ.LA.04.01.—	6396	RISI.LA.07.12.28	9497	RISI.LA.22.12.—?	10460
SIIQ.LA.04.02.13	10373	RISI.LA.07.12.—	9475	RISI.LA.22+.04.—	9228
SIIQ.LA.04.02.26	10344	RISI.LA.07.12D.12	9594	RISI.LA.23.05.—	7333
SIIQ.LA.04.04.25	9800	RISI.LA.08.01.xx	9589	RISI.LA.23.12.—	10385
SIIQ.LA.04.06.08	7090	RISI.LA.08.08.04	9585	RISI.LA.24.04.—?	10504
SIIQ.LA.04.09.17	9397	RISI.LA.08.12.—	5604	RISI.LA.24.05.—	9880
SIIQ.LA.04.11.13	9801	RISI.LA.09.07.—	5387, 5390, 6511, 9182	RISI.LA.24.06.—	7323
SIIQ.LA.05.02.12	11203			RISI.LA.24.08.30?	8985
SIIQ.LA.—.08.02	9398	RISI.LA.10.03.24	9426	RISI.LA.24.09.27	2104
Ṣilli-Adad		RISI.LA.10.03.—?	8936	RISI.LA.24.09.29	5305
SIAD.LA.01.09.01	7290	RISI.LA.10.04.10?	6793	RISI.LA.25.06.16	9468
Warad-Sîn		RISI.LA.11.06.—	8015	RISI.LA.25.07.18	5531
WASI.LA.03.03.—	9728	RISI.LA.13.10.19	8974	RISI.LA.25.09.04?	8805
WASI.LA.04.01.—	5570	RISI.LA.13.12.30	10508	RISI.LA.25.09.14	9664
WASI.LA.04.02.26	11318	RISI.LA.14.—.—	1235, 8561	RISI.LA.25.10.14	9587
WASI.LA.04.06.14?	8612	RISI.LA.16.01.12	9022	RISI.LA.25.xx.—?	9388
WASI.LA.06.03.05?	9783	RISI.LA.16.01.xx?	8988	RISI.LA.26.07.06	8656
WASI.LA.09.09.xx	6340	RISI.LA.16.03.—	9004	RISI.LA.26.07.—?	8705
		RISI.LA.16.04.23	10488	RISI.LA.26.12.05?	10398
				RISI.LA.27.10.27	8580

RISI.LA.28.03.16?	7316	RISI.LA.32.12.—	9322	RISI.LA.38.04.03	9615
RISI.LA.28.06.04	11157	RISI.LA.32+.03.08	9415	RISI.LA.38.04.04	9412
RISI.LA.28.06.18	5306	RISI.LA.32+.05.01	9643	RISI.LA.38.04.23	9638
RISI.LA.28.06.27	11148	RISI.LA.32+.07.08	9599	RISI.LA.38.04.30?	8821
RISI.LA.28.09.20	11156	RISI.LA.32+.07.—	9806	RISI.LA.38.04.xx	9238
RISI.LA.28.10.10	8573	RISI.LA.32+.11.—	6375	RISI.LA.38.05.17	9646
RISI.LA.28.??.—	6317	RISI.LA.32+.12.15	9702	RISI.LA.38.05.18	8816
RISI.LA.29.07.02	10447	RISI.LA.32+.xx.24	9454	RISI.LA.38.05.28	9641
RISI.LA.29.08.—	10440	RISI.LA.32+.xx.26	8661, 9433	RISI.LA.38.06.xx	9466
RISI.LA.30.04.05	5672	RISI.LA.33.04.—	10370	RISI.LA.38.07.—	9608
RISI.LA.30.04.15	8699	RISI.LA.34.10.—	10483	RISI.LA.38.10.03?	8822
RISI.LA.30.05.—	9065	RISI.LA.35.03.03?	9706	RISI.LA.38.11.08	6763
RISI.LA.30.06.xx	11565	RISI.LA.35.04.—	9788	RISI.LA.38.11.29	9413
RISI.LA.30.09.—	9887	RISI.LA.35.12.—	10072	RISI.LA.38.12D.xx	8818
RISI.LA.30.??.12	8078	RISI.LA.36.02.19	9694	RISI.LA.39.03.15?	11415
RISI.LA.30.??.16	8310	RISI.LA.36.04.10	7315	RISI.LA.39.04.—	8659
RISI.LA.30.??.24	8973	RISI.LA.36.07.xx	9240	RISI.LA.39.06.—	9792
RISI.LA.30+.03.—	8170	RISI.LA.36.11.02	9697	RISI.LA.39.07.25	9486
RISI.LA.30+.10.—	8609	RISI.LA.36.12.03	9489	RISI.LA.39.10.05	9263
RISI.LA.30+.xx.14	9892	RISI.LA.36.12.27	9417	RISI.LA.39.—.—	9755
RISI.LA.31.03.—	7288	RISI.LA.37.01.12	9704	RISI.LA.40.01.20	10481
RISI.LA.31.05.—	9063	RISI.LA.37.01.15	9629	RISI.LA.41+.06.15	9634
RISI.LA.31.07.06?	9003	RISI.LA.37.02.04	9186	RISI.LA.42.06.—	10077
RISI.LA.31.09.xx	10472	RISI.LA.37.02.16?	9708	RISI.LA.43.11.01?	9311
RISI.LA.31.12.xx	9277	RISI.LA.37.02.20?	9700	RISI.LA.43+.01.—	8998
RISI.LA.31.12.—	9675	RISI.LA.37.06.—	7335	RISI.LA.44.—.—	8997
RISI.LA.31.??.16	10466	RISI.LA.37.09.30	8812	RISI.LA.45.01.10	8986
RISI.LA.31.??.17	10080	RISI.LA.37.10.29	9644	RISI.LA.45.03.17	8984
RISI.LA.31.??.26	10068	RISI.LA.37.12.14	9645	RISI.LA.45.03.xx	9703
RISI.LA.31.??.30	10070, 10078	RISI.LA.37.12.24	9647	RISI.LA.45.04.01	9569
RISI.LA.31.??.30?	9086	RISI.LA.37.12.27	8806	RISI.LA.45.05.—	5316
RISI.LA.31.xx.30	9068	RISI.LA.37.12.xx?	9596	RISI.LA.45.10.—	9729
RISI.LA.31.xx.xx	10513	RISI.LA.37.12D.08	8891	RISI.LA.45.11.—	5454
RISI.LA.31+.01.01	10446	RISI.LA.37.12D.17?	9423	RISI.LA.46.01.—	5311
RISI.LA.31+.03.—	9071	RISI.LA.37.xx.01?	9416	RISI.LA.46.05.—	5321
RISI.LA.31+.10.—	10389	RISI.LA.38.01.27	8308	RISI.LA.46.08.—	9013
RISI.LA.31+.11.—	10528	RISI.LA.38.01.—	8591	RISI.LA.47.01.20	9069
RISI.LA.31+.??.05	10082	RISI.LA.38.02.01	6772	RISI.LA.47.01.—	6755, 7277, 11584
RISI.LA.31+.??.25	9006	RISI.LA.38.02.27?	8823		
RISI.LA.31+.xx.06	10454	RISI.LA.38.02.—	7727	RISI.LA.47.01.—?	10471
RISI.LA.31+.xx.24	10081	RISI.LA.38.03.20?	8799	RISI.LA.47.02.22	8620
RISI.LA.31+.xx.—	10467	RISI.LA.38.03.24	9414, 9642	RISI.LA.47.03.24	8641
RISI.LA.32.11.xx	9307	RISI.LA.38.03.30?	8817	RISI.LA.47.04.—	10526
RISI.LA.32.12.—	6787	RISI.LA.38.04.01?	9639	RISI.LA.47.06.—	9391

RISI.LA.47.07.26	5511	RISI.LA.51.04.—	7303	RISI.LA.58.04.08	7299
RISI.LA.47.08.01	8937	RISI.LA.51.10.09	8992	RISI.LA.58.04.10	7340
RISI.LA.47.08.10	9395	RISI.LA.52.04.—	7310	RISI.LA.58.05.01	5303, 5356
RISI.LA.47.08.—	7283	RISI.LA.52.09.17	9559	RISI.LA.58.06.—	9076, 9609
RISI.LA.47.10.08	9637	RISI.LA.53.01.30	10465	RISI.LA.58.07.26	9631
RISI.LA.47.10.13	8981	RISI.LA.53.01.—	10441	RISI.LA.58.08.08	9026
RISI.LA.47.11.16	9079	RISI.LA.53.03.—	9618	RISI.LA.58.10.30	7284
RISI.LA.47.11.27	7286	RISI.LA.53.03.—?	7709	RISI.LA.58.10.—	7294
RISI.LA.47.11.—	10487	RISI.LA.53.06.30	6748	RISI.LA.58.12.30	7298, 10332, 10496
RISI.LA.47.12.20	9087	RISI.LA.53.07.18	7282		
RISI.LA.47.12.—	6754, 8979, 9020, 9039, 11516	RISI.LA.53.07.—	7304, 11361	RISI.LA.59.01.14	7295
		RISI.LA.53.07.—?	10443	RISI.LA.59.01.—	6773, 9399, 10479
RISI.LA.48.01.24	9008	RISI.LA.53.09.—	8972		
RISI.LA.48.01.—	9045	RISI.LA.53.10.02	9602	RISI.LA.59.02.—	7275, 7293, 8640, 8689, 10453
RISI.LA.48.02.29	10463	RISI.LA.53.12.30	9046, 11555		
RISI.LA.48.03.xx?	9092	RISI.LA.53.—.—	9024	RISI.LA.59.03.08	8619
RISI.LA.48.04.01	8627	RISI.LA.53+.xx.—	9075	RISI.LA.59.03.13	9590
RISI.LA.48.04.—	10820	RISI.LA.54.02.17	9041	RISI.LA.59.03.—	10503
RISI.LA.48.05.07	8579	RISI.LA.54.02.20	8994, 9011, 9471, 10516	RISI.LA.59.04.—	8547, 9074
RISI.LA.48.05.24+	9626			RISI.LA.59.05.—	7285
RISI.LA.48.07.—?	9624	RISI.LA.54.09.—	9083	RISI.LA.59.06.01	9403
RISI.LA.48.08.30	9627	RISI.LA.54+.07.—	8967	RISI.LA.59.06.—	10458, 10491
RISI.LA.48.09.20	9711	RISI.LA.55.02.05	7278		
RISI.LA.48.10.14	10840	RISI.LA.55.08.—?	9799	RISI.LA.59.07.13	9093
RISI.LA.48.10.16	9479	RISI.LA.55.10.—	8935	RISI.LA.59.07.—	7291
RISI.LA.48.10.30	9705	RISI.LA.55.12.30?	9674	RISI.LA.59.08.01	9016
RISI.LA.49.01.26	9564	RISI.LA.56.04.15	8996, 9091	RISI.LA.59.08.16	10468
RISI.LA.49.01.30	9570	RISI.LA.56.04.16	8995	RISI.LA.59.08.17	8978
RISI.LA.49.05.09	9593	RISI.LA.56.06.01	7317	RISI.LA.59.08.29	8683
RISI.LA.49.05.—	11521	RISI.LA.57.01.10	8990	RISI.LA.59.08.—	5336, 7300
RISI.LA.49.06.10	7312	RISI.LA.57.01.11	9005, 9032, 10523	RISI.LA.59.09.17	5351
RISI.LA.49.09.30	7297			RISI.LA.59.09.—	8676
RISI.LA.49.09.—	9499	RISI.LA.57.01.15	9056	RISI.LA.59.11.30	10445
RISI.LA.49.10.—	10417	RISI.LA.57.01.18	8943	RISI.LA.59.11.—	8964, 9081
RISI.LA.49+.04.30	9080	RISI.LA.57.03.22	9555	RISI.LA.59.12.—	9088
RISI.LA.50.01.09	10382	RISI.LA.57.03.—	9027	RISI.LA.60.01.—	10512
RISI.LA.50.01.—	7289	RISI.LA.57.04.xx	9089	RISI.LA.60.02.—	7287
RISI.LA.50.03.—	6335	RISI.LA.57.05.xx	8894	RISI.LA.60.03.—	10456
RISI.LA.50.05.16	8803	RISI.LA.57.06.20	8649	RISI.LA.??.02.—	6757
RISI.LA.50.05.20?	9488	RISI.LA.57.12.11	10451	RISI.LA.??.12.—	9918
RISI.LA.50.08.28	11506	RISI.LA.58.01.—	10442	RISI.LA.??.xx.20	9693
RISI.LA.50.08.—	9422	RISI.LA.58.02.29	9017, 9563	RISI.LA.xx.xx.17	9418
RISI.LA.50.11.—	9009	RISI.LA.58.03.30	11561	RISI.LA.xx.xx.xx	9588, 10386, 11519
RISI.LA.50.12.20	9640	RISI.LA.58.03.—	8596, 11406		

RISI.LA.—.02.09?	9237	Ḫammurabi		Samsuiluna	
RISI.LA.—.03.08	9235	HARA.BA.01.02.—	9429	SAIL.BA.01.01.02	10913
RISI.LA.—.06.04	9787	HARA.BA.01.03.—?	9576	SAIL.BA.01.01.05?	10519
RISI.LA.—.10.13	9239	HARA.BA.03.04.06	10087	SAIL.BA.01.02.25	9767
RISI.LA.—.12D.25	9236	HARA.BA.05.07.08	1250	SAIL.BA.01.11.06	9581
RISI.LA.—.??.11	11520	HARA.BA.07.08.—?	6818	SAIL.BA.02.09.20?	1276
RISI.LA.—.??.17	9040	HARA.BA.10.—.—	5574	SAIL.BA.02.11.21	1275
RISI.LA.—.??.21	7844	HARA.BA.16.—.—	9679	SAIL.BA.03.07.22	5576
RISI.LA.—.??.24	9018	HARA.BA.24.10.25	8494	SAIL.BA.03.—.—	4118
RISI.LA.—.—.—	9275, 10065	HARA.BA.30.05.14	5453	SAIL.BA.04.03.08	6764
Rīm-Sîn II		HARA.BA.31.03.14?	8898	SAIL.BA.04.05.12	8738
RISI2.LA.01.04.—	11417	HARA.BA.31.08.12	10379	SAIL.BA.04.05.17	5363
RISI2.LA.02.12.30	1249	HARA.BA.31.09.—	10353	SAIL.BA.04.07.23	6261
RISI2.LA.03.03.16	9771	HARA.BA.32.03.15+	8606	SAIL.BA.04.08.16	8692
RISI2.LA.03.05.05	9574	HARA.BA.32.03.—	5299	SAIL.BA.04.08.22	1248
RISI2.LA.03.09.01	11464	HARA.BA.33.04.—	10500	SAIL.BA.04.12.05	5348
RISI2.LA.03.09.10	5328	HARA.BA.33.05.18	10394	SAIL.BA.04.12.20	1261
RISI2.LA.03.10.01	9791	HARA.BA.33.06.01	10057	SAIL.BA.04.12.24	5290
RISI2.LA.03.10.10	9768	HARA.BA.34.06.—	5320	SAIL.BA.04.—.—	4129
RISI2.LA.03.10.20	9769	HARA.BA.35.06.20	10230	SAIL.BA.05.01.—?	9789
Unknown		HARA.BA.36.03.01	1271	SAIL.BA.05.05.20?	9676
UN.LA.A.03.—?	9072	HARA.BA.36.08.14	10355	SAIL.BA.05.05.22	1263
UN.LA.B.02.05	10497	HARA.BA.36.12.17	6804	SAIL.BA.05.05.—	5358
		HARA.BA.37.06.01	11460	SAIL.BA.05.06.20?	9625
		HARA.BA.38.05.—?	8631	SAIL.BA.05.06.—	9621
BABYLON		HARA.BA.39.01.18	10229	SAIL.BA.05.08.10	8831
Sumu-abum		HARA.BA.39.01.24?	6759	SAIL.BA.05.08.26	9430
SUAB.BA.01.11.—	6318, 8671	HARA.BA.39.06.—	10231	SAIL.BA.05.11.01	8570
Sumu-la-el		HARA.BA.39.09.—	11472	SAIL.BA.05.11.13?	8874
SULA.BA.28.07.—	5066	HARA.BA.40.03.05	8697	SAIL.BA.06.02.22	8564
SULA.BA.30.07.24	4218	HARA.BA.40.03.15	10482	SAIL.BA.06.02.30	8589
SULA.BA.30.11.—	4217	HARA.BA.40.06.—	11474	SAIL.BA.06.02.—?	9786
SULA.BA.31.04.—	1236	HARA.BA.40.07.23	5369	SAIL.BA.06.03.20	8913
Sabium		HARA.BA.41.02.20	11504	SAIL.BA.06.04.06?	8729
SABI.BA.07.09.—	10345	HARA.BA.41.04.—	8704	SAIL.BA.06.04.28	8747
SABI.BA.14.03.20	1244	HARA.BA.42.04.—	8650	SAIL.BA.06.06.17?	8767
Sîn-muballiṭ		HARA.BA.42.05.—	8555	SAIL.BA.06.06.18	8723
SIMU.BA.03.04.—	10156	HARA.BA.42.06.01	5413	SAIL.BA.06.07.06?	8761
SIMU.BA.05.—.—	11455	HARA.BA.42.08.03	11461	SAIL.BA.06.08.01	8735
SIMU.BA.08.01.08	7687	HARA.BA.42.10.—	8546	SAIL.BA.06.09.22	8567, 8722
SIMU.BA.13.08.—	7350, 10066	HARA.BA.43.01.15	6802	SAIL.BA.06.09.28	8836
SIMU.BA.16.06.—	1247	HARA.BA.43.10.02	7308	SAIL.BA.06.09.—?	9208
		HARA.BA.xx.09.—	10093	SAIL.BA.06.10.01	11475

SAIL.BA.06.10.05	8877	SAIL.BA.07.07.05	8826	SAIL.BA.07.10.15?	8833
SAIL.BA.06.10.06	8848	SAIL.BA.07.07.07	8791, 8830	SAIL.BA.07.10.16	8793
SAIL.BA.06.10.10	8825	SAIL.BA.07.07.08	8869	SAIL.BA.07.10.17	8795
SAIL.BA.06.10.15	8764	SAIL.BA.07.07.09	8582, 8740,	SAIL.BA.07.10.19	6348, 8796
SAIL.BA.06.10.17	8728		8779	SAIL.BA.07.10.21?	8873
SAIL.BA.06.10.19	8530	SAIL.BA.07.07.11	8824	SAIL.BA.07.10.22	8745
SAIL.BA.06.10.26	1264	SAIL.BA.07.07.14	8718	SAIL.BA.07.10.24?	8532
SAIL.BA.06.10.—	7324, 9812	SAIL.BA.07.07.14?	8770	SAIL.BA.07.10.28	8742
SAIL.BA.06.11.03	8540	SAIL.BA.07.07.17	8647	SAIL.BA.07.10.xx	8879
SAIL.BA.06.11.18	8737	SAIL.BA.07.07.18	8765, 8787	SAIL.BA.07.10.—	8778, 8809,
SAIL.BA.06.11.26	8865	SAIL.BA.07.07.19	8850		8829
SAIL.BA.06.12.20	8749	SAIL.BA.07.07.20	8753, 8758	SAIL.BA.07.11.14?	8908
SAIL.BA.06.12.25	8760	SAIL.BA.07.07.21	8739, 8842	SAIL.BA.07.11.30	8743, 8775
SAIL.BA.06.12.26	8769, 8839	SAIL.BA.07.07.21?	8814	SAIL.BA.07.11.xx	6798, 8720
SAIL.BA.06.12.30	8741	SAIL.BA.07.07.23	8870	SAIL.BA.07.12.01	6752
SAIL.BA.06.xx.27	10147	SAIL.BA.07.07.25	8558	SAIL.BA.07.12.17	5407
SAIL.BA.07.01.16	8845, 8871	SAIL.BA.07.07.xx	8880	SAIL.BA.07.12.20	8768
SAIL.BA.07.01.25	8559	SAIL.BA.07.08.01	8713	SAIL.BA.07.12.30	9772
SAIL.BA.07.02.22	8910	SAIL.BA.07.08.01?	8868	SAIL.BA.07.xx.01?	8838
SAIL.BA.07.02.24	8732	SAIL.BA.07.08.08	8786	SAIL.BA.07.xx.10	6350
SAIL.BA.07.03.01	8698	SAIL.BA.07.08.18?	8754	SAIL.BA.07.xx.24?	8774
SAIL.BA.07.03.08	9749	SAIL.BA.07.08.19	8717	SAIL.BA.07.—.—	9270
SAIL.BA.07.03.27	6253	SAIL.BA.07.08.22	8553, 8750	SAIL.BA.08.01.14	8563
SAIL.BA.07.03.30	8556	SAIL.BA.07.08.24?	8552	SAIL.BA.08.03.01	6749
SAIL.BA.07.04.03	8827	SAIL.BA.07.08.25	8780	SAIL.BA.08.04.26	8571
SAIL.BA.07.04.04	8751, 8788	SAIL.BA.07.08.28	8783, 8867	SAIL.BA.08.05.01	6789
SAIL.BA.07.04.13	8834, 8841	SAIL.BA.07.09.02	8752, 8909,	SAIL.BA.08.05.xx	8942
SAIL.BA.07.04.15?	8875		8912	SAIL.BA.08.06.02	8539
SAIL.BA.07.04.21	8725	SAIL.BA.07.09.03	8719	SAIL.BA.08.06.16	8657
SAIL.BA.07.04.30	1272	SAIL.BA.07.09.07	8757	SAIL.BA.08.06.21	6799
SAIL.BA.07.05.13	7349	SAIL.BA.07.09.08	8759	SAIL.BA.08.07.03	8730
SAIL.BA.07.05.17	8744	SAIL.BA.07.09.10	8551, 8843	SAIL.BA.08.08.12?	8819
SAIL.BA.07.05.20	7307	SAIL.BA.07.09.20?	8911	SAIL.BA.08.10.01	6827
SAIL.BA.07.05.22	8726	SAIL.BA.07.09.24?	8844	SAIL.BA.08.12.20	8533
SAIL.BA.07.05.28	8560	SAIL.BA.07.09.25	8724, 8797	SAIL.BA.08.xx.30	8662
SAIL.BA.07.06.01	8798	SAIL.BA.07.09.—	8792	SAIL.BA.08.—.—	6290
SAIL.BA.07.06.07	8538	SAIL.BA.07.10.01	8731	SAIL.BA.10.12.20	1243
SAIL.BA.07.06.08	8849	SAIL.BA.07.10.04	8766	SAIL.BA.10.12.—	5567
SAIL.BA.07.06.11	8568	SAIL.BA.07.10.05	8785	SAIL.BA.11.04.12	9672
SAIL.BA.07.06.15	8554	SAIL.BA.07.10.06	8781	SAIL.BA.11.05.20?	5392
SAIL.BA.07.06.20?	8693	SAIL.BA.07.10.07	8588	SAIL.BA.11.08.02?	9584
SAIL.BA.07.06.xx	8846	SAIL.BA.07.10.08	8835	SAIL.BA.11.08.—	5334
SAIL.BA.07.07.01	8610, 8763	SAIL.BA.07.10.10	8663	SAIL.BA.11.09.01?	8180
SAIL.BA.07.07.02	8762	SAIL.BA.07.10.12	8866	SAIL.BA.11.12.xx?	9737

SAIL.BA.12.03.07	5333	SAIL.BA.22.02.21	9572	SAIL.BA.27.01.07	10067
SAIL.BA.12.06.—	6758	SAIL.BA.22.10.14	8642	SAIL.BA.27.02.10	1256
SAIL.BA.12.08.—	5315	SAIL.BA.22.11.01	9628	SAIL.BA.27.04.09	8270
SAIL.BA.12.10.01	5571	SAIL.BA.22.11.10	8283, 9583	SAIL.BA.27.04.22	1259
SAIL.BA.12.12.20	10096	SAIL.BA.22.12.10	8584	SAIL.BA.27.05.01	5324
SAIL.BA.13.05.18	6777	SAIL.BA.22.xx.xx	9726	SAIL.BA.27.05.16	7276
SAIL.BA.13.11.10	9669	SAIL.BA.23.02.15	10142	SAIL.BA.27.08.01	9655
SAIL.BA.13.xx.xx	10084	SAIL.BA.23.03.01	5458	SAIL.BA.27.08.10	9467
SAIL.BA.14.07.23	5573	SAIL.BA.23.05.15	5327	SAIL.BA.27.08.17	6823
SAIL.BA.14.08.10	9744	SAIL.BA.23.11.01	8228	SAIL.BA.27.08.21	9747
SAIL.BA.15.05.07	5541	SAIL.BA.23.11.13	9682	SAIL.BA.27.09.xx	9226
SAIL.BA.15.06.04	5310	SAIL.BA.23.11.23	8801	SAIL.BA.27.10.10	5532
SAIL.BA.15.10.20?	9735	SAIL.BA.23.12.—	5493	SAIL.BA.27.10.14	9407
SAIL.BA.15.10.25	9709	SAIL.BA.24.01.12	8577	SAIL.BA.27.10.20	9561
SAIL.BA.16.06.16	5565	SAIL.BA.24.02.01	6824	SAIL.BA.27.11.04	5385
SAIL.BA.16.09.12	5353	SAIL.BA.24.02.20	9202	SAIL.BA.27.12.14	5564
SAIL.BA.16.12.30	9605	SAIL.BA.24.03.20	9297	SAIL.BA.27.12.24?	8782
SAIL.BA.17.06.05	6786	SAIL.BA.24.03.—	4082, 9490	SAIL.BA.27.12D.19	9200
SAIL.BA.17.06.20	6337	SAIL.BA.24.06.08	5365	SAIL.BA.27.12D.21	9264
SAIL.BA.17.12.14	5568	SAIL.BA.24.06.21	5534	SAIL.BA.27.12D.22	5360
SAIL.BA.17.xx.xx	10351	SAIL.BA.24.08.29?	9690	SAIL.BA.27.xx.xx	9742, 10363
SAIL.BA.18.06.26	10378	SAIL.BA.24.10.04	4117	SAIL.BA.28.01.14	8815
SAIL.BA.18.xx.30	10457	SAIL.BA.24.10.21	6329	SAIL.BA.28.01.16	9225
SAIL.BA.19.04.01	1234	SAIL.BA.24.10.23	5361	SAIL.BA.28.02.11	1262
SAIL.BA.19.04.16?	5540	SAIL.BA.24.11.30	6795	SAIL.BA.28.02.25	9975
SAIL.BA.19.05.20	10140	SAIL.BA.24.12.01?	9795	SAIL.BA.28.03.02	9885
SAIL.BA.19.06.06	9632	SAIL.BA.25.03.—	1237	SAIL.BA.28.04.06	9813
SAIL.BA.19.07.12	6325	SAIL.BA.25.04.26	9617	SAIL.BA.28.04.06?	9832
SAIL.BA.19.07.29	9696	SAIL.BA.25.05.08	9779	SAIL.BA.28.04.12?	8804
SAIL.BA.19.08.15	8601	SAIL.BA.25.05.21?	9300	SAIL.BA.28.05.01	10160, 10175
SAIL.BA.19.10.02?	9315	SAIL.BA.25.05.30	10169		
SAIL.BA.19.10.22	6324	SAIL.BA.25.09.10	9810	SAIL.BA.28.05.23?	9692
SAIL.BA.19.11.07	10051	SAIL.BA.25.12.03?	10188	SAIL.BA.28.05.xx	9478
SAIL.BA.20.08.01	5578	SAIL.BA.25.12.28	9833	SAIL.BA.28.07.09	9201
SAIL.BA.20.08.02	6466	SAIL.BA.26.02.09	10189	SAIL.BA.28.09.10	1255
SAIL.BA.20.11.25	10144	SAIL.BA.26.04.13	10165	SAIL.BA.28.—.—	10126
SAIL.BA.20.11.—	9899	SAIL.BA.26.06.05	10150	SAIL.BA.34.05.01?	6761
SAIL.BA.21.02.06	9654	SAIL.BA.26.06.30	10141	SAIL.BA.35.06.05?	5569
SAIL.BA.21.04.01	6333	SAIL.BA.26.08.01	6830	SAIL.BA.??.01.01	8543
SAIL.BA.21.04.21	8885	SAIL.BA.26.10.01	1239	SAIL.BA.??.01.02	8578
SAIL.BA.21.07.01	5492	SAIL.BA.26.10.18	5391	SAIL.BA.??.04.02	8872
SAIL.BA.21.07.10	10113	SAIL.BA.26.11.05	8294	SAIL.BA.xx.01.14	10107
SAIL.BA.22.01.20	9730	SAIL.BA.26.12.03	8273	SAIL.BA.xx.01.15	10058
SAIL.BA.22.01.28?	9736	SAIL.BA.26.12.—	9834	SAIL.BA.xx.02.10	6819

SAIL.BA.xx.02.22?	9699	
SAIL.BA.xx.03.07	9777	
SAIL.BA.xx.04.14	8756	
SAIL.BA.xx.06.xx	9756	
SAIL.BA.xx.07.03	10172	
SAIL.BA.xx.08.—	9222	
SAIL.BA.xx.12.22+	8651	
SAIL.BA.xx.xx.xx	8832, 8878, 9722	
SAIL.BA.—.07.20	1269	

Abī-ešuḫ
ABEŠ.BA.01.07.21	1245
ABEŠ.BA.02.09.06	11511
ABEŠ.BA.K.08.05	1238

Ammiditana
AMDI.BA.05.04.01	4986
AMDI.BA.06.04.20	11454
AMDI.BA.26.08.22	6305
AMDI.BA.30.01.09	8899

Ammiṣaduqa
AMSA.BA.10.05.20	5575
AMSA.BA.13.12D.04	5301, 5456
AMSA.BA.15.12.06	5355
AMSA.BA.17.02.10	5294

EŠNUNNA

Ipiq-Adad
IPAD.EŠ.D.—.—	8274, 9158

Narām-Sîn
NASI.EŠ.11.12.19?	10103

Dannum-taḫaz
DATA.EŠ.02.—.—	8271

Unknown
UN.EŠ.AB.08.—	6263
UN.EŠ.AB.11.—	5646
UN.EŠ.P.12D.05	8545

KAZALLU

Ibni-šadum
IBŠA.KA.F.—.—	7342

KISURRA

Itūr-Šamaš
ITŠA.KI.C.12.—	9280
ITŠA.KI.F.04.—	8036

Manabaltiel
MABA.KI.J.—.—	7305

Ubaya
UBAY.KI.01.04.—	9855

Unknown
UN.KI.A.12.—	7179

MANANA

Manana
MANA.MN.A.11.—	6775
MANA.MN.F.—.—	1246

Sumu-Yamutbala
SUYA.MN.??.06.03	7302

Unknown
UN.MN.A.—.—	7330

NEREBTUM

Dannum-taḫaz
DATA.NE.03.12D.25	8548
DATA.NE.03.—.—	5359, 5382

ŠADLAŠ

Unknown
UN.ŠL.H.—.—	8293

ŠADUPPÛM

Waqrum
WAQR.ŠA.A.—.—	8236

Ḫammi-dušur
HADU.ŠA.B.—.—	8281

Ipiq-Adad II
IPAD2.ŠA.A.05.27	9207
IPAD2.ŠA.A.—.—	8289
IPAD2.ŠA.J.—.—	7309

Narām-Sîn
NASI.ŠA.B.—.—	5367
NASI.ŠA.E.—.—	5386
NASI.ŠA.F.—.—	5335, 5368, 5376, 5383, 5467, 5498, 8715, 9159, 10362
NASI.ŠA.I.12.14	9762
NASI.ŠA.I.—.—	5347, 5388, 5499, 8604, 9151, 9160, 9161, 9753, 9829
NASI.ŠA.J.03.—	5373
NASI.ŠA.J.10.08	6751
NASI.ŠA.J.—.—	5403, 9152
NASI.ŠA.xx.—.—	9761

Iqīš-Tišpak
IQTI.ŠA.01.—.—	5494, 9162

Dannum-taḫaz
DATA.ŠA.C.—.—	8603

Daduša
DADU.ŠA.B.—.—	9807
DADU.ŠA.C.—.—	8616
DADU.ŠA.xx.xx.xx	7930

Ibāl-pī-el II
IPE2.ŠA.03.—.—	8272
IPE2.ŠA.07.—.—	8290
IPE2.ŠA.08.08.01	9193
IPE2.ŠA.08.—.—	7325, 8287
IPE2.ŠA.08.—.—?	5304
IPE2.ŠA.09.—.—	8280
IPE2.ŠA.10.07.30	8684
IPE2.ŠA.10.—.—	9206
IPE2.ŠA.B.02.19	10179
IPE2.ŠA.B.—.—	8258, 9191

IPE2.ŠA.H.05.20	8263	TUTUB		URUK	
IPE2.ŠA.H.—.—	8262	Abdi-Eraḫ		Sîn-irībam	
IPE2.ŠA.—.02.02	10092	ABER.TU.A.06.—	6820, 6821	SIIR.UK.01.09.10	7327
Unknown					
UN.ŠA.M.—.—	8291				
UN.ŠA.N.—.—	6791